Endangered Liaisons

Endangered Liaisons

DON SHAY

alarus

For Estelle
who struck the spark,
and for Jerry
who fueled the blaze,

and
in memory of my dad,
Frank W. Shay
who, to my great and lasting sorrow,
left this mortal world while I was
off adventuring in Africa.

ISBN 978-0-615-21345-3

Printed in the United States of America

Alarus Press
P.O. Box 20027
Riverside, California 92516

www.alaruspress.com

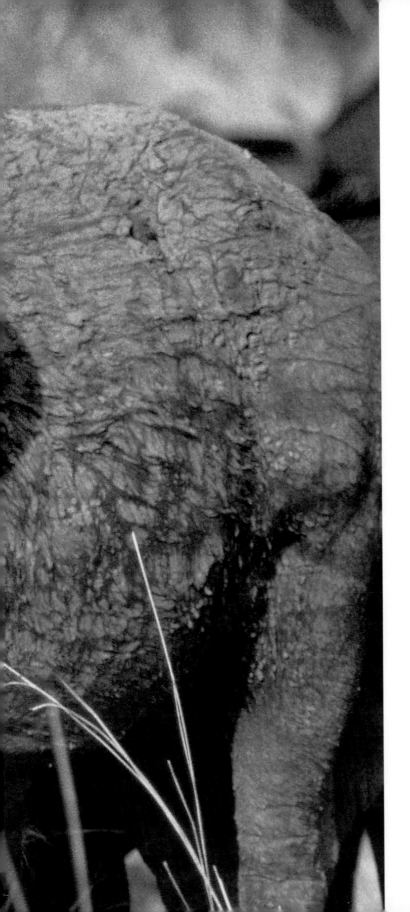

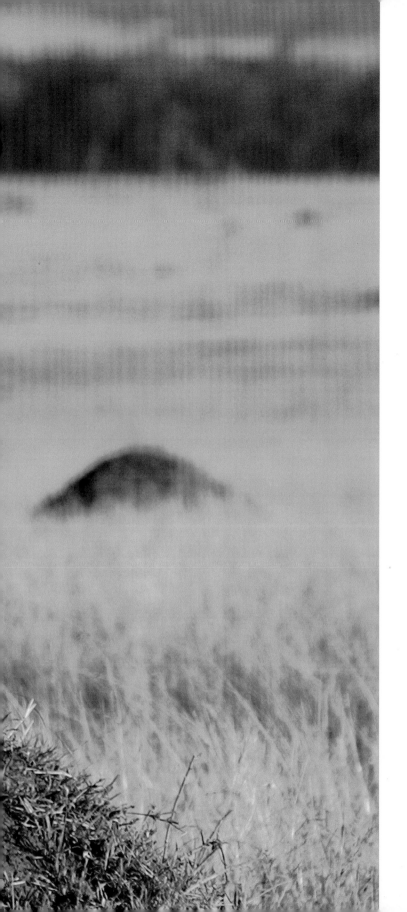

Call of the Wild

A map of Africa hangs on the wall in our library. Estelle and I came upon it some years ago in an antiquarian bookshop overlooking the plaza in Santa Fe and thought it would be a fine memento of both that trip and the several we had already taken to Africa. Intricately engraved and hand-tinted in the manner predating color printing, the map had been extracted from a mid-nineteenth-century atlas. The outline of Africa is estimably precise – a tribute to the mapmakers of the day – but beyond the coastal perimeter, dotted with maritime trading settlements, much of the continent is a cartographic void. Even Lake Victoria, larger than many modern-day countries, lies unrevealed within a vast white expanse bearing the legend 'Unexplored Region.' The map is a graphic reminder of just how long Africa withheld its innermost secrets from the outer world.

All that would change – and rather quickly. Most of the continent had been explored, settled and tamed, colonized, exploited, fought over and freed long before I ever set foot on it. But for a boy growing up in America, a mere one hundred years after this vintage map was drawn, Africa was still very much unexplored region. Travel and wildlife documentaries were not ubiquitous at the time. There was no Discovery Channel and no Animal Planet. *National Geographic* was still decades from becoming a television entity. In its seminal print form, however, it was then – as it is now – a gilt-edged passport to faraway lands. From a young age, I can recall poring over copies during summer stays at my grandparents' house, losing myself between games of croquet and canasta in page after glossy page of incomparably photographed places and people – and wildlife. Even then it was the wildlife that most engaged me.

My appreciation of that wildlife was heightened in the wilds of Manhattan. Once or twice a year, my parents would treat my sister and me to an outing in New York – often around our birthdays, just two days apart. We would drive sixty miles to the city, park the car, and embark on a day of high adventure seeing the sights and riding the subway and, best of all, lunching at one of the Horn & Hardart Automats that were always nearby. Often we would separate for part of the day in various gender-centric pursuits. My mom and sister might go shopping or catch the high-kicking Rockettes at Radio City Music Hall, while my dad and I would take in a show at one of the Times Square movie palaces or a ball game at Yankee Stadium. More often than not, however, we would roam the hallowed halls of the American Museum of Natural History – my perennial first choice.

In those days, when my boyish aim was to follow in the footsteps of Roy Chapman Andrews, I was ever drawn to the great dinosaur halls whose fossil remains of creatures long extinct never failed to awe me. Of almost equal interest, however, was the hall of African mammals with its imposing herd of elephants on a central dais surrounded by other exotic animals displayed behind glass in diorama habitats. The hall was a testament to the art of taxidermy and a tribute to the memory of its namesake creator, naturalist Carl Akeley, who designed the innovative exhibits and collected the wildlife for them at a time when doing so in the service of education was still praiseworthy. Each perfect specimen was meticulously stuffed and groomed, and posed as in life within settings authentically detailed to the last blade of grass. I felt I could have walked to the far horizon in any one of them.

A pride of lions lounging beneath a thorn tree. Zebras and antelope mingling on a vast open plain. Giraffes stooping to drink at a waterhole. Mountain gorillas feeding in a lush rainforest. I moved from one vibrant tableau to the next, taking in every detail, convinced in my mind that these marvelous re-creations were somehow more alive than their flesh-and-blood counterparts caged in the penitentiary-style zoos of the day. This was what Africa must be like. In the viewfinder of my trusty Brownie Hawkeye – framed tight to eliminate walls and floors – the illusion was uncannily complete. I must have taken the same shots on every visit. Those counterfeit wildlife images were scarcely in the same league as the photos I so admired in *National Geographic* – but they were mine, and I could almost imagine having captured them on safari.

I had occasion to revisit those memories some thirty years later. My passion for paleontology as a career had gone the way of most pre-pubescent dreams, but my love of the natural world and its photographic depiction had survived into adulthood. I seldom went anywhere without a camera. My old Brownie Hawkeye had long since been retired, replaced by a succession of Pentaxes and Nikons – even a Hasselblad for a spell – and I was now shooting with a brand-new Minolta Maxxum, which was then the only 35mm single-lens reflex with an integrated autofocus system. I had splurged on two pricey bodies and a couple of lenses, plus enough film to send Kodak stock soaring, all in advance of what promised to be my most exciting travel adventure ever. Now I was home, sorting through the mounds of photographs I had taken. As with my childhood museum shots, they were scarcely in the same league as the photos I so admired in *National Geographic* – but again they were mine, and this time they had been captured on safari.

I was stricken with safari fever during my trip to Africa. There is no medical explanation for this common malady, and no cure, but it affects the heart and mind in powerful ways, causing an irresistible urge to replicate the infecting experience. In the twenty years since my initial exposure, I have succumbed willingly and often to this seductive impulse. I blame it all on the woman who came into my life shortly before that transformative first trip.

Most of our friends see Estelle as adventurous. Our travels through the years would support such a notion, as she shares with me a love of experiences and places that are outside the mainstream. Tourist hotspots seldom attract us. We have walked the black-sand beaches of the Galápagos, for example, but never the white-sand beaches of Hawaii. For a devotee of exotic travel, however, Estelle is often out of her comfort zone, her game derring-do masking a swarm of chronic fears. Fear of flying. Fear of water. Fear of disease or injury or death. To name a few. Yet she refuses to be hobbled by them. Her fear of missing out trumps all others. A textbook white-knuckle flyer, anxious from takeoff to landing, she has nonetheless logged a quarter of a million air miles in everything from jumbo jets to light aircraft to hot-air balloons – even, on a lark that astonished us both, an ultralight. A minimal swimmer, wary of deep water even in our backyard pool, she has joyously snorkeled amongst the coral reef denizens of the Caribbean, had hands-on encounters with whales in Baja California, and braved world-class whitewater rapids in the Grand Canyon – and been helicoptered out. No matter that insects and snakes make her flesh crawl – spiders warrant a spousal 911 – she has trekked through Central American rainforests and scaled ancient Mayan pyramids. And she has been steadfast at my side on all but three of my safaris to Africa, which have taken her to some of the most daunting places on earth. Only once or twice has she had a teary meltdown.

Our travels together have seasoned our lives, strengthened our bond, and defined us as a couple in the eyes of others. But that came with time. At the start, all Estelle wanted was a weekend in Santa Barbara. She knew and liked the city, had a longtime friend who lived there, and wanted to share it with me. We were in the third trimester of what would prove to be a full-term relationship, spending most of our free time together, and for some months Estelle had been trying to spirit me away for a romantic getaway up the coast. A publisher in the early years of building a business, I always had some occupational excuse for putting it off. How could I possibly leave my work for three whole days?

So imagine my surprise when she asked me one evening if I might consider going on a photographic safari to Africa with her. And imagine hers when I promptly said yes. Was this a test of my work resolve – a pop quiz? Or was her overture rooted in sentiment, since the sumptuous *Out of Africa* had been our very first date movie? Or was it kismet? Whatever the underlying reasons, the impetus came from a colleague at the hospital where Estelle was working at the time. Dick Tichy had been to Africa several times, was enthralled by it, and had shared some of his photos and recollections with her. Another trip was in the offing, and the fellow who was organizing it was going to be in town for a visit. We asked to meet with him.

Twenty years ago, safari chic was not yet in vogue, so when a white-haired man in multi-pocket khakis entered Estelle's outer office, we had little doubt that this was Jerry Dale. A former minor league pitcher and major league umpire, with a doctorate in education and psychology, Jerry was now living his dream in a world far removed from both sports and academia. During his early years as an umpire, he had fulfilled a lifelong ambition by journeying to Kenya during the off-season, and was so taken by the experience that he went again the next year, this time with a couple of friends. Other trips followed. Other friends joined him. Soon he had a network of contacts at the best safari lodges in the choicest wildlife areas. Africa was an annual getaway. When he retired from baseball in the mid-1980s, Jerry decided to formalize his role as a safari operator, and was now personally leading three to five trips a year. After fifteen years and dozens of safaris, Jerry was an impassioned ambassador for the African bush, as excited by the thought of his next trip as he had been by his first. His enthusiasm was infectious, and in twenty minutes we were sold. Jerry Dale would introduce us to Africa.

At the time, Kenya was the default destination for anyone contemplating a first safari to Africa, and Jerry had a well-honed two-week itinerary that covered five of its celebrated national parks and reserves. Nowhere else on the planet exceeded it in terms of diversity and sheer numbers of free-ranging animals. After interminable months of anticipation, we stepped off an Air France plane in Nairobi, passed through a gauntlet of customs and immigration officials, and emerged into a world that would change the course and character of our lives. We overnighted at the Hilton in the bustling city center, met our fellow travelers, and set out the next morning in a pair of pop-top minivans that afforded everyone a window seat.

I had seen a bit of the world through travel, and had spent a year in the Philippines during my military service, so I had a sense of what to expect of a country whose scenic beauty and natural riches stood in sharp contrast to the prevalent human condition. I can scarcely imagine the effect it must have had on Estelle, who had never been out of the United States and was traveling on a virgin passport. We had come to see the animals, but the long dusty drives between game reserves, over wretched roads and through desperately poor townships, were perhaps more enlightening, raising our consciousness and heightening our understanding of the often conflicting relationship between the land and the wildlife and the people.

With a showman's aplomb, Jerry had arranged the itinerary so that each stopover surpassed the last. Within a few days we had seen most of the flagship animals of Africa. Our accommodations were in safari lodges that were spacious and comfortable and architecturally unique. Jerry knew everyone by name, from managers and desk clerks to chefs and waiters, treated them like old and valued friends, not servants, and consequently got the very best of everything for his clients, from room assignments to dining room seating. With Jerry it was not an act, however. He loved the African people. As our friendship progressed over time, I learned that he had been quietly supporting a number of charities and orphanages, and for years had been paying for the schooling of a young girl – the daughter of a friend – who has since graduated and become a teacher, enriching other lives as he enriched hers.

To say that we were smitten by our maiden trip to Africa would be a colossal understatement. For weeks – make that months – after our return, we could think or speak of little else, and I had a terrible time getting back into my workaday routine. I recall writing to Jerry in the afterglow, thanking him for an extraordinary experience and noting that the only thing preventing me from proclaiming our safari the trip of a lifetime was the certainty that there would be others. And, indeed, within a few months, Estelle and I were planning our return to Africa.

We agreed that the only way to improve on our first safari would be to do one with a group of friends. So we arranged with Jerry to reserve one of his peak-season Kenya trips entirely for us, and before long had ten people signed up to join us on it. They were the first of many friends we would introduce to Africa over the years. Africa became a passion – and then an obsession. Three years would pass before Estelle and I finally got that weekend getaway to Santa Barbara. By then, we had already been to Africa twice – with a third trip in the planning.

Although Jerry had refined his Kenya itinerary to perfection, and for years to come would consider it the gold-standard safari for most of his clients, in his personal travels he was beginning to find more exclusive and intimate experiences elsewhere on the continent, and before long was offering them to some of his more devoted acolytes. Under Jerry's wing – and then later on our own – we began visiting less-traveled regions of Africa, seeking out rarer and more endangered species, and discovering the sublime pleasures of small tented camps in areas far removed from the crush of fellow tourists. The magnetic pull intensified with each new exposure. What began as a one-off adventure evolved into a biannual pilgrimage and then an annual one. More was never enough.

As of this writing, I have been to Africa fourteen times, having visited nine countries and dozens of wildlife preserves. In two- to four-week increments, I have spent more than nine months on safari. Why do I keep going back? That question has been posed, by friends and family and others, more times than I care to recall. My practiced response is that Africa is a big place, half again as large as the United States and Europe combined, and incredibly diverse. Much of it is still wild, and I am trying to experience it all. A fair answer, if none too illuminating.

I used to think that my photographs spoke to the larger question. They certainly did to me. I could glance at any image I had captured through the years and be whisked straightaway to the time and place it was taken. Every aspect of every moment came rushing back. In attempting to share those moments with others, however, I came to realize that even the best of my photos failed to represent the addictive intensity of the safari experience. Something more inclusive was needed. And so this volume began percolating in the back of my mind. If a picture is worth a thousand words, then my travels through Africa have netted me the equivalent of some 20 million words – enough to fill an encyclopedia. But could those visual surrogates convey both the experience and the appeal of safari? I thought not. Like an encyclopedia, my photos of wild places and wild creatures imparted an objective truth stripped of its subjective context. To adequately address the question of why I have felt so compelled to revisit Africa over and over, I knew I would have to delve deeper. I would need to sift through twenty years of hard recollections and soft impressions, and from there come up with just the right words to encompass and bridge the two. What would I discover on the way? I had to find out.

And so I embarked on another long journey …

WILDEBEEST AND ZEBRAS
Masai Mara National Reserve, Kenya

DELTA WATERWAY
Moremi Game Reserve, Botswana

DESERT PAN AND DUNES
Namib-Naukluft Park, Namibia

SODA LAKE GEYSER
Lake Bogoria National Reserve, Kenya

WOODED SAVANNA
Tarangire National Park, Tanzania

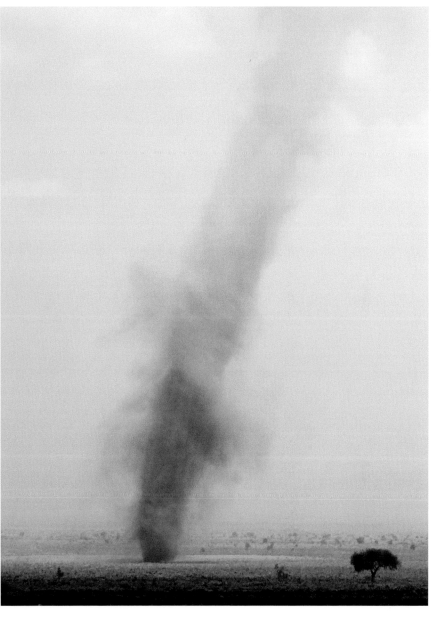

DUST DEVIL
Amboseli National Park, Kenya

AFRICAN LION
Masai Mara National Reserve, Kenya

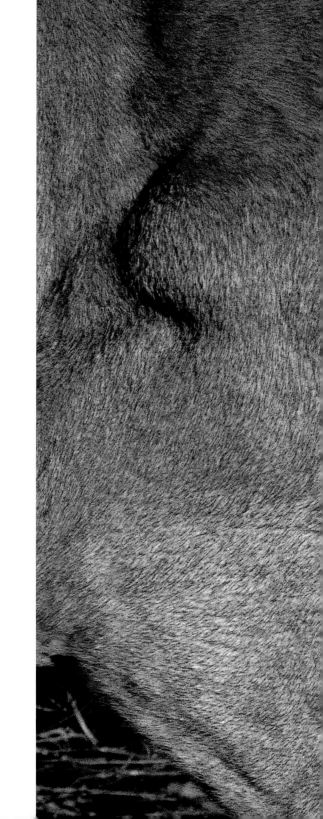

LIONESS STALKING
Savuti, Chobe National Park, Botswana

CHEETAH
Masai Mara National Reserve, Kenya

LEOPARD

DEFASSA WATERBUCK
Masai Mara National Reserve, Kenya

IMPALAS
Samburu National Reserve, Kenya

VERVET MONKEY
Tsavo West National Park, Kenya

SYKES' MONKEY
Mount Kenya National Park, Kenya

MOUNTAIN GORILLA
Parc National des Volcans, Rwanda

OLIVE BABOONS
Lake Manyara National Park, Tanzania

AFRICAN ELEPHANTS
Amboseli National Park, Kenya

ELEPHANTS AND BUFFALO
Mount Kenya National Park, Kenya

GEMSBOK
Sossusvlei, Namib-Naukluft Park, Namibia

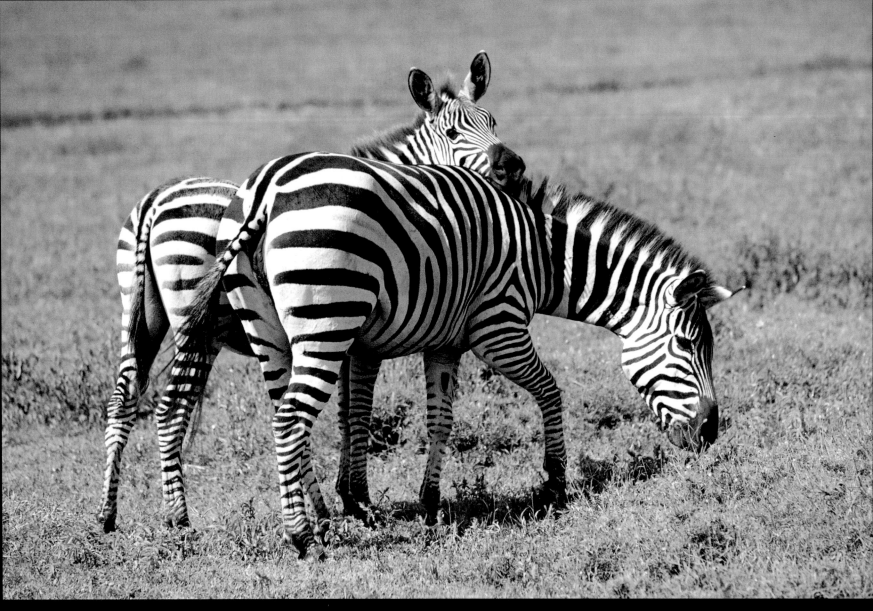

ZEBRAS
Ngorongoro Crater, Tanzania

MATING LIONS
Masai Mara National Reserve, Kenya

Close Encounters

Anyone who thinks getting there is half the fun has never been to Africa. At least not from the western United States where, even with today's planet-shrinking modes of transport, 12,000 miles and eleven time zones must still be spanned before one can set foot on the ancient plains where man first stood erect to challenge his environment. What awaits, however, is more than worth the creature discomforts of being strapped into an airplane for two or more days and then jounced over god-awful roads for another to reach places of such sublime remoteness that any road at all is an aesthetic affront. For the allure of Africa today is akin to that which drew the great European explorers to its uncharted interior a scant century and a half ago. Indeed, the vast empty spaces of Africa, largely unchanged, seem to resonate still with the footfalls of Richard Burton and David Livingstone and others whose travels and writings first introduced the Dark Continent to a world of mannered gentility hungry for accounts of primitive peoples and exotic beasts. Though the romantic notion of Africa has been tarnished over the years – first by the oppression and exploitation of colonialism, then later by the corruption and conflict of undisciplined self-rule – the attraction of Africa remains much as it must have in those bygone days. For the ultimate wilderness experience, there is simply no other place to go.

A repository of Guinness records, Africa lays unchallenged claim to the largest, the tallest, the fastest, the most animals of any place on earth. More than a thousand species of land creatures coexist on the continent, each providing a vital link in the overall ecosystem. All animals are equal, of course, but some are more equal than others – at least in the judgment of tourists who journey from distant lands to see them. As with tabloid celebrities, however, even the anointed can diminish in appeal over time – for we humans are a fickle lot. Unfailingly, the first game sighted on any safari – even a lowly wildebeest – is greeted with great enthusiasm and expenditure of film. A week or two later, the most winsome of antelopes warrants barely a passing glance.

Predators rarely suffer such slights. Not just because there are few of them relative to prey animals, but because something in their essence strikes a common chord with us, the preeminent predators on the planet. By nature and of necessity, predators are smarter and craftier than the creatures they hunt, their behaviors more intriguing and easy to read. They never fail to fascinate – and we gravitate toward them.

Of the African predators, the big cats are clearly the most charismatic. The smallest and most delicate of the three is the cheetah, a daytime hunter whose sparse numbers make spotting one an always welcome treat. The leopard, though widely dispersed and highly successful, is a creature of the night, sly and shy and rarely seen. The most emblematic of Africa, and the one most readily encountered, is the lion. As top dog among the African cats, the lion fears almost nothing and does little to conceal its presence. If a lion wants to nap at a waterhole, other thirsty animals stay clear. If a lion wants to nap on a road, vehicles wait or go around. If a lion wants to nap, it simply naps – when it wants and where it wants – often for as much as twenty hours in any given day. This propensity for somnolence makes lions a frustrating object of affection. For while it is common enough to find lions, it is difficult to find them doing anything.

We experienced one memorable exception to this general rule during our fifth visit to the Masai Mara in Kenya. At the time, almost all of our Africa trips began with Kenya. It was the safari destination Jerry Dale knew best, and he had spent more than a decade sorting out the best lodging and best game viewing the country had to offer. It was not his only destination, however, and Estelle and I had, by then, accompanied him on exotic side trips into several other African countries. But Kenya had a lingering hold on our hearts. So even though this particular excursion was to center on South Africa and Botswana, where we were meeting up with friends we had induced to make their first visit to the continent, Estelle and I convinced Jerry to fly over a week early so we could spend some time at a couple of our favorite Kenya game haunts before heading south to join the rest of our party. Accompanying us on the warmup were Bill and Sally Snyder, good friends whom I had met on an earlier Jerry Dale safari. To be sure, not all good friends make good traveling companions, but the Snyders' interests and temperaments mesh nicely with Estelle's and my own, and over the years we have enjoyed each other's easy company on regular outings to Africa – a mutual passion – as well as other destinations at home and abroad.

We had left Nairobi just after breakfast and driven five hours over punishing roads to the Masai Mara National Reserve, arriving in time for a late lunch at Keekorok Lodge, our customary accommodation in the park. Situated in southwestern Kenya, along the border shared with Tanzania, the Masai Mara is a region of open plains and rolling hills adjoining the Great Rift Valley – a mammoth trough in the earth's crust defined by jagged fault lines and towering peaks – which slices through Kenya on its indirect course from Ethiopia to Mozambique. Though universally regarded as a five-star wildlife sanctuary, the Masai Mara is modest in size, representing less than a tenth of the vast Serengeti-Mara ecosystem spanning Kenya and Tanzania. The core of the reserve – about a quarter of its 700 square miles – is unblemished by human settlement. The rest is an ecological buffer zone where creatures of the wild share space and resources with traditional Maasai tribespeople. The annual migration of grazing herd animals from the Serengeti to the Masai Mara and back is widely recognized as one of the paramount wildlife spectacles of the world, and during the period spanning July and October, when the itinerant wildebeests and zebras and gazelles are predominantly in Kenya, the Masai Mara has the highest density of resident and transient wildlife anywhere on the planet.

A torrential downpour had swept through just after lunch – coming and going in an hour, as is typical of the place and season – and the moist air was clean and crisp as we embarked on our first game drive of the current safari. Our vehicle, like most in use throughout Kenya, was a Nissan minivan, retrofitted with a hinged pop-top roof that afforded unobstructed open-air views of the terrain and its denizens. I stood in the back with the wind in my face, like an exhilarant dog with its head out the window, and surrendered myself to the sights and smells and sounds of Africa that linger in my soul, beckoning, from journey to journey. Although it was August and the migration was in full swing, late rains had delayed the passage from Tanzania into Kenya. As a result, the grass, which by now should have been chewed to the ground throughout most of the southern Mara, was still tall and lush. We wove through vast herds of wildebeest and zebra grazing their way northward.

Before long, we sighted our first lions – a male and two females lying in the grass a few yards off the road. Our guide, Peter Mwangi – a last-minute replacement for Paul Kariuki, Jerry's regular guide whose young daughter had died in a tragic drowning accident just days before our arrival – pronounced at once that they were mating, though their current level of activity was on par with just about any other lion we were likely to encounter in the daytime. While mating lions are a common enough sighting in Africa, by happenstance we had seen this particular behavior just once, on our first safari, and then only fleetingly and from afar. Sex among lions is a process, not an event. When a lioness comes into estrus, she and her consort seek seclusion from other pride lions for the full four or five days she is ovulating. They do not hunt, they do not eat, they do not leave each other's side. All they do is copulate copiously and rest in between. So what was the second lioness doing here? Was this ambitious male seeking to impregnate two partners at once?

Most often it is the female who initiates the reproductive act. So we were not surprised when one of the lionesses stood and circled the male, then stretched provocatively before plopping down again. The male hauled himself up and grimaced, sniffing for signs of sexual receptivity, and approached her with interest – but the tawny coquette sprang to her feet and darted away. Disinclined to press the matter, the male returned to the other female, who was still in repose, and nuzzled her face and neck. She presented herself compliantly. He mounted her for a few quick thrusts, ritually biting the nape of her neck at the climax, then disengaged without the mutual snarling and swatting that often marks the completion of lion intercourse. The lioness rolled onto her back – instinctively enlisting gravity to aid in the transit of sperm to her ovum – and the spent lion stood for a moment, surveying his domain, before collapsing onto his side to rest up for the next round.

One of the pleasures of traveling with the Snyders is that any topical question can be answered with authority on the spot. While nearly all safari vehicles come equipped with standard-issue field guides for identifying common birds and mammals, Sally comes equipped with a full research library tailored to our itinerary – books on wildlife behavior and geography, national and cultural histories, detailed road maps, and more than anyone cares to know on the subject of plants and trees and even grasses, all stuffed into a bulging backpack that Bill dutifully lugs about from place to place.

The lions had barely hit the turf before Sally was digging through her pack for just the right reference. Moments later she was reading aloud a compilation of facts and figures on the finer points of lion courtship.

Despite their unquestioned strength and vitality, lions are hardly efficient when it comes to reproducing. Only one estrus in five results in offspring – and then only after prodigious effort. Citing her learned source, Sally noted that day and night during mating, lions copulate an average of 2.2 time per hour – an amusingly precise calculation, it seemed to me. We checked our watches. Only twenty minutes till the next performance. Soap opera scenarios ran through our minds. Would the lion be true to his mate? Would he succumb to the other female? We could only stay tuned and see.

After half an hour, we began to suspect that our lions were unaware of the statistics Sally was citing. None of the three was showing the slightest inclination to do anything more energetic than brushing away flies. With little else to command our attention, we scanned our field of view with binoculars, and, to our surprise, discovered a second pair of mating lions a few hundred yards away. Considering their proximity, it was almost certain that the females were from the same pride, thereby related, and that the males were members of a coalition. Coalition partnerships are common among male lions, affording strength in numbers during the often-bloody pursuit and defense of pride territories, thereby insuring coalition vanquishers – often blood relatives, but not necessarily – exclusive breeding privileges with resident females until such time as they themselves are driven away or slain by the next generation of younger and stronger rivals. For the pride male intent upon insuring the continuance of his genetic imprint – the prime directive of all species – no opportunity can afford to be wasted, since even those in coalitions will rarely command a pride for more than two to four years.

We considered driving over to check out the newly spotted duo, but opted to stay put and see what developed with our presumptive ménage à trois. We were coming up on 45 minutes, though, and there was still no sign of anything salacious in the offing. Just shy of the one-hour mark, the male must have realized he was 1.2 copulations behind schedule and could wait no longer for one of his females to make the first move. He stood and approached the one with whom he had earlier mated. She rose to meet him, then turned and crouched accommodatingly into position as he mounted her for another grimacing coital encounter, topped off with a few low growls and a bite on the neck.

We were up and out before sunrise the next morning. Our objective was the Mara River, which cleaves the park from north to south, isolating a region to the west known as the Mara Triangle. Although forage is plentiful to the east and north, many of the migrating herbivores are drawn to the river and the promise of prime grazing beyond, and the fording of the Mara at several habitual points is the dramatic highlight of the months-long trek. In the mad frenzy to cross the often treacherous waterway, hundreds, even thousands, of animals perish every year through drowning and predation by voracious crocodiles lurking beneath the surface. Although the river passage rarely conforms to a reliably predictable timetable, with animals crossing and recrossing in herds or clusters over a period of weeks, the majority of the migrants ought to have crossed long before our arrival in the region. However, since the off-season rains had delayed the migratory advance this year, we were hopeful that we might witness some latecomers making the attempt.

Only a minute or two into our drive we came upon two lions – a male and a female – just a few yards off the access road to the lodge. We could have walked to the spot from breakfast. The lions were sitting side by side in the dew-drenched grass – clearly another mating pair – and as we slowed to a stop before them, the big male glared at us and growled menacingly. Since most lions react with indifference to approaching safari vehicles, we were somewhat surprised by the chilly reception. Vehicles have been a benign presence in the game parks of Kenya for so long that lions and others generally consider them a nonthreatening part of the environment. Jerry observed that he had never had a lion growl at him in the Mara. This one was not having a good day.

We parked a bit farther away than we ordinarily might and the lion settled down. As the sun peeked over the horizon, we heard the distant blast of propane burners firing and turned to watch a hot-air balloon rising above the trees, carrying a basket-full of tourists skyward for a rapturous view of the Mara at daybreak. Our attention returned to the lions when the male got to his feet, stretched and yawned, then circled behind the female and sniffed impolitely. The lioness rose and stepped away from her suitor. He followed close behind, crowding her, obviously intent upon mating. She spun around and snarled at him, then loped away. Unfazed by the rebuff, the lion kept in step with her, his massive head towering

above her slinking hindquarters. Suddenly the lioness dropped to the ground, but rather than presenting herself to him in the customary position, she rolled over on her back in passive rejection. The lion stepped away and roared in frustration.

Usually lion roars are heard from afar – most often at night when the mighty beasts express themselves in a succession of reverberant grunts to warn off territorial intruders or maintain contact with roaming pride members. A full-throated roar can carry for miles. We had heard roaring lions on many occasions, of course, but this was the first we had heard from only twenty feet away. The sound was raw and unattenuated – a paralyzing call of the wild – and with each angry bellow, I could feel the ground vibrating through the tires and frame of our minivan. The display continued for the better part of a minute, each roar expelling a whoosh of vapor from the lion's lungs that hung on the chill morning air before fading away.

Despite this fearsome exhibition, the lioness made no conciliatory response. Having expressed his displeasure to no avail, the lion sought out a nearby bush and scent-marked it with a spray of urine, identifying it and all around it as his, then pawed the ground with his hind legs and lay down a distance apart from the unreceptive female.

Embarrassed for the poor fellow, we left and drove on toward the river, stopping along the way to watch a giraffe and her gangly month-old calf stroll stiff-legged, as though on stilts, across an open pasture. Further on, we encountered a small herd of elephants, including a pair of teenage bulls who sparred playfully and energetically, tusks and trunks intertwined, as others in the family browsed the coarse vegetation nearby. And – to no great surprise by now – we came upon still more mating lions. Were *all* of the Mara lions intent upon copulating for our viewing pleasure? In theory, no. While lionesses within a given pride often come into season synchronously – a common trait among mammalian species whose females live in close society – there is no fixed time of the year when estrus is universal. Our serial encounters with libidinous lions were strictly coincidental.

We continued on to the river where we found no sign of the herds we had hoped to find massed on the bank, ready to cross. Not that we expected to, really, but it was disappointing nonetheless. We stayed for

a while, observing a pod of placid hippos bobbing in the shallows and a couple of crocodiles sunning at the water's edge, then headed back northward in search of more stimulating fare.

The fraternal order of safari guides is a close one. Or so I supposed when we first started ranging through the game parks of East Africa. No matter where we were – on whatever excuse for a road – if we came upon another vehicle on a similar search-and-photograph mission, our guide and his opposite would invariably pull up next to each other, exchange a choreographed secret handshake and converse for a minute or two in an alien tongue before driving on. To a vigilant vulture, aloft on the thermals, we must have looked like a procession of ants, scurrying to and fro with great apparent purpose, yet stopping for an arcane interaction with every passerby along the way.

We realized soon enough, of course, that our guides were exchanging intelligence, sharing notable sightings and locations with each other to help meet the exalted expectations of their clients. But they were cagey about it, rarely sharing with us what they had learned, and any probing on our part was met with genially evasive response. It was a benign conspiracy – a game. We knew it and they knew it. The object for our guides was to convince us that they were near-prescient in their ability to find wildlife. The object for us was to figure out what they were saying to each other and anticipate the next miraculous discovery.

Usually the palaver was in Swahili – the unifying tongue of East Africa that enables scores of tribes, each with a language of its own, to communicate with one another – but our guides were cryptic in its use. Since many tourists pick up at least a smattering of local words and phrases – some of which have passed into the popular lexicon thanks to a beloved Disney movie and stage show – our guides inventively avoided giveaway words in their private exchanges. A favorite guide we used often in Tanzania finally broke the code for us, explaining that he and his fellows eschewed such commonly known appellations as 'simba' in favor of whimsical sobriquets unlikely to be part of a non-native's toddler-level vocabulary. Lions, for example, were denoted by the Swahili word for 'mustache' or 'beard' while leopards were referred to as 'spots.' The subterfuge was good-natured, but the brotherhood of safari guides – in the upper echelon of working-class Africans, due in no small part to the largesse of impressed and gratified clients – had ample incentive to maintain the bread-and-butter myth of individual gamespotting acumen.

The man – or, in rare instances, woman – behind the wheel of the typical safari vehicle is no mere driver. Though the best of the breed can dodge potholes and worse with the aplomb of a slalom medalist while navigating a tangle of unmarked roads and open terrain without getting lost – or letting on, if they do – there is much more to the job than such straightforward skills. To be recognized and licensed as a safari guide, a candidate must be demonstrably proficient at locating and identifying indigenous flora and fauna, be studiously versed in the mysteries of spoor and dung, be both knowledgeable and conversant on wildlife behavior and conservation topics, and, perhaps most important, be able to 'read' a potentially dangerous animal and react in a manner certain to put neither the client nor the creature at risk. In addition, when happenstance warrants, a safari guide must be confidently adept at emergency first aid treatment and makeshift auto mechanics. Guiding is no slouch job.

All of that training and expertise is easily neutralized, however, at least in such tourist meccas as the Masai Mara where time-honored traditions of tracking and gamespotting often give way to something far more mundane. Even a rank novice can scan the horizon for gatherings of safari vehicles, and it is often in this manner that major sightings are revealed. Someone has to be first on the scene, of course, but like the cheetah who must bolt its hard-won kill before the scavengers arrive to usurp it, those first to discover a trophy sighting must relish the solo moment before others arrive to sully the experience.

Vehicular convocations can be ranked by numbers. One or two minivans parked together might be anything or nothing – hardly worth going out of the way to investigate. Three to five ups the ante – could be lions lounging in some shade or scavengers on a carcass. Or possibly elephants – always a favorite – though their size tends to take guesswork out of the equation. Six or more signals a prime attraction – a cheetah on the move, perhaps, or a leopard in a tree, or even the top draw of any safari, a hunt in progress. A purist would reject such second-hand sightings and go for something fresh, but the temptation to investigate what others find captivating is hard to resist. No one lines up to see wildebeest.

And so, near the end of our morning drive, we reacted with interest when, topping a small rise, we sighted several vehicles jockeying for position around a bushy hillock a quarter-mile away. We had been scouring the savanna northwest of Keekorok in search of cheetahs. With most of the migrating herbivores near the park's southern boundary, grass was still tall throughout much of the Mara, but the particular region we were combing had been mowed to the ground by an advance party of grazers that had left behind vast naked areas with just enough surface irregularities to provide cover for stalking predators. Classic cheetah terrain. In amongst lingering wildebeest and zebra we had spotted many Thomson's gazelles – prime cheetah prey – but, as yet, no cheetahs. Had someone else? From afar, we were unable to discern what had drawn the clustered safari vehicles, but as we watched, a stream of others began converging on the spot from all directions. Our cheetah had been found. We were certain of it.

We should have just left. Anyone with an ounce of compassion for the hapless animal whose cover had been compromised would have resisted the lynch-mob urge to throw in with the procession of vehicles bearing down on it. We had done just that on our previous visit to the Mara. Happening upon a dozen or more minivans arrayed like an embattled wagon train around a lone cheetah, we had opted – with an air of righteousness – to continue on without stopping. We had taken the high road.

This time we took the low road. Perhaps it was because we had seen nothing of note in the past hour or so. Perhaps it was to confirm our deduction as to what had been found. Perhaps we were just insensitive louts. Whatever the reason, we set course for the cluster of parked vehicles. Hitherto unseen competition kept streaming into view. We were like stray stars being sucked into a cosmic black hole. A safari romantic at heart, I work to preserve the notion, however illusory, that each wildlife encounter is an intimate and personal gift for me alone. I find it possible to sustain that unlikely fantasy in the presence of others in my vehicle – perhaps even others in a nearby vehicle or two. But the illusion is rather hard to sustain amidst a veritable traffic jam. We pulled up as close to the assemblage as we could, craning to see what was beyond the blockade of early arrivals, and finally spotted a young lioness sitting upright in the tall grass staring back at the paparazzi before her.

Despite the attention, unwanted and unwarranted, the lion showed no signs of distress or agitation – lions rarely *do* – but I felt distress and agitation watching seasoned safari guides, spurred on by pressures to please, pushing their lurching minivans forward and past the creature in cruel determination to afford their clients a fleeting, if memorable closeup. It was the photographic equivalent of a drive-by shooting. Why and how a lion had drawn that much attention was a mystery, a quirk of happenstance, but the onslaught was wholly contemptible – a violation of rules and decency – and we withdrew in distaste and drove away. Would we have done the same had it been a cheetah? I thought so. But I pondered the question as we made our way back to the road.

Though we were finding lions behind every blade of grass on this visit, my only unnerving encounter was with a fellow primate roughly the size of our family dog. We were back at Keekorok, shortly after lunch, and with an hour or more to kill before our afternoon game drive, I grabbed my camera and strolled out to the rustic boardwalk that meanders through the marshy woodland behind the lodge. During previous stays, I had found it a good place to observe monkeys and baboons, which reside in the trees and use the boardwalk and its supports as an ersatz jungle gym.

As a species, we tend to anthropomorphize the creatures around us, ascribing human attributes based upon our interpretation of appearances and behaviors that may have nothing to do with what we suppose. While this tendency might be frowned upon in the scientific community, it is both forgivable and inevitable when the subjects at hand are primates, whose every expression and gesture seem to mirror our own. Monkeys and baboons are the primates most commonly sighted on safari. Though in the wild they are likely to be cautious and aloof, darting aloft or away when approached, they can often be observed openly around lodges and camps, where temptations abound.

I have watched vervet monkeys steal towels and soap left untended by a housekeeper. I have entered a room where companions lay napping to find a blue monkey, which had gained entrance through an open window, gleefully rummaging through their open suitcases. I once saw an olive baboon scale a ten-foot wall in a split second to snatch a dinner roll off the plate of a startled diner. And I have watched others climb stealthily

into parked vehicles and make off with entire box lunches. While such larcenous shenanigans are invariably entertaining, it is disturbing nonetheless to see these creatures corrupted by exposure to humans. More natural behaviors can be seen in the wild, where an hour with a troop of monkeys or baboons is likely to reward the patient observer with poignant displays of feeding and grooming, playing and fighting, mating and parenting – the full gamut of primate behaviors, all echoing our own.

I walked the full length of the boardwalk, out to a small thatched bar which is rarely used as such, and looked back over the open marshland toward the lodge. Our party had stood in the same spot the night before, peering into the darkness with night-vision binoculars, observing little, but being amply entertained by tiny lovelorn frogs performing a mellifluous recital that, in another context, might have been taken for the tinkling of a thousand glass bells. Today there was little to see or hear on the boardwalk, primate or otherwise, so I headed back toward the lodge.

There I discovered why the boardwalk had been vacant. Ranging across the grounds, combing the lawn and flower beds for nourishing plants and insects, were some three dozen olive baboons. Most conspicuous was the dominant male – perfectly coiffed like a best-in-show poodle – attended by two adult females half his size. In wide orbit around him were other subordinate adults, a few subadults of both sexes, and a passel of rambunctious youngsters. I was not surprised to find Estelle among them, camcorder in overdrive as she captured on tape the antic interactions of her favorite video subjects. Estelle is incapable of lowering her camera whenever primates are about – especially the young.

Baboons can be volatile and dangerous, but those around the lodges are accustomed to humans, so I felt somewhat secure in approaching them carefully, watching for any signs that my intrusion was unwelcome. Several youngsters, including a few infants, were cavorting on some rocks bordering one of the flower beds. I unshouldered my camera and crept to within shooting range, then sat on the grass to appear less obtrusive, my knees steadying the lens as I zoomed in on my subjects.

One of the youngsters – a year or so old – must have found my presence intriguing, because he broke away from his playmates and sidled over to me, curiosity tempered with caution. Uncertain of what to expect,

I glanced around to see if I had drawn any other unwelcome attention. This was really closer than I cared to be to a baboon – regardless of age – and I felt a bit vulnerable sitting on the ground, but I thought it unwise at this point to rise and withdraw. The young animal advanced to within arm's reach of me, extended a tiny hand and clasped the toe of my tennis shoe. Not wishing to encourage further interspecies bonding, I retracted my foot, ever so slowly, but the youngster started and leaped back in alarm – and before I was even aware of his proximity, the dominant male charged at me and screeched, his flashing three-inch canines looking like a sabertooth cat's from my eye-level perspective. Had there been time to react rationally, I would have remained still and done my best to look non-threatening. I was certainly in no position to get away. Without thinking, however, I dug my heels into the grass and scuttled backwards, leaving skid marks on the lawn as I sought distance from the angry male. For-tunately, the baboon had made a mock charge, and once he determined that I was sufficiently intimidated by his display he promptly returned to the business of gathering foodstuffs. It took longer for the flash flood of adrenaline that had swept through my system to subside. I decided I had enough baboon photos for the day.

We set out on our afternoon game drive. Just down the road from the lodge stood three vehicles huddled around a large boulder. Atop it was the grumpy lion whose petulant tantrum we had witnessed that morning. Next to him was the lioness whose disinterest had enraged him. Both were asleep. We took a quick vote and determined we could live with-out witnessing another lion assignation. Enough was enough ... or maybe not. We were about to continue on when Estelle noticed the lion's eyes opening. She thought we should wait and see what developed. We agreed – but only after hazing her a bit. No sooner had we selected a vantage point than the male got up and nuzzled the female, who responded much more obligingly than she had at dawn. She stood and brushed past him, flicking her tale in his face, then turned and presented herself for coupling. Oblivious to the ogling spectators encircling the boulder, the earnest ex-hibitionists engaged in a typically brief tryst accompanied by whispered love-growls from both participants. When the male withdrew, the female turned on him with a snarl and delivered a sharp swat with her forepaw.

Then she collapsed on the rock and rolled onto her back. The lion stood for a bit, posing for photos and approbation, then flopped down nearby. Scarcely five minutes had passed from the time we pulled up. We had seen displays of lion lust at almost every turn. Where next, I wondered? On the verandah at the lodge?

Anxious to avoid a repeat of the morning's sorry spectacle, we set out for an expanse of parkland Peter considered unlikely to be overrun with safari vehicles. With no particular objective in mind, other than to have a more uncorrupted wilderness experience, we drove for quite some time without seeing much of anything, animal or human. Then, up ahead, we spotted the dust-cloud signature of an approaching vehicle. Even from a distance we could tell it was not the rolling shoebox we were accustomed to seeing in these parts. This was something far more iconic – a Land Rover. A real Land Rover. Not one of those prissy designer models more at home in a Beverly Hills driveway than on the plains of Africa, but a battered old-style classic, rugged and angular, stylelessly functional, dressed with jerry cans, winches and shovels and a textured patina of powdery dirt, splattered bugs and caked-on mud. Now here was a safari vehicle. John Wayne could have roped rhinos from this baby.

The Land Rover slowed to a stop as we closed on it. From his accent, I took the driver to be either an expatriate Briton or a white native Kenyan who, based on demeanor and appearance, had spent much of his life in the bush – quite likely a guide. He conversed with Peter in fluent Swahili, then – aware that we would otherwise be kept in the dark – addressed the rest of us. A mile or so back, he revealed, was a lioness on the hunt – and she had just missed a kill. At last, we thought, a lion with something on its mind besides sex.

Off-road driving is forbidden in most of Africa's national parks and reserves. The reason is evident, the logic unassailable. Animals and plant life, even insects and soil essential to sustaining the delicate ecosystems, would not be well served by convoys of safari vehicles chomping through grasslands and woodlands like threshing machines. In some places, however – like the Masai Mara and the Serengeti – where vast open spaces are deemed resilient enough to withstand a degree of vehicular trauma, cautious off-road driving is permitted, except within a specified radius around lodges and campgrounds where high-volume traffic would quickly pound the area to dust.

Upon casual consideration, it seems reasonable to assume that environmental harm might be minimized if off-road vehicles followed in the tracks of others that have ventured before them – but such is not the case. Experienced guides recognize that nature will heal a single tire trail in reasonably short order, but repeat passages over the same bruised terrain will soon produce a permanent scar. Better to leave a reparable, if temporarily unsightly, network of single-use tracks than forge, in effect, a whole new system of secondary roads. That being the prevailing wisdom, as we approached the area to which we had been directed, we were not surprised to see several fresh tire trails cutting through the tall grass abutting the roadside. Two, presumably, had been made by our informant – one in and one out – but another vehicle or two had evidently followed or preceded him.

At least it was not a mob scene. We set a course and plunged into the waist-high grass. From a short rise just off the road, the savanna spread out before us and we could see a dusty brown mass of grunting wildebeest, many hundred strong, salt-and-peppered with clusters of zebras. Presumably this was an advance party that had only recently trekked into the region, since the area showed little evidence of the mass nonstop grazing that would, in a few short weeks, reduce a year's growth of forage to little more than ground-stubble throughout much of the Masai Mara.

Zebras and wildebeest often frequent the same grazing areas and show little hesitance to intermingle. Zebras find security in numbers in the company of the much more plentiful wildebeest, and wildebeest – not the brightest link in the food chain – benefit from their striped brethren's heightened alertness to predatory dangers. Also, there is little or no competition for food, since zebras prefer the stalky upper parts of the plains grasses while wildebeest opt for the leafier lower portions left behind. For this reason, it is typically zebras that lead the migration into new areas.

Prowling the open expanses around the herd were two minivans, almost certainly on a quest for the lioness that had been reported to us. As they had obviously not found her, we joined in the search, sweeping in a wide arc around the grazing herbivores and peering into the tall grass that, at this time of year, was virtually the same golden-orange color as our quarry. Before long we spotted her. Or she spotted us. As we inched our way through the veil of camouflage, the lioness popped up no more than ten feet in front of us. She had been sprawled in the grass, invisible before she announced her presence. The lioness rose quickly, loped out of our path, then flopped down again to resume her siesta. If this was the one that had attempted a kill, she was obviously in no hurry to try again. A failed hunt can be exhausting. Once we came to a stop, it was evident to those in the other vehicles that we had found something, and they soon pulled up beside us to gaze down on the lazing cat.

Daytime hunting is uncommon among lions, which customarily opt for cool night air and the cover of darkness to boost their chances of securing a meal. But with every somnolent lion sighting comes the lingering hope that, perhaps just this once, the indolent beast will get up from its nap and go find something to kill. More often than not, however, midday exertion comes principally in the form of ear waggles or flicks of the tail aimed at shooing away irksome insects. Having spent far too many hours observing lions engaged in such soporific inactivity, we decided to abandon this particular stakeout and see what else was about.

Up the road a mile or more, we succumbed to the lure of two parked vehicles and stopped to investigate. A narrow stream had sliced a ditch along the roadway, about ten yards away, and on the near bank was a bushy tree with a fresh wildebeest carcass tucked underneath. Only the partially severed hindquarters showed evidence of having been eaten. Also on the near bank stood a lioness, her back to us, peering into the tall grass on the opposite side of the stream. We did the same — and were rewarded with fleeting glimpses of a second lion and what would soon be confirmed as four young cubs. We were still trying to determine an exact count when the curtain of grass parted and all five animals trooped into view. The lioness in the lead stepped gingerly through the shallow water and joined her companion on our side of the stream. The year-old cubs padded back and forth at the water's edge, wanting to follow but lacking the nerve. After a few minutes, the adults crossed back over and all of the lions vanished into the grassy thickets on the opposite bank.

The minivans that had been on the scene before us soon departed, but we remained behind, thinking it odd that lions would abandon a kill that had barely been touched. We speculated that the adults — usually unflappable, but cautious perhaps with their cubs in tow — might have been startled off the kill by the arrival of the first vehicles. Hoping the lions would return to feed if given sufficient space, we backed off a few car lengths and parked on a rise with a clear view of the carcass. We waited. And waited. But the lions did not return.

Our patience unrewarded, we doubled back in the direction of the lodge, thinking we might make a short detour to check on the slumbering lioness we had abandoned earlier. The sun was dropping toward the horizon, and a hungry predator might well conclude that it was time to get started on the night's quest for food. We could always hope. A few minutes later we were surveying the grassy plain we had quit an hour before. The wildebeest and zebras were still grazing in tight formation, seemingly undisturbed, but there were no safari vehicles anywhere in sight, only paired tire trails radiating from the area where we had last seen them parked. Did this bode well for us — or not? At the point where the tracks converged we had our answer. The lioness was gone.

Hoping to see a hunt — perhaps even our first-ever kill — we began combing the open expanse between us and the herd, stopping often to scan the obscuring grass with binoculars and the naked eye for signs of our lioness on the prowl. We focused most on the likely approaches to any wildebeest, especially young ones, that had wandered apart from the main body of the herd. During one of our stops, I happened to notice that the light breeze fanning the grass was coming from behind us. Supposing that a lion, given the choice, would approach its prey from the downwind direction, I suggested that we circle around the herd and continue our search from there.

Within minutes of doing so, we spotted the lioness sitting upright in the gently undulating grass, scrutinizing the herd from about fifty yards away. Were it not for the distinctive black patches behind her ears — a genetic adaptation that helps lions keep tabs on one another during cooperative hunting — we would never have spotted her. The line of her form was obscured by the shimmering grass, and her coloration was all but identical. It seemed a perfect scenario for a successful hunt.

No one, not even our guide, had challenged my proposal that we reposition. Only later would I learn that no evidence exists to suggest that hunting lions pay any attention to wind direction, despite the fact that field studies confirm a higher success rate when they do approach prey from downwind. Either I was lucky or this lioness was smarter than the average bear.

Hunting is not a sport for lions, or any predator, so a lion scouting a herd of prey animals will not be looking for the most worthy opponent. Somehow aware that the nutritional value of a strong, healthy animal is no better than that of a weak, sickly one, the prudent predator will spend time studying a herd in order to single out the very old, the very young, the injured or the ailing. Our lioness was doing just that — and we did the same, scanning the herd with binoculars in an effort to predict which animal, if any, would be chosen as a target. But vulnerability is not the only governing factor. Though opportunistic hunters in general, lions often demonstrate decided preferences when it comes to prey — and frequently these preferences are at cross purposes with the notion of selecting an easy mark. Whether because of habit or training or taste, many lion prides show a collective preference for Cape buffalo, among the largest and meanest animals in Africa, seeking them out even when less hazardous prey is abundant. Others seem to favor warthogs — formidable opponents and a minimal meal to boot — often spending hours trying to dig them out of their underground dens. One pride we encountered even specialized in taking young elephants — very risky business considering how protective the adults are of their offspring. The lioness we were watching here evidently had preferences, as well. After thoroughly measuring her prospects, she elected to pass on any number of likely wildebeest targets and instead began circling the herd in the direction of a dozen zebras grazing somewhat apart on the far side.

Once we established where the lioness was heading, we made a wide loop around the herd and headed for the zebras, hoping to position ourselves at a good vantage point from which to observe how the drama would play out. Though we could not see it until we were upon it, a seldom-used vehicle track — two hard-packed ruts through encroaching grass — ran between the main herd and the target splinter group. We pulled onto the track and eased our way toward the zebras, coming to a stop about thirty yards from them. We stood and gazed out from the open rooftop with anticipation. The wildebeest, blithely unaware that a predator was nearly in their midst, continued grazing. The zebras, generally more alert than their wildebeest companions, also continued grazing.

We scoured the approach, looking for signs of the huntress moving in our direction. But there were none — only the hypnotic swaying of the tall grass. Patience was clearly in order, but we were already questioning our intercept strategy. Had we misread the lion's intentions? Had she resumed her nap or targeted another animal? Should we go looking for her? No — best to stay put. Any other course might disrupt the hunt — if there was a hunt. Which for us was looking unlikely. The sun was just above the horizon now, and park regulations required that we be off the roads and in our lodge well before dark. The lioness had no curfew and no reason at all to hurry. She would wait for full darkness and better advantage — and we would be far away. It was a familiar scenario.

Then we saw her. Head down, eyes locked straight ahead, she was moving slowly and deliberately, in a ground-hugging crouch, toward the zebras bunched behind us. Without the black ear patches viewable from the rear to signal her presence, it was difficult to follow her progress, especially in the dwindling light. Only the faint line of her arched back was visible through the grass. Every few yards, she stopped and peered ahead cautiously.

When the lioness reached the track, twenty yards away, she veered onto one of the worn tire trails and crept in our direction. With an unobstructed course and tall grass all around, she could close the distance between herself and the zebras quickly and with minimal chance of detection. She was still in her tight crouch position, intensely focused, and as she advanced toward us, I had the eerie sensation that it was we who were being stalked. Then I realized that she was using our vehicle as a blind, keeping it between her and her prey. Peter whispered for us to close our windows. As I was in the rear of the vehicle, closest to the lioness, I ducked down slowly to avoid startling her and gently slid the side window closed just as she stepped off the track and passed by, only a foot or two from me. I stood up again and faced forward. The lioness crept back into the grass-lined ruts just ahead of us and laid down, head erect like a golden sphinx, listening for signs that her movement had betrayed her to the zebras. She lay very still for several minutes.

Most seasoned safari guides have seen just about everything, so even the prospect of a successful lion kill is not always enough to command their full attention. Often as not, while clients are engrossed in a prolonged sighting, the compleat guide will be focused elsewhere, proving his worth by casting about for the next big attraction, or even a lesser one that might otherwise be missed. So I was not altogether surprised when Peter turned to us and announced quietly that he had spotted a rhino in the far pasture. Hesitant to divert our attention from the lioness for even a moment, we nonetheless grabbed our binoculars and sighted along Peter's pointed finger. Sure enough, there was a black rhinoceros browsing on a cluster of small bushes some 200 yards away. Ordinarily a rhino would be the highlight of any game drive. Once common throughout much of Africa, they had, in recent decades, been poached to the brink of extinction for their signature horns. Only thirty remained in the whole Masai Mara. In previous trips to the region, we had seen rhinos on only two occasions. Now, with daylight on the wane, we had to choose between the critically endangered herbivore and the common carnivore about to make a kill. It was really no contest.

After a few moments, the lioness rose slightly and peered through the grass. The zebras, still only thirty yards from us, were oblivious to the predator stalking them. The lioness studied them for several minutes, perhaps determining which would be the most vulnerable. Then she crept forward a bit, just a few feet, and laid down again. After a long pause, she repeated the maneuver. She was now halfway between us and the zebras, inching her way closer and closer to her quarry, intent upon getting to within striking distance without losing the element of surprise. No one in the vehicle spoke or whispered or even breathed. We were riveted.

Still, we were barely prepared when it happened. In a flash, the lioness was afoot and bounding through the grass. The zebras, instantly aware, bolted in all directions. In three or four giant strides, the lioness halved the distance between herself and the nearest zebra – and then it was over. For no discernible reason, she broke off the charge and stopped dead in her tracks. Tasting failure but nothing else, the huntress watched impassively as her quarry danced out of reach. Then she turned and walked away.

We pondered what we had seen all the way back to Keekorok. The hunt had been a drama of the highest order, one of the highlights of our Africa adventures, but with a less than gratifying outcome. The lioness had been so diligent in her stalking and so close to her quarry that a kill seemed inevitable. Yet she had halted in midstride without, it appeared, having given it her full effort. It was difficult to fathom. We could only suppose that something about the unfolding action had convinced her, within seconds, that her next meal would not be at the expense of this particular group of zebras. Thus aware, she had stopped at once to preserve her energy for another, more fortuitous, attempt.

By now, the afterglow of sunset had dissolved into twilight, draining our surroundings of color and leaving only a textured monotone in its place. We were a good half-hour from Keekorok, and the time remaining until the park curfew was considerably less than that. Risking a harsh reprimand if caught out after hours, Peter nonetheless detoured across the gray grassland toward the browsing rhino, pulling up close enough for us to get a good view without annoying the beast. With the bulk and functionality of a tank, the black rhino has a reputation for short-fused aggressiveness not to be ignored, but this dusty old bull, sporting a formidable pair of horns, showed little interest in our arrival. Aged enough to have recalled the days when hundreds of his kind roamed the Masai Mara, he was now a rare and endangered relic of a bygone era. We paid our respects to the old survivor and set a hurried course through the gathering darkness toward our lodge.

MATING LIONS
Masai Mara National Reserve, Kenya

LIONESS
Ngorongoro Crater, Tanzania

SPOTTED HYENA
Masai Mara National Reserve, Kenya

LION ON WILDEBEEST KILL
Masai Mara National Reserve, Kenya

VULTURES ON WILDEBEEST CARCASS
Masai Mara National Reserve, Kenya

WHITE-HEADED VULTURE
Masai Mara National Reserve, Kenya

MARABOU STORK
Mount Kenya Safari Club, Kenya

HYENA NURSING CUBS
Masai Mara National Reserve, Kenya

BAT-EARED FOXES
Serengeti National Park, Tanzania

ZEBRA STALLIONS SPARRING
Serengeti National Park, Tanzania

BURCHELL'S OR PLAINS ZEBRAS
Masai Mara National Reserve, Kenya

GREVY'S ZEBRAS
Samburu National Reserve, Kenya

GERENUKS
Samburu National Reserve, Kenya

ELEPHANT AND DOUM PALM
Samburu National Reserve, Kenya

AGAMA LIZARD
Masai Mara National Reserve, Kenya

CROCODILE FISHING
Tsavo West National Park, Kenya

CHEETAH FEEDING ON
PREGNANT THOMSON'S GAZELLE
Masai Mara National Reserve, Kenya

ELEPHANT AND CATTLE EGRET IN MARSH
Amboseli National Park, Kenya

ELEPHANTS
Masai Mara National Reserve, Kenya

LIONS ON KOPJE
Serengeti National Park, Tanzania

LIONESS
Masai Mara National Reserve, Kenya

YELLOW-BILLED OXPECKERS ON CAPE BUFFALO
Masai Mara National Reserve, Kenya

ELEPHANTS AND CALF NAPPING
Amboseli National Park, Kenya

Where the Antelope Roam

No one embarks on a trip to Africa without some notion of what to expect. Certainly not someone whose dreamy-eyed youth had been spent in the thrall of Edgar Rice Burroughs and H. Rider Haggard and many a homegrown Hollywood potboiler set in the jungles and swamps and plains of that beckoning far-distant place. Africa was not my only passion, to be sure, and somewhere along the way, in the manner of most childhood obsessions, it disappeared, with dinosaurs and Flash Gordon and movie monsters, into the dusty attic of my maturing psyche – treasured in a nostalgic sense, never to be discarded, but of no perceivable import in the future I envisioned. It remained up there, dormant and moldering for twenty-some years, until Estelle and I began planning our first safari and I rediscovered its potent hold on me. I was under no delusion, of course, that I had ever known the real Africa, only a wildly romanticized likeness of it, but in the countdown months before our departure, I made a conscious choice not to recast my lingering youthful impressions by immersing myself in the geography and the culture and all of the things serious travelers seem to do before a serious trip. I wanted Africa itself to do that. I wanted the experience to wash over me, undiluted, rather than have my perceptions of it directed by someone else's. Whatever unfolded, I knew that Africa would not – could not – disappoint.

On that first trip, we journeyed overland through the game parks of Kenya, sampling a diversity of scenic splendors, from rolling savannas and snow-capped peaks to dense bush country and terra-cotta deserts and sprawling soda lakes. And whatever the surroundings, hostile or hospitable, wildlife was everywhere. We saw all of the signature beasts of the realm, plus a remarkable number that were previously unknown to me – a cornucopia of mammals and birds and reptiles. What I failed to interpolate was the interconnectedness of it all. Even at that time, I nurtured a degree of disdain for checklist tourists who gauge the success of a safari by the number of confirmed sightings logged in the pages of their trusty field guides – but, in a sense, perhaps because of my opting to let Africa reveal itself to me on its own terms, that first safari was somewhat of a checklist experience. I was just unaware of it.

I returned from that venture with a suitcase full of books and maps, and promptly established the Africa wing of my already overstuffed home library. I began haunting the nature and travel sections of bookstores far and wide. I searched through television listings for programs and documentaries on Africa. I rooted through aging stacks of *National Geographic*, too precious to share the fate of lesser magazines, for anything on the continent and its photogenic wildlife. My childhood passion for Africa had been rekindled. By the time I returned to Kenya for a second outing, I was better prepared to see Africa as much more than the sum of its parts.

A grim encounter underscored my awareness. We were on a morning game drive in the Masai Mara. Our route took us west from Keekorok Lodge toward the Mara River, past and through herds of wildebeest and zebra extending out to the horizon. High above the river ahead, from a distance, we noticed dozens of vultures circling purposefully and, with wings outstretched and talons dangling, plummeting earthward like paratroopers. We continued on to the river crossing, a narrow concrete bridge with no railings, and eased out onto its crumbling surface. Just below us, on the opposite bank, were some two dozen wildebeest carcasses lodged along the river's edge, most attended by hungry vultures tearing at the remains and squabbling noisily amongst themselves. Marabou storks strode on stilt-legs through the shallows, trolling for bits of carrion but kept at bay by the vultures' uncharitable aggressiveness. Other vultures of various species lined the riverbank, watching and waiting with seeming politeness for an opportunity to partake of the grisly repast. As the skies emptied, there would be more. We knew at once that we were witnessing the aftermath of a mass river crossing somewhere upstream, early that morning or the previous day, and that these sodden wildebeests were among those trampled and drowned in the attempt.

At the time, I was oblivious to anything but the moment, fascinated by the spectacle. Only later, on reflection, did it challenge my perception of Africa. There was the Africa I had gleaned from books and magazines and films, and there was the Africa I had gleaned from observation and experience – and somehow I had failed to marry the two into an aggregate view. I had known from the first day of my first safari that I would return to Africa. But my initial conviction that I could be wholly content revisiting, over and over, the same gloriously remote places and embracing whatever each presented to me was abruptly overturned by the sight of screeching scavengers feeding on what, mere hours before, had been vibrant and robust antelopes. I was now compelled to recognize that for all of its stand-alone wonders, Africa was much more than a succession of picture-perfect tableaux, neat and discrete. It was a vast stage upon which great, messy dramas were enacted. With our two visits to the

Masai Mara, we had observed tantalizing segments of one such drama. I wanted to witness it all – and for that, we would have to migrate south with our principal players.

Migration is a worldwide phenomenon driven by collective memory and instinctive response. Birds do it. Mammals do it. Even fish and amphibians and insects do it. Triggered by seasonal changes and a range of environmental stimuli, organisms of every classification and description undergo choreographed journeys – often long, often arduous, often deadly – in mass pursuit of sustenance or breeding opportunities or more temperate climes. Although certain species of birds are the undisputed front-runners in terms of navigation and endurance – one makes an annual transpolar round trip – only one mass migration has captivated the human imagination enough to have earned upper-case designation, and that is the annual Great Migration of wildebeest and zebra, nearly two million strong, looping endlessly through the Serengeti ecosystem of Kenya and Tanzania.

I first set foot on Tanzanian soil during a game drive in the Masai Mara. Had there not been a concrete obelisk to denote where Kenya ended and Tanzania began, I would never have known. There was no gate, no fence, no guard post, not even a sign – only tacit understanding on the part of our guide that we could go no further. Although the adjoining nations do nothing to obstruct the flow of migrant herbivores – as has been done with disastrous consequences elsewhere in Africa – no such consideration is shown to tourists for whom the border has been closed for almost thirty years. Anyone wishing to legitimately stand on both sides of the invisible line I straddled that day would have to endure a succession of charter flights or a minimum of two long days of difficult driving. We decided to do just that on our next trip to Africa.

My first foray into Tanzania proper was to have been the first for Jerry Dale, as well, a trial-run addendum to one of his customary Kenya safaris, and we had planned it together. At the last minute, however, Jerry had to back out when the Tanzania government refused him a visa because his passport had reflected previous visits to apartheid South Africa. So I, as the only one remaining who had ever been in Africa prior to this outing, became the de facto leader of our tiny expeditionary contingent, which consisted of Bill and Sally Snyder – on the first of our many trips together – plus my friend and colleague Bill Lindsay. It was a whirlwind extravaganza of the sort I refuse to do now – five destinations in seven days, with a lot of rough driving in between – and it was not even a choice time of year since the migration was in Kenya. But the Tanzania sampler was as exhilarating as it was exhausting, and it cemented my resolve to return with Estelle, who, recuperating from recent surgery, had withdrawn from the long-planned trip while insisting persuasively that I go without her.

The Serengeti plain owes much of its topographical character to the chain of extinct volcanoes that defines its southeastern boundary. A prolonged period of volcanic activity some three million years ago blanketed the region with a thick layer of ash and debris that leveled out the surrounding landscape and left an 'endless plain' from which, in the language of the Maasai, the Serengeti takes its name. Only clusters of weathered granite outcrops, scattered throughout the region, disrupt the utter flatness of the southern plain, which supports seasonal grasses in abundance, but little else in the way of vegetation. Farther to the north and west, where distance diminished the geomorphic influence of the volcanoes, broad expanses of bush country and woodland coexist amongst seasonal and permanent waterways.

Seasons in the Serengeti are distinguished, not by temperature, but by precipitation. Typically there are two wet seasons each year. The short rains of November and December draw the great herds of wildebeest and zebra to the southern short-grass plains whose rich volcanic soil erupts with nutritious new growth. There they remain, giving birth to their young, until the grasses are grazed to stubble. With the coming of the long rains in March and April, the herds move north into the central Serengeti and then, after a spell, into the western corridor which extends almost to Lake Victoria. In the open areas, they forage and fight and mate before pushing through the northern woodlands and across the Mara River into Kenya, where they subsist on the bounty of the Masai Mara until the year-end short rains draw them south once again.

Many books and films have chronicled the Great Migration – most by writers and photographers and documentarians who have had the good fortune to follow the spectacle for at least one, often many, complete cycles. Certainly no two- or three-week safari could be expected to reveal the full spectrum of an epic pilgrimage that unfolds over the course of an entire year. But with persistence and planning, I hoped in time to witness the elements I thought would at least capture its essence. Key among these was the wildebeest calving season in which nearly every female wildebeest of age gives birth within just a few short weeks. This synchronized calving insures that, by virtue of overwhelming numbers alone, the next generation of wildebeest will survive the intense predation of the young and vulnerable that occurs during this time of plenty for the region's many carnivores. Our first attempt to witness this pivotal event was too early by a matter of weeks. A second attempt was likewise premature. Trying to time a few days' visit to a particular short-term occurrence – half a world away and months in advance – was a fool's exercise, as I was well on my way to recognizing. Just about anything – an errant rainstorm – could disrupt nature's tentative timetable. On three separate occasions we tried planning safaris in Kenya to coincide with the migrant herds' spectacular crossing of the Mara River, a churning melee in which wildebeest and zebra by the thousands risk terrible death drowning or flailing in the jaws of resident crocodiles. Despite this being an intermittent, ongoing event of considerable duration, we managed to miss the mark all three times. This was hardly grounds for serious disappointment, however. Jerry Dale, who has spent more time on safari than anyone I know, once observed that even after a hundred or more outings, he never failed to see or experience something exceptional for the very first time. I found the same to be true.

Still, it was always tempting to plan an African safari with the hope, if not the expectation, of witnessing a signature event. Having consistently missed the river crossing in Kenya and the calving season in Tanzania, I decided for our next sojourn to revisit Tanzania, but at a different time of the year, in the hope of seeing the elusive river crossing from the Tanzanian side as the great herds pushed southward in October and November. Estelle and I had honeymooned in Africa, spent a couple of anniversaries there, plus a birthday or two – any occasion would do – but this particular trip was to be a wedding gift to our son and daughter-in-law who had married a few months earlier. Two years prior, recognizing that his days as a single man were numbered and wanting him to share in something that had come to mean so much to me, I had introduced Gregg to Africa. It had been just the two of us – one of those father-son bonding things – and I was pleased that he had responded to the experience as enthusiastically as I. Near the end of our stay in Tanzania, he had told me he was planning to ask Rachael, his longtime girlfriend, to marry him, suggesting that the Africa experience had somehow prompted the decision. The romance of Africa prevailed, and with Rachael set to join our family of inveterate safariphiles, Estelle and I convinced ourselves that it would be downright unwelcoming for our new daughter-in-law to be the only one with nothing to say when talk turned to Africa.

The cornerstone of our three-week family safari was to be an eleven-day excursion through the Serengeti, during which we would – to the extent possible – trace the full course of the Great Migration in Tanzania. Like most of our African trips, this one was planned almost a year in advance – which, in this particular instance, imposed even more than the usual measure of uncertainty. For a period of nearly five months ending earlier in the year, East Africa had been deluged with rain as a result of the worst El Niño in a century. Resistant to meaningful forecast, El Niño phenomena occur every few years when shifting warm-water currents in the eastern Pacific Ocean alter climatological conditions worldwide, often severely, bringing torrential rains to some regions and extreme drought to others. This most recent occurrence brought widespread flooding and mudslides to the California coast, evoking relentless media coverage of local misfortunes, but only the sparest footnote mentions of equally grave happenings elsewhere in the world. I wondered what effect El Niño would have on our safari. We had planned it so as to be in the Serengeti at the start of the short rains, when the herds typically begin trekking south into Tanzania, but with the glut of off-season precipitation this year, would 'typical' still apply?

We began to get a sense of what El Niño had wrought when we arrived at our first destination. Lake Manyara – one of four soda lakes in the central Rift Valley whose algae-rich waters nourish flamingos by the millions – lies midway along the principal driving route connecting Arusha, our point of departure, and the vast Serengeti ecosystem to the north-

west. The smallish national park that adjoins the lake is noted for its abundance of elephants and buffalo and baboons, and for its lions oddly disposed to lounging in trees. But the Manyara we had known from previous visits was now strikingly different. By this time of year, at the end of what would normally have been a long dry season, the lake should have evaporated down to its smallest size – but it was still very much larger than I had ever seen it. That was apparent as we approached from atop the Rift Valley escarpment. Upon entering the park below, however, we discovered the full consequence of the lake's extraordinary state. After passing through the tropical forest beyond the main entrance we emerged onto what had heretofore been acacia woodlands and grassy floodplains to find that the aberrant overflow had swallowed just about everything. The network of driving tracks that wound through the wildlife habitats was largely underwater – as were the bases of most of the trees. Much of the wildlife had vanished – including the flamingos – and before long, the woodlands, too, would be gone. When we next returned to the area, a few years later, the water had withdrawn to its customary confines – but not before the majestic acacias had perished. Only their skeletal remains still stood. The park had been eerily transformed.

Our first view of the Serengeti was from atop Ngorongoro where the road tracing the crater rim slips off the western slope and plunges into a primal world of unspoiled beauty and superabundant wildlife. Due to generally more rugged terrain, the two-wheel-drive minivans that prevail throughout Kenya are rarely seen in Tanzania. Instead, we were installed in a spacious new Toyota Land Cruiser accessorized with removable roof panels and other accouterments of the safari trade. At the wheel was Gervas Lubuva, a personable and resourceful young guide who had served us well on our first two Tanzania outings. At the end of our last safari together, I had given him one of my cameras and a telephoto lens, and he had kept in touch by mail, sending me photos from time to time. When he left the safari company we customarily used in Tanzania and, with a partner, set out on his own, he wrote urging me to utilize his new company when we next returned to Tanzania. And so we did. Pleased to see us again, and anxious to make an especially good impression, Gervas was determined to surpass our expectations at every turn.

We descended toward the Serengeti plain, past traditional Maasai villages comprised of mud-and-stick huts arranged in circles and fenced with thorn brush to discourage predators from abducting cattle at night. On the slopes outside these enclosures, young boys tended family herds, which are the principal measure of wealth in Maasai society. Men, draped in bright reds and blues and leaning on spears, loitered in the shade socializing, while women and girls, adorned with colorful beadwork, toted water or firewood to and from the compound. An enterprising few, in full tribal regalia, stood at the roadside, signaling their willingness to pose for photos – for a suitable fee. We gave them a friendly wave, but continued on, not stopping until we leveled out past the Ngorongoro foothills and beheld our first eye-level view of the fabled Serengeti.

The most distinguishing feature of the southern Serengeti is its utter lack of distinguishing features. Flatness prevails in all directions – so much so that from choice vantage points the earth's curvature is discernible at the far horizon. The lower portion of the plain lies within the Ngorongoro Conservation Area – a limited-use reserve where the semi-nomadic Maasai share the land and its resources with resident wildlife – while the upper portion, free of human settlements, lies wholly protected within Serengeti National Park.

Our last two visits had been timed to the great herds' presence in this region, when the range was lush and green and animals could be seen from horizon to horizon. Unlike the vast expanses farther north, where tall grasses predominate, the southern Serengeti, hampered by subsurface hardpan, produces only a short carpet of shallow-rooted grass, quickly renewable by rotational grazing which stimulates growth. Now, even with the extreme rains months before, the plains were parched and hostile to all but a few dry-season denizens such as Grant's gazelles and ostriches. Only the bleached bones of large herbivores, strewn about like jacks, suggested that for nearly half of every year the region bounteously supports the million or more wildebeest and zebras that now stood poised, somewhere to the north, awaiting the seasonal short rains that trigger the long journey back. With barely a stop, we motored across the dusty expanse, passed under the archway signpost into Serengeti National Park, and continued on another dozen miles to the official park entrance at Naabi Hill.

Anywhere else it would scarcely warrant a name, but in these parts Naabi Hill is a landmark rivaling Mount Kilimanjaro. Rising out of the interminable flatlands, it is a beacon of nonconformity, an oasis of rock and foliage from whose squat summit much of the lower Serengeti can be surveyed. While Gervas attended to park fees and other formalities, we broke out the box lunches we carried and settled onto a low stone wall to eat.

After lunch, we continued along the main road toward the central Serengeti. Though the region was still predominantly flat, taller grasses now prevailed, making it seem less like a tabletop environment. The landscape began to take on real character when a cluster of kopjes came into view. These curious granite outcrops – shaped by wind and rain – are the protruding summits of ancient hills interred long ago in volcanic ash. Varying in size from meager to mammoth, they support a diversity of vegetation and provide both habitat and refuge for a wide range of creatures.

We were nearing the kopjes when we came upon our first large predators. Just off the road, in the sparse shade of a thornbush thicket, a pride of seven lions eyed us disinterestedly as we pulled to a stop. Though they were full-grown, or nearly so, all but the two ranking females were subadults, still bearing remnants of the spots that serve as camouflage for young cubs. One was a male. While he had not yet attained the body mass of a mature male lion – which can weigh half again as much as a female – his head was already larger than his pride mates' and he was beginning to grow the mane that would fully distinguish him.

One of the pleasures of sharing Africa with others is experiencing it anew through novice eyes. Estelle and I – even Gregg – were safari veterans. Sleeping lions? No big deal. But for Rachael, each experience was pure and fresh, and it was a delight sharing her excitement at seeing these formidable felines in the wild, just a few steps from our vehicle. Even though they were doing little more than napping and passing time until the cool of evening, every tail flick and ear twitch was a captivating event. If one took a playful swat at another, as happened, or gnawed on a twig, or simply shifted to make use of a rock as a chin rest, that was high drama – or as close as we would come to it. By sundown, when the

real drama commenced, we would be long gone.

A mile or two up the road we had a second significant sighting. On a termite mound, a dozen yards away, lay a female cheetah in a stock cheetah pose – flat on her side, head upright, relaxed yet alert. Daytime hunters, cheetahs often use termite mounds as lookout posts when seeking prey, but this one seemed no more inclined to imminent exertion than the lions we had left. She was simply resting. We watched for a while and then noticed some peripheral movement. A cheetah cub – only three or four months old – emerged from behind the mound and, with a measure of effort, scrabbled up the side to join its mother.

The canopy above had been shifting from blue to gray all afternoon, and the photographer in me was mourning the loss of sunshine. Beyond that, I gave it little consideration until Gervas pointed out a bank of storm clouds racing across the plain behind us. Curtains of rain rippled beneath. As the storm progressed, shards of lightning snapped to the ground, followed by waves of reverberant thunder. Nothing about this seemed terribly unusual. Weather in the Serengeti is mercurial, particularly in the afternoons. Out of nowhere, dark stormy clouds swallow sunny blue skies. Heavy rains fall and then stop. Sunny skies return. All in an hour or less. That was common. But Gervas thought what was advancing on us had the makings of a serious storm – the first of the season – and he said we should hasten to our lodge. We were still far away.

The storm overtook us just before sundown, or what would have been had there been any sun. Under the best of circumstances, the sun sets early in Tanzania and, absent the lingering twilight of latitudes farther from the equator, darkness soon follows. In our veil of eclipsing storm clouds, the transition was precipitous.

Heavy raindrops splatted on the windshield and pummeled the roof of our vehicle. Visibility dropped to a few yards, even with headlights, and Gervas, peering through fogged glass and flapping wipers, struggled to maintain safe and steady progress. Lightning flashed with alarming frequency, accompanied by near-simultaneous thunderclaps. There was no need to count the seconds between flash and crash to gauge the distance. I saw one lightning bolt strike the ground less than a mile away. Estelle, who numbers thunder and lightning among her primal fears, burrowed deep into my shoulder, eyes closed tight and ears covered. A feeble gesture. We were in the middle of a celestial fireworks display that would not be ignored. Then it started to hail.

With hailstones pinging off our vehicle like buckshot, we left the main road and started down a dirt track that the rain had transformed into a mud slick. Gervas announced that our lodge was just a few miles up ahead and plunged on through the darkness. We were now in open woodland. The hailstorm lasted only a few minutes, but the rain continued unabated, as did the thunder and lightning. In the fading glow of one staccato flash, I saw something we had not yet seen in the Serengeti. White stripes — lots of white stripes. Just off the road, standing fast in the storm, was a herd of zebras. I wondered what to make of it. Was the Great Migration underway? I knew that zebras often take the lead, acting as a vanguard, days or more in advance of the wildebeest. But we were still many miles from the Mara River. Had the herds already crossed over and progressed this far south?

Suddenly there were lights up ahead, smeary through the windshield, then shadowy architectural shapes in the darkness. Deliverance was at hand. A burst of acceleration closed the gap. Gervas ground to a halt in front of the Serengeti Serena Lodge and a troop of uniformed greeters rushed forth to welcome us with umbrellas and helping hands.

Just seven years before, when I first visited Tanzania, the only permanent accommodation in the central Serengeti was Seronera Wildlife Lodge, ideally located in a wildlife corridor of exceptional beauty. I have little doubt that the place, in its day, was a beacon of luxury in an area where overland tent-camping was still the norm. But those days were gone. Traces of its former allure remained, in the lounge and dining areas nestled into the native rock of a giant kopje, but the government-owned lodge had suffered from twenty years of neglectful management and the rooms had the charmless appeal of a discount motel.

Construction of the Serengeti Serena Lodge and the Serengeti Sopa Lodge dramatically upscaled the available options. Gregg and I had stayed at the Sopa during our previous visit, and though impressed with its spacious rooms and cavernous communal areas, I questioned whether its jaw-dropping opulence was appropriate to the place and the experience. In planning our current trip, Gervas had suggested the Serena as an equally sumptuous alternative, but with a measure of restraint and a more African ambiance.

Morning brought clear skies. Awakened by nature's alarm clock, we stepped out onto the deck of our dome-shaped dwelling — one of about twenty patterned after the thatched huts of traditional African villages — and took in our first view of the rolling savanna that extended out past the far horizon. To the naked eye, the lightly wooded expanse seemed oddly unoccupied from our hillside elevation, but with binoculars and a steady hand, we soon picked out and identified a variety of herbivores grazing and browsing in the gathering light. Down a flagstone path, past flowering plants and shrubs, stood the lounge and dining areas of the lodge which echoed the guest quarters, but on a larger and grander scale, with interconnected dome structures supported by carved wooden pillars. Furnishings were stylish and comfortable — and very much in tune with the place. We had a fine breakfast on the verandah and then set out to explore the region.

Although we were now in a woodland habitat, open meadows were numerous, and even before we reached the main road we saw zebras by the dozens — even hundreds. Since there are populations of zebras and wildebeest that remain year-round in the Serengeti rather than trekking to and from the Mara like their more convention-bound brethren, we could only speculate as to whether these particular animals were permanent residents or an advance party of migrant returnees.

Unlike wildebeest, which have no social hierarchy within the herd structure, most zebras belong to stable family units comprised of a single stallion and up to five or six mares and their offspring. Within each unit, the mares have a ranking based on seniority, with additions to the harem being made whenever the stallion successfully abducts a filly from her natal family. Usually this occurs when the filly comes into her first estrus, and only after the interloper prevails in combat over his intended's sire and any fellow suitors. Once won and bred, the filly remains with the victor's harem, usually for life. Maturing colts join small bachelor herds until they are strong enough to abduct a filly of their own or, less common, challenge a stallion for his harem. Stallions are fierce defenders of their chattel, against both predators and challengers, and will often retain their dominant station for a dozen years or more. Harem units

and bachelor herds remain discrete, even when merged together in con-
glomerate herds numbering into the hundreds or thousands.

Our objective for the day was to drive south along the main road
to one of the secondary tracks that wind through the clustered kopjes
of the eastern Serengeti flatlands. It was an off-road area, very picturesque, and Gregg and I, on our previous safari, had spent many hours
there being entertained by a pride of lions with three rambunctious
cubs. It had been a highlight of the trip.

We had no particular expectations this time, but since the greater
kopjes had shaded areas for lounging, and elevated vantage points for
searching out prey, it was not unreasonable to presume that any of the
big cat predators might be found among them. As it was, we discovered
our first before the kopjes were even in sight. Just after we had left the
woodlands and started across the tall-grass plains, we came upon a
black-maned lion lying by the roadside. Fewer in number than their tawny-
maned cousins, black-maned males are reputedly considered by females
to be especially desirable breeding partners. This handsome fellow had
been in a recent fight, probably a territorial dispute with a rival. A scarlet
slash furrowed his snout, and his left rear paw was deeply lacerated and
bleeding. He licked at it intermittently, but otherwise seemed stoic about
the injury, though he did walk with a painful limp when he rose to seek
shade under a nearby thorn bush. We wondered what would become of
him. Had he been the victor or the vanquished?

Moving on, we drove past several herds of Thomson's gazelles. Small
and agile, with perpetually switching tails, the side-striped Tommies are
among the most abundant and gregarious of the East African antelopes.
Often they occupy areas being grazed by wildebeest and zebras, eating
the leafier short grasses left behind by the larger herbivores. Tommies,
too, participate in the Great Migration, though their route differs somewhat from the wildebeests' and zebras' and does not extend into the
Masai Mara. Most of the Serengeti's other antelopes – twenty-some
species ranging from the massive eland to the tiny dik-dik – are essentially nonmigratory, occupying specific ranges throughout the year.

We spent the afternoon ranging around and through the eastern
kopjes – my favorite area in the park. Clustered in three main groups,
the weathered outcrops range in height from several feet to several hun-

dred. The larger ones, in particular, are self-contained ecosystems, with trees and vegetation and populations of rock hyraxes and agama lizards and other small animals that live their entire lives on these islands in the grass. Numerous other creatures – baboons and birds and felines – use the kopjes more incidentally.

We would have been happy spotting any large predator, but we were hoping for a leopard – the most elusive of the big cats. We circled the major kopjes, binoculars trained on ledges and crevices and shaded areas under trees and shrubs, but saw nothing larger than a troop of baboons. Near the base of one formation, however, we came upon three spotted hyenas lazing in the grass. Despite its reputation as a loathsome scavenger, the hyena is a fierce and efficient hunter, second in size only to the lion among Africa's predatory mammals. One of the three – its nap disturbed by our presence – rose and sauntered past us to a puddle where it lapped a quantity of muddy water before rejoining its companions.

On our way back to the lodge, we encountered a bachelor herd of impalas and stopped to watch the spirited jousting of two young bucks who, heads down and horns locked, muscled each other back and forth like opposing linemen in a bowl game. Others in the herd ignored the action. This was not a fight, only a sparring exercise to gauge strength and sharpen skills. For one of these two to leave the fold and one day claim a breeding herd, often comprised of females by the dozens, he would have to defeat, in earnest, that herd's existing dominant male. He would then have to drive away all male rivals, including the herd's own maturing juveniles, keep his copious harem safe and intact, and mate prodigiously to insure continuance of his genetic line before he, too, is ousted by a more powerful successor. Not many bucks are up to the task for more than a few weeks or months. Then back to the bachelor herd they go.

As the long rains progress into May, the migrating herds march from the central Serengeti into the park's western corridor where fresh forage is still abundant. On the vast wooded plains of this land-locked peninsula, the incessant grunting of wildebeest bulls and the reverberant cracks of head-butting rivalry mark the start of the rutting season. In the weeks to come, lusty males compete to the point of exhaustion to acquire, and keep, a substantial harem of breeding prospects. By the time the herds move on again in July, nearly every female of age will have been impregnated.

I had never been to the western corridor. During much of the rainy season its roads and tracks are impassable, and soon thereafter the herds cut north through a restricted area outside the park en route to the Mara River and beyond. Only resident animals remain behind, and those could be seen anywhere. There had seemed little reason to go. But since our stated objective on this safari was to trace the route of the Great Migration, within reason and possibility, we had included that distant region of the park in our itinerary.

Our course took us along a stretch of the tree-lined Seronera River where we slowed to a crawl to scrutinize the towering sausage trees for signs of leopards which are apt to be found draped over the stout lower branches. Not today. As we continued on into the alternating plains and woodlands of the western corridor, however, we began seeing considerable numbers of wildebeest, often intermingled with zebras. Whether they were residents or transients was still impossible to determine, but they seemed to be settled in for the present. And why not? Water and forage were abundant, and there was safety in numbers – or the perception of it. On the periphery of one mixed herd, we watched as a pair of hyenas and a handful of vultures picked over the day-old remains of a hapless wildebeest that had proven the exception.

The main road through the western corridor parallels the Grumeti River, a permanent, though fluctuating, source of water for the region's wildlife. The Grumeti is not much of a river as rivers go – maybe twenty yards wide and a few feet deep – but it presents a significant obstacle for the migrating herds, since most of them cross it on a shortcut route to the northern Serengeti and the Masai Mara. Imperiling the passage are countless resident crocodiles, up to eighteen feet in length, whose principal sustenance for the entire year is the seasonal smorgasbord of solids and stripes that splashes pell-mell into their midst when the urge to move onward impels the great herds. Just one of these monster reptiles can seize a full-grown wildebeest or zebra, even from the riverbank, and drag it underwater to its death.

Though we were well out of sync with the migration, we stopped at one of the herds' favored crossing spots, a narrow break in the tangle of undergrowth that lined the river. One of the giant crocs, sunning itself open-mouthed on the sandy embankment, slipped silently into the water as we approached. Others, including a few small ones, held their positions on the opposite bank. A wildebeest carcass – cause of death unknown – drifted in the current. Curiously, the crocs were ignoring it. Since crocodiles cannot chew, but instead swallow their food whole in great gluttonous gulps, they tend to feed cooperatively and in a frenzy, tugging and twisting the carcass until it is torn into manageable mouthfuls for all – but this ready-to-eat meal was intact. Perhaps these great carnivores, unevolved since dinosaurs walked the earth, were simply not hungry.

We were, though, and lunch on safari was a treat. Not the food, to be sure – subsistence fare at best – but the venues were outstanding. Wherever we ventured, Gervas found just the right picnicking spot – usually with a panoramic view and not another soul in sight – and we would break out our rations and sit on the roof of our Land Cruiser for the ultimate in alfresco dining. On this notably splendid day, having left the river and its denizens behind, we parked in the shade of a welcoming acacia and had our midday repast surrounded by a dozen giraffes that seemed every bit as engaged by our presence as we were by theirs. Presentation is everything.

After lunch, we continued westward, slowing a mile or so up the way to see why a lone vehicle was parked off the road, its occupants peering intently into a bushy tree. Birders, I supposed. Gervas exchanged a few words with his counterpart, then edged off the road and approached the tree. Perhaps because I was expecting something small, or because my view was obstructed by leaves and branches, it took me a while to realize what was there. Then I saw the eyes – amber eyes – and everything else snapped into focus. Deep in the enveloping foliage was a full-grown male lion. And he did not appreciate the intrusion. I craned for a better view, and he met my gaze with a penetrating go-away look and a rumbling subwoofer growl of annoyance.

Although tree-climbing is a signature behavior of the Lake Manyara lions – which are thought to do so in order to catch cooling breezes or escape biting insects or simply avoid being trampled by passing elephants – it is largely uncommon among lions found elsewhere. Whatever the reason this one had for hauling his considerable bulk into a scrawny tree

whose branches bowed in protest, I just wish I could have been there to watch him do it.

At the end of our day's drive was Kirawira Camp, near the westernmost extreme of the park. To anyone whose camping history has been of the pup-tent and sleeping-bag variety, the term 'luxury tented camp' must seem oxymoronic, but Estelle and I had spent enough time in such camps in Botswana to know better. Most were every bit as luxurious as the upscale lodges we had visited throughout Africa, but with an immediacy to the sights and sounds of the wild that made them even more appealing. Kirawira, our first such camp in East Africa, was no exception. The open-air lounge and dining areas, though under canvas, were spacious and inviting, with polished hardwood floors and faux period furnishings that recalled the bygone colonial era. Oversize sleeping tents, similarly appointed and with elegant bathrooms, were dispersed over the hilltop grounds. Meals were excellent and the service impeccable.

We were up and out before daybreak, hopeful as ever to witness a hunt before the nighttime predators, abundant in the area, sought respite from the sun's withering rays. In conversations with the resident guides, Gervas had learned that a large pride of lions, with cubs, was a regular attraction in the area, and so we set off along the Grumeti River in the direction it had last been seen. The adjoining savanna, stripped of low vegetation by dry-season wildfires, was now luxuriantly renewed with short green grass that had sprung from the ashes within days of the recent early rains. More and more wildebeest and zebras seemed to be infiltrating the western corridor, sharing the fresh forage with smaller numbers of year-round ruminants such as topis and hartebeest and Grant's gazelles.

Giraffes were everywhere – not in concentrations, but singly or in small herds around widespread acacias, browsing amongst the stiletto thorns with long prehensile tongues. Apart and in the open, two of the patchwork giants stood shoulder-to-shoulder, legs locked, necks entwined or swaying like charmed cobras. Years earlier, when I first witnessed this behavior, I took it to be a robust courtship ritual – necking at its most literal – a kabuki-esque prelude to intercourse. Not so. These were bull giraffes in competition for bragging and breeding rights. During such contests, heads may clop together or cudgel an opponent's chest and neck, but rarely is serious injury intended or sustained. Most often, the sparring is only a test of strength to establish dominance within the male hierarchy. To me it seemed almost balletic – a distinctly genteel form of pugilism.

The morning sun was already toasting the savanna. With no sign at all of the lions we were seeking, and little chance of their hunting now even if we found them, we decided to head back to camp – and breakfast. Along the way, we spotted a mother cheetah with four young cubs still sporting the tufted white dorsal fur that disappears a few weeks after birth. We tried to approach as unthreateningly as one can in a two-ton vehicle, but the wary mother chirped a sharp summoning call to her brood, and they vanished into a thicket.

We had almost reached camp when we passed a vehicle whose driver informed us that a lioness up ahead had just suffered her third failed attempt at a kill. Ever optimistic, Gervas deviated from our course and within a few minutes found the hapless carnivore panting under a thorn bush. Tawny spots on her whitish belly told us she was young, and perhaps inexperienced as a hunter. She was hungry, but also fatigued, and we supposed she would sleep through the heat of the day and resume her thwarted pursuits at nightfall. She yawned a few times, as if in confirmation, and we were about to leave when something behind us drew her attention. We followed her line of sight to a Kirawira safari vehicle parked a few dozen yards away. In it were three American women we had met at dinner the night before. Why would the lioness be interested in them? Then I saw. Standing near the vehicle on wobbly legs was a young topi not more than a few days old.

Minutes after birth, herbivore calves are up and walking, and thereafter remain close to their mothers. If, for whatever reason, a mother has to leave her calf for a spell, the youngster knows instinctively to lie still and wait. Staying out of sight is the only defense a newborn has against any number of predators that would make an easy meal of it. This young topi, perhaps in response to the attention it was being paid, had made a fatal error in standing up. The lioness, eyes locked on the tiny target, rose into a ground-hugging crouch and crept forward. The topi was oblivious, and so were the women cooing over it. Anticipating

the inevitable, Gervas put our Land Cruiser in reverse and eased back toward the other vehicle. Only then did the women realize what was happening. With a final burst of speed, the lioness closed on her prey and snatched it up like a floppy plush toy. One plaintive bleat and the calf's neck was snapped. The lioness, eager to conceal her prize from possible challengers, carried the dangling carcass into a thicket and lay down to catch her breath before feeding. The women, appalled by our dispassionate interest in the tiny tragedy, left at once and avoided us for the rest of our stay.

Our next two days in the western corridor were rich with predators and prey. The region I thought would be the least satisfying turned out to be the most. We could happily have spent the rest of our safari there, but we had our own personal migration to complete. And so we departed Kirawira on the morning of our fourth day and returned to the Serengeti Serena for a stopover en route to our next destination. We were greeted like old friends. As it was to be our last night there, Estelle inquired if a special 'newlywed' cake could be made for Gregg and Rachael and presented at dinner as a parting surprise. But of course.

Who has not borne witness to put-upon waiters droning through a birthday ditty while the mortified honoree feigns surprise and delight? This was nothing – at all – like that. No sooner had we finished our main course than we heard a chorus of hoots and whoops accompanied by rhythmic clanging and banging. Then from the kitchen came a procession of cooks and waiters – twenty or more – drumming long-handled spoons on pots and pans and singing a rousing rendition of "Jambo Bwana," an insidiously catchy Swahili tune that in moments had everyone in the room clapping hands and fudging the lyrics. At the head of the line was a large man in white, with an oversize chef's hat and a booming baritone voice, bearing a heart-shaped cake on a platter. The procession took a circuitous route through the dining room before zeroing in on our table. Only then did Gregg and Rachael – clapping and singing with everyone else – realize it was all for them. The performers gathered around our table, presented the cake, and sang a quieter song of farewell. Then, launching into a reprise of "Jambo Bwana," they filed out of the room to boisterous applause.

We set off in the morning for the final leg of our journey. We were headed north to Migration Camp, the closest permanent lodging to the Mara River, where we still harbored hopes of intercepting at least some of the migrating wildebeest. On the way, we stopped at a hippo pool where we were invited to exit our vehicle and clamber down a rocky embankment for a closeup view of these amphibious giants bobbing and jostling in the water. As hippopotamuses remain mostly submerged during daylight hours, there is usually little to see at a hippo pool except eyes and nostrils and wiggling ears. There is often much to hear, however, as hippos express themselves noisily with resonant honking that carries over great distances. Though they are herbivores, hippos are disagreeable when disturbed, and are purported to kill more humans than any other animal in Africa – a curious claim since the park services of Kenya and Tanzania, which have stringent rules barring extravehicular activity on game drives, seem to have no qualms about waiving those rules at hippo pools.

Just before the turnoff to Migration Camp, we noticed a pair of lions under a shade tree – a mating pair. With all of our lion sightings to date, Gregg and Rachael had yet to see mating behavior, so we pulled up to within a few yards and stopped. The male was a battle-scarred warrior with a missing right eye. His peripheral vision and depth perception may have been compromised, but nothing about him suggested weakness or infirmity. The female was enormous – almost as big as the male. These two would have formidable offspring.

We were there for only minutes before the lioness roused her obliging mate, who responded to her amorous advances in business-as-usual fashion. Sparing him the snarl and claw-swipe that often punctuates coupling, the lioness crossed in front of our vehicle and lay down nearby. The lion flopped onto his side and went back to sleep. About fifty yards away, four buffalo bulls stopped grazing and looked our way. They had just spotted the lions. Or they had just spotted us. Or perhaps they had simply caught a scent. Buffalo have poor eyesight and hearing, but an acute sense of smell. Whatever the stimulus, they began moving slowly in our direction. They had halved the distance when the lioness, sensing their approach, stood up and faced them. The lion awoke and padded over to her side. The buffalos froze.

Anyone versed in the African bush will attest that a buffalo bull is

the most dangerous animal to encounter on foot. In a mixed-herd situation, bulls are perennially alert and protective, but otherwise fairly placid, seldom going out of their way to make trouble. On their own, however, bachelor bulls – usually old-timers who have been evicted from the breeding herds – are notoriously irritable and belligerent. These were clearly of that sort.

With the entire Serengeti to roam, the bulls chose to take issue with the lions' presence on this tiny parcel of grazing land. After a lingering standoff, they fanned out like gunslingers and continued to advance, strength and numbers clearly in their favor. The lions were unintimidated. Their disdainful response was to lie down again – the male facing away. Was this some kind of game? The bulls narrowed the distance between themselves and the cats in small increments, continually chewing their cuds. When they were within a dozen yards, the lion rose to his feet and eyed them with his good eye. Three of the challengers stopped and turned away, opting for discretion over valor, but the largest and most determined continued on a few more paces. The lion stood his ground – and the battle of wills was won. With a head-shake and a grunt, the bull swung about abruptly and trotted off with his companions.

Migration Camp is the most remote – and thus least frequented – accommodation in the Serengeti. A permanent tented camp, it sits on a huge overgrown kopje in a wooded area at the end of a long secondary track. Just below it is the Grumeti River, which cuts across the northern Serengeti and then flows out of the park and in again, traversing the western corridor before spilling into Lake Victoria.

We were greeted by the camp managers, Antony and Jennifer Tooley, who showed us around the open-air common areas and then saw us to our spacious tents, which were perched on wooden decks extending out from the rocky hillside. Though not as luxurious as Kirawira, the camp had a rustic charm that was even more intimately African. We lay in bed that first night, awash in the surround-sound harmonies of countless insects, and listened to the faraway roars of lions and the whooping of hyenas close-by. It was magic. Colonies of baboons, nesting in the treetops along the river, chattered and screeched well into the night.

Those same baboons awakened us at dawn. Our morning activity was

to be a Migration Camp exclusive – forbidden elsewhere in the Serengeti, but permitted here because of the area's remoteness and low-density tourism. Shortly after breakfast, we set out on foot for a game walk guided by Antony. The objective of a game walk is not really to observe game. That can be done far more efficiently from a vehicle. In a national park setting, most animals consider vehicles to be familiar and harmless, just part of the environment, but a human on foot is something to be feared and avoided. There are, as always, worrying exceptions to the rule – most notably buffalo – so accompanying us on our walk was a veteran park ranger, David, a comforting presence with an AK-47 slung across his shoulder.

What makes a game walk special is not the prickly allure of possible danger – though that is part of it – but the discovery and appreciation of things that typically go unnoticed from a vehicle. We encountered a few antelopes, and a great many birds, but Antony was most in his element imparting his knowledge of trees and plants, and their medicinal uses among traditional peoples. He also gave us a field primer in tracking and identifying wildlife by their spoor. And he showed us more than we really cared to know about the distinguishing characteristics of animal excrement. All of it – even that – was fascinating. With many stops to look and learn, we trekked all morning through the bush and along the river, eventually looping back toward camp – or so we supposed. Jennifer had promised us a 'proper bush picnic' at the end of our walk – but as we had no idea when that might be, or where, we were surprised when Antony led us into a glade a few hundred yards from camp. There, under a large shade tree, sat five beckoning camp chairs and a cloth-covered table set with china and glassware. The dining staff met us with a choice of cold beverages and, once we were settled, placed a fine assortment of meats and salads before us. I doubt if Karen Blixen and Denys Finch Hatton could have had it any better.

A few hours later we were back in our Land Cruiser heading east toward the rocky bush country around Lobo Wildlife Lodge – Seronera's more fetching sister – which is situated on a landmark kopje and integrated so completely into the setting that it is virtually invisible beyond the parking lot. Along the way we saw zebras in the woodlands – including a nonconformist that was entirely black except for a few thin strips of white on his underside. Just above Lobo, we encountered our first Serengeti elephants. And a leopard.

Since the start of our safari – now half over – Gervas had been trying his best to find a leopard for Rachael. On our last game drive out of the Serengeti Serena, he had learned from another guide that one had been sighted in a tree along the Seronera River. As chances were good that the cat would remain there until nightfall, Gervas had set a course for the spot. An hour and a half later, after a stop or two along the way, we found it. Unfortunately, it was within the no-off-road perimeter around Seronera Lodge – and word of the sighting had ricocheted through the guiding community. A half-dozen safari vehicles were already encamped along the nearest roadway, with eager tourists peering through binoculars at a tiny speck in a distant tree. As it turned out, there was not one leopard, but three – a mother and two cubs – and there was an impala carcass draped over a branch near them. Of the major predators, only leopards have the strength to drag their prey into a tree to protect it from the thievery of others. Leopards in a tree would have been a great sighting at twenty yards, but at this range, and with this many vehicles around, it was a checklist sighting at best.

Now, two days later, we were driving through the kopje fields around Lobo when Gervas spotted something on a brush-covered boulder and drove over to investigate. Lying on the rock, its roseate coat blending into the sun-dappled vegetation, was a young male leopard – almost at eye level with us as we stood in the vehicle. We watched each other for quite some time. When his interest in us waned, the leopard stood and stretched, then climbed off the back side of the boulder and vanished into the tall grass.

Only one thing left to see ...

We set out before dawn. Up front with Gervas was David with his AK-47. His presence was warranted, not because of a perceived threat from the wildlife we might encounter, but because we were venturing into a little-trafficked area of the reserve where bands of armed bushmeat poachers were known to be active, despite a controversial shoot-to-kill edict issued by the government.

I had a feeling we were going through the motions. After months of interminable rainfall over much of the continent, compounded by early seasonal rains that had already drawn substantial numbers of zebra and wildebeest back into Tanzania, I thought it highly unlikely that the Great Migration would be on anything resembling its normal schedule. At every stop we asked for news – but information was scarce and equivocal. The camp manager at Kirawira shared a suspect report that the big herds had crossed over from Kenya and were now massed in one of the controlled areas outside the park – heading *north!* The managers at Migration Camp, meanwhile, offered up a seemingly more plausible report that thousands of wildebeest, recent arrivals, were loitering just inside the northeast corner of the park, near the Kenya border. Either or neither report could be true. The situation at the Mara River was unknown.

Then there was the issue of access. Migration Camp was the closest permanent accommodation to the river – a mere twenty-five miles as the vulture flies – and it had been my thought, in booking five days there, that we might go out each day and simply station ourselves at the river if it looked like a crossing was imminent, or even possible. But with marginal roads, plus en-route diversions, twenty-five bush miles could mean a five-hour trek, as I should have suspected and would soon discover.

We motored out to the main road and headed north toward the border. Although it had been our intent to cover the distance as fast as we could, just a mile or so up the way we spotted a cheetah moving through the patchy terrain. Passing up a cheetah sighting is unthinkable, so we pulled over and watched as the young male disappeared into a clutch of blackened boulders. We eased off the road and circled around until the cat came into view. He was crouched on a low rock, head down, haunches aloft. I had seen cheetahs feeding in that stance, and thought perhaps this one had caught a newborn antelope or other small prey, but as we inched forward, I realized that he had simply stopped to lap rainwater from a shallow depression. After slaking his thirst, the cheetah paced around on the rocky perch, surveying the terrain, then hopped down and strode off toward a herd of Grant's gazelles grazing in the distance. Tempting though it was, following was not an option. We were on a mission. We pronounced the sighting a good omen for the day, and doubled back to the road.

Halfway to the border, we left the main thoroughfare again and headed northwest on a secondary road that was little more than two faint depressions in the grass. The route was used primarily by ranger units posted throughout the remote northern sector of the park. The terrain was rocky, but open and picturesque, with gently rolling hills and valleys, and vegetation that varied from mile to mile, grassy plains alternating with thicketed brush and savanna woodlands. We passed through acres upon acres of whistling thorn acacias growing in rows so precise that they seemed to be planted. Few stood taller than eight or ten feet, and with scrawny branches adorned with silvery thorns and dark bulbous growths they looked rather like piteous Charlie Brown Christmas trees. Although some species of acacias secrete a bitter alkaloid to fend off browsing herbivores, the whistling thorn has no such chemical defense. Its distinguishing growths, however, which form at the base of thorn pairs, make inviting homes for stinging ants, whose aggressive response to the slightest disturbance serves as a sharp deterrent to probing snouts and tongues. Tiny access holes in the hollow spheres, created by the ants, produce a shrill whistling sound in the wind.

From a hilltop vantage point we watched a herd of eland trotting across the plains at a measured clip. I had rarely seen more than a handful of eland at any one time – and then usually from the rear since these habitually shy antelope are quick to take flight – but this herd numbered nearly a hundred. With spiraling horns and a bulky, ox-like physique, the eland is the largest and slowest of the African antelopes, yet possesses remarkable strength and agility. From a standstill, and with evident little effort, it can leap ten feet into the air.

We drove on into the day, passing sizable numbers of herbivores – mostly gazelles. A herd of giraffes warranted a stop, as did a mother ostrich with a dozen half-size chicks in tow. But we saw no predators and we saw no sign of humans – friend or foe. It was as though we were wholly removed from the world of man. As we drew closer to our destination, we saw more and more zebras and wildebeest on the move, including an enormous herd that stretched out – in virtual single file, as is often the case – for what seemed like miles along a switchback course through a shallow valley. Though the procession was orderly, with each animal in line mindlessly following the one ahead, the pace was evidently too plodding for the occasional few. At intervals, one or two would break ranks,

galloping and leaping and bucking with abandon in what could only be viewed as high-spirited displays of wildebeest joie de vivre.

Later on, a smaller herd ambling across the road broke into a full run as we approached. We came to a stop and waited for them to pass. Wildebeest can run for hours without stopping to rest, so there was no slackening of the pace, even after we yielded the right of way. Our route was nearly cleared when suddenly, and for no apparent reason, the entire herd turned in a great dusty cloud and thundered back in the opposite direction – before pulling yet another reverse and resuming its original heading. The same 200 animals passed us three times in almost as many minutes.

It was nearly midday as we approached the riverine forest abutting the Mara River, which meandered from horizon to horizon. As we drew closer, David told us there was a guard post in the woodlands nearby, and that we would check in with the rangers there to let them know we were in the area. Best not to be mistaken for poachers was the unstated message, though I wondered how many of those were plying their trade in late-model Land Cruisers. But it soon became evident that the Tanzania park service took the poaching threat very seriously. I had seen ranger outposts elsewhere in the Africa bush, and they were customarily tented enclaves or rustic huts – nothing the average tourist would find at all inviting, but adequate shelter from the elements and the wildlife. This one may have been the same on the inside – but from the outside it was a concrete fortress, roughly ten feet tall, without windows, and with only one way in and out that we could discern. We waited inside our vehicle as David walked over to the gate, announced himself, and was admitted to the central compound.

He emerged a few minutes later and rejoined us. The news was not encouraging. The rangers inside reported no big herds in the vicinity. The stretch of river up ahead, a common crossing point for the migrating animals, had seen little activity so far this season. Moreover, the bridge spanning the Mara River, also up ahead, had been washed out in the pervasive El Niño flooding six months earlier, and had not yet been repaired. No surprise there.

We drove on to the river to see for ourselves. The road vanished at the water's edge, and beyond, in the rippling current, stood the concrete footings that had formerly supported the narrow bridge that accessed the otherwise isolated northwest corner of the park. There was not a wildebeest or zebra to be seen on either side. We drove east along the river to where the tributary Bologonja flowed in from the south. Gervas noted that the spot was a habitual crossing point for the great herds – and it would have been a perfect place to watch – but there were no herds in sight, only hippos and crocodiles lazing in the shallows where the river widened out and slowed at the juncture. Along the riverbank, however, there was clear evidence that substantial numbers of ungulates had crossed not long before.

Following the muddy spoor, we continued eastward, eventually cresting a rise from which we could see, on the grassy plain below, thousands of wildebeest and zebra running full throttle through a maze of rocky outcrops. The level of activity seemed particularly manic, I thought, as if the beasts were running on adrenaline after a frenzied river crossing. From the same vantage point, looking across both the Bologonja and the Mara, we could see another mass of animals gathering on the approach to a crossing point that was maddeningly hidden from view by the dense vegetation lining both waterways.

Gervas was not about to give up. He knew of a bridge on the Bologonja. If it had survived the diluvial onslaught, we could double back to the Mara and perhaps catch the next crossing. Unsure of exactly where the bridge was, Gervas cut over to the river and followed its course for a mile or more until we came upon another set of concrete footings that now served as monuments for the erstwhile span that, like the other, had been swept away earlier in the year. Frustratingly, the Bologonja was only about ten feet wide at that point, and shallow enough that we could have crossed it on foot, but the banks were steep and cut away, and even with four-wheel drive Gervas was not about to risk it. If we were to get stuck out there, in this area of the park, it could be a long time before anyone found us. It was time to admit defeat. We were not going to see our river crossing.

Gervas circled back to the open area where the herd we had left was still cavorting. We discovered almost at once that the great migration of wildebeest and zebra coincided precisely with the great migration of flies. Even before we came to a stop they descended upon us in clouds. Most of them, fortunately, were the African equivalent of the common housefly – but masquerading among them, adding injury to insult, were just enough tsetse flies to keep us flailing and cursing. Slightly larger than the common fly, the tsetse is a stealthy bloodsucker whose staple-gun bite, which can penetrate even denim, leaves an angry, itching welt that lingers for days. Some species transmit parasitic trypanosomes that have ravaged populations of wild animals and domestic livestock and which, in humans, can cause African sleeping sickness, a lethal form of encephalitis. Tsetse flies are most predatory at midday in dry-season bush country – but they adhere to no strict rules of engangement. At one point during our previous visit to Tanzania, Gregg and I were attacked so mercilessly by these vicious assailants that Gregg took to clouting them with an empty water bottle and taping them to the window of our vehicle as trophies.

We had eaten nothing since our predawn departure, and it was now mid-afternoon. Only somewhat fazed by the prospect of sharing our box lunches with a million pestering flies, we drove out into the parting mass of wildebeest, parked near a granite outcrop, and sat atop a choice boulder munching dry sandwiches and cold chicken while we pondered the events of the day. Our quixotic quest was at an end. We had sought and failed, once again, to see the iconic river crossing. My expectations had been low, but my hopes had been high. It was disappointing. But our objective was not entirely unattained. We had reached the river. We had seen the great herds on either side. The migration was clearly underway. Now we were sitting on a rocky island in a sea of grunting wildebeest, having our midday repast as they were having theirs. Our journeys had merged. Despite all of the forces that had been brought to bear, the wildebeest were crossing the river. Our planning had been perfect. But we had not – and would not – be witness to the mythic running of that treacherous course. Maybe next time.

CHEETAH
Serengeti National Park, Tanzania

CHEETAH AND CUB

VERVET MONKEY
Serengeti National Park, Tanzania

MASAI GIRAFFE
Serengeti National Park, Tanzania

WILDEBEEST AND NEWBORN
Ngorongoro Crater, Tanzania

WILDEBEEST CALF
Ngorongoro Crater, Tanzania

CHEETAH AND CUB
Masai Mara National Reserve, Kenya

WILDEBEEST BULLS
CLASH DURING RUTTING SEASON
Amboseli National Park, Kenya

ZEBRAS
Tarangire National Park, Tanzania

WILDEBEEST
Serengeti National Park, Tanzania

WILDEBEEST SKELETON
Amboseli National Park, Kenya

VULTURES FEAST ON DROWNED WILDEBEEST

HYENA ON BUFFALO CARCASS
Serengeti National Park, Tanzania

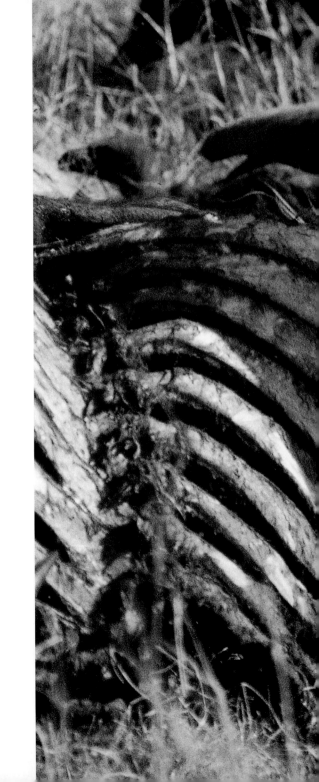

HYENA WARDS OFF COMPETITION
Serengeti National Park, Tanzania

HYENA CUB AT DEN ENTRANCE
Serengeti National Park, Tanzania

BAT-EARED FOXES
ROUST HOODED VULTURES
Serengeti National Park, Tanzania

ZEBRA AND FOAL
Ngorongoro Crater, Tanzania

LION CUBS AT PLAY
Serengeti National Park, Tanzania

LION CUB WITH WILDEBEEST SKULL
Serengeti National Park, Tanzania

LIONESS AND CUB
Serengeti National Park, Tanzania

LIONS ATOP KOPJE
Serengeti National Park, Tanzania

ZEBRAS

LIONS AND CUB IN ACACIA
Serengeti National Park, Tanzania

Star of Africa

Since the chance discovery in 1866 of a twenty-carat diamond on a riverbank in South Africa, that region and the lower continent overall have come to be known as the planet's most abundant source of gem-quality diamonds. Raw diamonds were soon being dredged from rivers and clawed from the ground — mountains of diamonds in near-endless supply. An exceptional few, those of extraordinary size and quality, were bestowed upon royalty and cut into magnificent creations — the evocatively named Star of Africa foremost among them. Weighing more than five hundred carats, and cleaved from the largest diamond crystal ever unearthed, the incomparable Star of Africa remains to this day the centerpiece of the British crown jewels.

An immeasurably larger jewel, equally worthy of celestial appellation, nests in a highland setting a few degrees south of the equator in Tanzania. A product of the same geological forces that created diamonds — intense heat and pressure over time — Ngorongoro is thought to have once surpassed Kilimanjaro as the tallest peak in Africa. No more. Today it is but one of ten major mountains in the region, all formed as a consequence of the Great Rift that split the continent about 20 million years ago, fracturing the earth's crust and allowing magma to surface and evolve, over successive eons, into towering volcanoes. Ngorongoro lost its superlative stature some 2.5 million years ago, when solid rock plugged its main lava vents causing the molten material within to escape more voluminously elsewhere. As the magma chamber emptied, the volcano collapsed, forming an enormous caldera known popularly, if imprecisely, as the Ngorongoro Crater.

There is little to distinguish Ngorongoro on a ground approach. It is merely one of several adjoining peaks — not even the tallest — serving as a natural obstacle to anyone seeking access to the Serengeti via the principal driving route from the south. From the market town of Karatu, the last outpost along the way, a gravel road makes a gradual ascent through abundant farmland cultivated in wheat and maize and dotted with small rustic dwellings. Past the gated entry into the Ngorongoro Conservation Area, at the wooded base of its namesake volcano, the road winds steeply upward and the topography transforms into dense montane forest. Much of the precipitation that falls on the mountain is deposited on its southern and eastern slopes, resulting in a lush rainforest environment. Wildflowers and broad-leafed plants abound, as do towering trees draped with vines, and everywhere there are signs of the elephants and buffalo and lesser creatures that make this realm their own.

At the summit rim of the ancient caldera, a mile and a half above sea level, the road levels out and promptly delivers an unobstructed view of the Ngorongoro Crater. Roughly ten miles in diameter and more than a third of a mile deep, the scenic wonderland within spans an area four times the size of Manhattan. With rivers and streams, lakes and swamps, forests and grasslands, and one of the densest and most diverse animal populations on earth, the Ngorongoro Crater is Africa in microcosm – wild and resonantly beautiful.

Estelle and I had sampled the crater on previous outings, as had Gregg on his first safari, but for Rachael it was still an unknown. To a degree, even I wondered what to expect. Since my first visit only seven years earlier, three new lodges had been constructed on the crater rim, more than doubling the number of available rooms. I hated the thought of it. The Ngorongoro Crater had already been one of the few places in Tanzania where major wildlife sightings were certain to draw crowds. At just over a hundred square miles, with unobstructed views in most directions, it was simply too small and too open to expect otherwise. What would it be like with twice the number of tourists and vehicles? Much the worse, I was certain. But the crater experience, even diminished, was not to be missed.

We were near the end of a long safari. We had gorged ourselves on game viewing and had seen everything of note – everything but rhinos. There had been none of those in the places we visited – only a handful in the Serengeti under constant armed guard in a tightly restricted area. Most of the others had been poached off the map. The prodigious black rhinoceros, however, still had a toehold in the Ngorongoro Crater, where about fifteen of the horned giants lived in relative security. While seldom observed doing anything more than feeding or plodding across the plains – which scarcely sets them apart from other large herbivores – their status as one of the planet's most critically endangered species makes rhinos a prime trophy sighting. On every prior visit to the crater we had seen one or more of these great beasts at close range, and this was certain to be the only place on our current itinerary where Rachael stood a chance of viewing one in the wild.

Although most organized tours spend only a day in the crater, we gave no consideration to such an abbreviated sojourn. Our plan was to spend our arrival night at the new Ngorongoro Serena Lodge – which commanded a spectacular view from the southwest rim where most of the crater lodges were arrayed – then game-drive through the crater all the next day, exiting on the opposite side for another two nights at the Ngorongoro Sopa Lodge, perched in isolation on the east rim.

We were up and out early. In visits past, accessing the crater from the southwest rim had entailed following the perimeter road for several miles to a turnout on the northwest rim where spare vegetation contrasted sharply with the lush greenery a few minutes away to the south. From there, tracing an ancient route worn into the downslope by generations of itinerant wildlife and Maasai livestock, a narrow descent road plunged steeply into the crater bowl. To exit, it was necessary to cross to the southwest wall where an equally torturous ascent road returned vehicles to the rim amongst the lodges. For years, these one-way passages were the only vehicular routes in and out of the crater. Since our last visit, however, someone must have suggested that it made little sense to have a one-way exit road early in the day. Who, after spending the better part of an hour getting to the bottom, would zip across the crater floor and drive back out again? Whatever the actual reason – no one seemed to know for certain – the former ascent-only road was now an alternate descent route during the morning commute.

We were not the first to reach it. As we left the main road and stopped at a gate manned by a uniformed Maasai ranger, we could see below us a procession of safari vehicles inching down the narrow switchback carved into the upswept wall of the caldera. We passed through the gate and joined the migration. As we wound our way down, Ngorongoro revealed itself in ever-shifting perspective. Ahead and below us, where the road opened up onto the crater floor, a stream of wildebeests flowed in the direction of Lake Magadi, the collapsed volcano's dominant feature when observed from above. The caldera should have been a dustbowl. We were at the end of the dry season when, in any typical year, the plains would be parched and depleted and the shallow soda lake evaporated to a quarter of its maximum size, leaving caustic mineral deposits whipped by winds into searing particulate clouds that assault both eyes and lungs. But as we had already learned, this was no typical year. Record rains in the previous wet season had so flooded the crater that now, five months into the nominal dry season, the grassy plains were still remarkably green and the lake was larger than it often is at the height of the rainy season.

Due to the volume of traffic in the crater – a diminutive ecosystem by any standard – a strict and necessary ban on off-road driving is vigorously enforced to prevent vegetation and wildlife from being ground to bits. With a hundred miles of interconnecting roads and tracks, however, and quite possibly the greatest density and diversity of wildlife anywhere in the world, the lack of absolute access is only moderately inconducive to game viewing at very close range.

The winding descent road spilled out onto a gently sloping plain and, after a mile or so, leveled as it approached the caldera's central grasslands through a narrow passage between a dense wooded area to the left and vast marsh to the right. Anxious to part company with the vehicle convoy – which in emulation of the wildebeests was proceeding in a column toward the lake – we took the first possible offshoot road and entered the forest.

Perennially lush and green, the Lerai Forest is comprised largely of yellow-barked acacias – enduringly known as 'fever trees' since the early days of African exploration when these distinctive thorn trees, generally found in the same marshy areas where mosquitos breed, were thought to somehow cause malaria. As the only spot in the crater offering day-long sanctuary from the sun – as well as most predators – the Lerai Forest is home to several antelope and primate species rarely glimpsed in the open. We stopped to enjoy the playful antics of a small baboon troop, and thereafter watched as vervet monkeys groomed one another and attended to their young. Several waterbuck grazed near one of the streams that feed the forest with runoff from the crater rim. Multicolor songbirds performed all around while, high above, marabou storks with hang-glider wingspans traced circles in the sky.

Just past the forest stood a strangler fig some eighty feet tall and nearly as broad. I recognized it at once. Years before, on my first trip to Tanzania, I had camped beneath that very tree. I recalled pulling up to it for the first time – Gervas Lubuva, then as now, was at the wheel – and

seeing three overland camps in the classic style. The most inviting was a vision in canvas, with spacious walk-in tents, folding camp chairs and tripod wash basins, individual toilet and shower tents, and a mosquito-netted dining tent with real china and stemware. The other two were less opulent, but no less charming, and I remember thinking that any one of them would be splendid for our two-night stay in this extraordinary setting. But Gervas motored past them all to a previously unnoticed cluster of tiny nylon igloos erected by our predispatched camp crew. Nearby was a sputtering cook fire and a few mismatched chairs around a rickety aluminum table set with plastic plates and cups. Hardly in the grand tradition. The public washroom serving our no-frills encampment was blessedly downwind in a cinder-block construct that I suspect may have doubled as a research station for advanced entomological studies. Contentedly unaccustomed to roughing it – unlike my traveling companions, campers all – I think I put on a pretty good show of rising to the occasion, going so far as to invite cardiac arrest with a daring ice-water shower. But I confess to popping an industrial-strength anti-diarrheal tablet for no other reason than to stave off the need for a perilous balancing act over the putrescent black hole that passed for a toilet. Our crater camp was an early lesson in not leaving the details of safari planning to a tour operator.

Not until we bedded down for the night did I begin to savor the experience. Curled up in a ball – other options were few – I rejoiced in the sounds of the African night. Above the polyphony of myriad insects came the ululant whoops of hyenas on the prowl and the strident barking of baboons in the treetops. Lions – thrillingly close – rumbled and grumbled. At one point during the night's a cappella revue, Bill Lindsay and I ventured warily out of our tents and shone flashlights into the rustling darkness. A few dozen glowing eyes mirrored back. Nothing alarming – just a small herd of antelopes. Bill and Sally Snyder, wedged into a single igloo apart from ours, stayed zipped in their tent, convinced they were in the company of lunatics. In the morning we found lion tracks in camp.

Had we not camped on the crater floor we would have missed our predawn drive through mist-shrouded shapes that resolved into animals as the residue of low-lying clouds dissipated with the warming sun. And we would have missed the impromptu comraderie of a noontime softball game that developed among campers and camp staff – many of whom had never played the game – when Bill Lindsay broke out the bat and ball, even a couple of mitts, that he had for some curious reason brought along on safari. It was an oddly incongruous highlight of our stay. Whatever its shortcomings in terms of basic comforts, our humble tent camp was forgiven for the compensatory opportunity it afforded to experience and embrace one of the world's great natural wonders in a very intimate way. None of us would have passed on it. Just how singular that opportunity would be was not apparent at the time. Only seven months after our visit, the Tanzania government, citing concern for the environment, terminated all camping within the Ngorongoro Crater.

Seven years later the old campground looked much as I remembered. Gervas pulled up under the colossal fig tree and we all piled out to gawk at its immensity and stretch our legs a bit. Intent upon preserving the moment, I strode off with my camera, soon to realize that it was almost impossible to get the entire tree in frame and still be able to discern the tiny human forms beneath it – an apt metaphor, I suppose, for our place in the grand scheme of things.

Despite its high concentration of predators and prey, and the statistical probabilities inherent therein, the Ngorongoro Crater has not, in my experience, been the place to see the dramatic intertwining of life and death that seems to typify Africa in the minds of so many. Too many vehicles, coupled with vast open spaces and no off-road access, conspire against it. Rather, it is a place of charm and beauty that works its magic in subtle ways, a place that can be seen in a day, every mile of its roads and tracks traversed, but never fully known. Most of all, it is a place that rewards those who are patient and attentive to detail. With that in mind, it was our intent to embrace the crater on its own terms. Near the end of an exceptionally bountiful safari, we could afford the luxury of passing up lions or other big-ticket attractions, particularly if there were vehicles all around, and instead seek out more precious rewards.

Having cruised the acacia forest and tarried at the giant fig tree, it was mid-morning before we worked our way out onto the grasslands that blanket much of the crater floor. The caravan of vehicles had long since dispersed into far-flung ones and twos, now perceivable only in

motion by the clouds of powdery dust churning in their wakes. We drove in the direction of Lake Magadi, where scattered groups of wildebeest and zebra, intermixed with gazelles, could be seen along the northern shore, even from a distance. Though the lake water has a high soda content, rendering it caustic and unsuitable for drinking, freshwater springs flowing in from the north make that region a favored gathering point for all manner of thirsty animals. Also visible was a pinkish fringe around the lake periphery denoting the presence of thousands upon thousands of greater and lesser flamingos. As we neared the honking mass, we could distinguish individual birds striding through the shallows on spindly legs, the greater variety stirring the muddy bottom in search of snails and crustacea while their lesser cousins – smaller and more colorful – swept the surface with inverted heads, filtering the brackish water through their bills to extract the microscopic algae that comprise their diets.

Sharing the shoreline were flocks of crowned cranes, monochromatically plumed in whites and grays and blacks, but with prominent red wattle and a bristly straw-colored headdress lending a touch of color and distinction. Sandpipers and other small shorebirds darted in and out of the water. Crowds of Egyptian geese paraded about on land.

As we edged around the lake, we came upon a young zebra apart from any others, which in itself was unusual since foals tend to remain close to their mothers for the first year. Still wearing her fuzzy-brown baby stripes, she was standing by the roadside with her right foreleg awkwardly elevated. Drawing near, we could see that the limb was severely broken in two places – ugly compound fractures below the knee that we supposed must have come from a wrenching fall or a bad stumble into a hole while running. The young mare was making a brave show of going about her normal routine, grazing on tufts of coarse grass growing out of the alkaline soil surrounding the lake, but whenever she attempted to advance a step to the next inviting clump, she lurched and hobbled in evident pain, unable to put any weight on the shattered limb.

This was not the first injured animal we had seen – only days before we had encountered a zebra whose raked and bloodied hindquarters attested to a lucky escape from lions – but it was the first with injuries so grievous that we knew it stood little chance of surviving the coming night and no chance at all of surviving to maturity. It is an axiom of the wild that some must die so that others might live. Everyone accepts that – even relishes it in the context of an African safari where bloodlust runs high and most seem to favor predator over prey in life-and-death contests. We were no different. Yet none of us wanted to put a face on the next to perish. None of us wanted it to be this poor animal.

Our compassion for the preyed-upon vanished a few hundred yards up the shore when we happened upon a pair of golden jackals lazing in the grass. Though they appeared to have no pressing agenda, one in particular was keeping an eye on a few stray flamingos sweeping the shallows nearby. Estelle and I have always had a special fondness for jackals, which remind us in appearance and behavior of the coyotes that inhabit the hills behind our California home. Both are unjustly maligned. The common view is that jackals – like hyenas and vultures, with whom they share a housekeeping role vital to the well-being of the ecology – are contemptible thieves and scavengers, unworthy of respect or consideration. Although a small portion of their diet is indeed comprised of carrion and other off-putting fare they can acquire with minimal effort, jackals are in fact wily and intelligent hunters adept at catching anything from insects and lizards to rodents and birds and even young gazelles. It would not be unlike them to try for a flamingo, so we decided to wait and see what transpired.

After a while the jackals rose and stretched a bit, then ambled to the water for a drink. Though the flamingos made no show of alarm, the nearest among them sidled comfortably out of reach and continued feeding. A flotilla of ducks and geese paddled past, seemingly within range, but the jackals showed little attention. Having slaked their thirst, they instead nuzzled fondly and licked each other's faces. Then one lay down while the other patrolled the shoreline looking for foodstuff. Before long we became aware of a sharp clicking sound, vaguely metallic in nature, coming from a spot not far from our vehicle. We identified the source as a blacksmith plover, a common bird equally at home on lakeshores and grasslands, that was strutting about agitatedly as the jackal meandered back and forth. Evidently the plover, which nests in shallow depressions on the ground, had eggs or chicks in the vicinity and was voicing her displeasure at the predator's presence. As the jackal moved in her general direction, seemingly oblivious to the commotion, the alarm calls became more frequent and shrill. When it moved away, they became less so. The plover was like an avian Geiger counter.

As it was now past noon, we completed our loop around the lake and headed to the Ngoitokitok Springs picnic area, one of only two places on the crater floor where visitors are permitted to leave their vehicles. The central feature of the site is an azure freshwater lake, replenished year-round by underground springs. The setting is a magnet for birds of all description, but the ones most certain to make an impression are the black kites. These crafty bandits render any thoughts of an idyllic lakeside picnic out of the question. From a hundred yards aloft, the hawk-size raptors can target a piece of cold chicken or a sandwich and in a flash come tearing out of the sky like warplanes on a strafing run. Wings spread wide and talons extended, they descend in force upon anyone ignorant or foolhardy enough to suppose that a picnic lunch should be eaten in the open. With a deft snatch, hands are emptied and claws are filled, often with a morsel of torn flesh to compound the affront. Having dined in this impolite manner for years, with human complicity at times, the black kites of Ngorongoro have lost all fear of people and become extremely aggressive – a mutually dangerous situation that underscores the dimwittedness of feeding animals in the wild. Even the finest Tanzanian lodges have yet to master the art of assembling an appealing picnic lunch – ours was no exception – but we had no desire to share our meager offerings with a bunch of thieving birds. We ate in the vehicle.

Birds of another sort occupied our attention after lunch. Traversing the open plains in the eastern sector of the caldera, we pulled over to spend some time with a trio of ostriches feeding just off the road. Larger in the extreme than any living bird – up to eight feet in height and 300 pounds – the ostrich is incapable of winged flight, but can run tirelessly at racehorse speed on legs that can also deliver a crippling blow to any predator. And it has – as we were to discover – one of the most hilarious courtship rituals on the planet.

None of our previous safaris had happened to coincide with the ostrich mating season, so neither Estelle nor I was alert to the signs. To us, these were just ordinary ostriches – a male and two females – feeding in the usual manner, seizing on leaves and seeds with rapid-fire

pecking, tossing them back into their gullets, then lifting their heads from time to time to swallow the accumulation in baseball-size globs that bulged all the way down their long slender necks. That in itself was enough to warrant a lingering stop, but Gervas pointed out that something even more interesting might be in store since the male's customary black-and-white livery was now stylishly accessorized with bright pink neck and thighs signifying his seasonal readiness and suitability to claim a female.

While the male's flashy plumage enhances his attractiveness to the plain-Jane brownish females, it also makes him more attractive to a range of predators. Consequently, female ostriches outnumber their male counterparts – an actuarial imbalance agreeable to the breeding male who has only to stake out a territory and wait for aspiring mates to come calling. As we watched in anticipation, one of the females did just that, presenting herself by crouching with her wings spread outward and her neck and head low to the ground. The object of her affection exhibited little interest, however, continuing to feed without interruption. Ignoring the rebuff, the female capered about seductively with her wings still extended, then repeated the invitation. This time the male took notice. He arose from his feeding stance and strode over to the female, posturing and strutting. Then he dropped to his knees and went into his courtship routine. Wings splayed into circular fan shapes, he rocked from side to side in a rhythmic solo dance, his head and neck tracing broad figure eights – like Stevie Wonder on muscle relaxants. The female lowered herself to the ground, head and neck outstretched, and the male rose to his feet, tip-toed daintily into position, and mounted her. Then, as the female stared ahead impassively, the male launched into his grand finale, all the while continuing to sway back and forth, wings out and head flailing. In a minute it was over. The male rose to his feet. The female did the same. And they walked off in opposite directions as though nothing at all had happened.

Sundown found us dragging into the Ngorongoro Sopa Lodge, the first of the crater's new luxury accommodations and the only one on the eastern rim. Everything at the Sopa was on a grand scale – from its spacious view suites with dual queen-size beds and private balconies to its cathedralesque lounge and dining room overlooking the crater. I marveled at the logistics involved in crafting such a structure in this most remote of places, where every timber and stone and panel of glass had to be trucked from afar over spectacularly awful roads.

The principal attraction of the Sopa was not manifest until the next morning when we found that ours was the only vehicle waiting on the access road when a park ranger unlocked the gate shortly after sunup. In minutes we were on the crater floor. We owned it. Vehicles disgorged from the western lodges were just beginning their slow descent on the opposite side. It would be hours before they encroached upon us.

Our day commenced with a drive past the Gorigor Swamp where we stopped to admire three bull elephants feeding on the tall marsh grass. Identifying crater elephants by sex, even at great distance, is simple enough since cows and calves almost never venture into the caldera, preferring to remain in the wooded areas along the rim, presumably for security and better browsing. Males move freely back and forth. Two of the three before us sported ivory of the sort seldom seen in today's Africa where most of the magnificent bulls of old have been shot, either for sport or profit, and their great tusks mounted on trophy walls or carved into curios and jewelry. One was a particularly impressive specimen, fully twelve feet tall or more, with massive tusks that extended to within inches of the ground before curving gently upward. Had they not, he would have left furrows with every step. Very few elephants in the wild have tusks even a third as large. Together they must have weighed some 500 pounds – a ponderous load the majestic old bull carried proudly and without apparent effort.

A mile or so up the way we spotted some scurrying shapes in the middle of the road and slowed to avoid scaring them away. As we drew nearer, we identified them as black-backed jackal puppies, roughly two months old. Similar in size and physiology to the golden jackal, though more common and arguably more handsome, the black-backed jackal is easily distinguished by a saddle of black and white fur that extends from head to tail. These youngsters – four in all – were just beginning to get that maturing coloration.

The pups scampered aside as we eased to a stop, but did not run away. With cautious curiosity, they peered at us through the grass, then crept forward a few steps, bobbing and weaving with fear and excitement, ready to flee at the slightest alarm. One ventured so close that we had to lean out the windows even to see him. As there were no adults monitoring this risky business, we could only suppose that the parents were off on a morning quest for food, secure in the supposition that their offspring were safe in the family den, where they had always been left at such times. But the pups were now of an age where the lure of adventure prevailed over caution. One of the wayward youngsters, evidently having decided that our presence was unworthy of further attention, leaped without warning onto his nearest sibling, prompting a four-way bout of play-fighting. For a quarter of an hour they ran about furiously, stalking and jumping on one other, wrestling and biting and generally acting out. Then one darted off in the direction of a dry mud wallow – possibly the den site – and the others followed close behind. In a moment they were out of sight.

As we worked our way west, we began to see signs of oncoming traffic – our first of the morning. We would soon be sharing sightings. A string of parked vehicles drew us to a marshy area where, despite obscuring vegetation, it was clear that something substantial had been killed in the night. No sooner had we come to a stop than a hyena loped past us and plunged into the tall grass and reeds, creating an explosion of vultures and marabou storks routed by the sudden intrusion. More winged scavengers lined the branches of nearby trees. A second hyena arrived from a different direction than the first. While fellow clan members could certainly have made the kill, with these two simply being late arrivals, we thought it more likely that lions had done the deed and then abandoned the carcass after gorging themselves. Unable to leave the road, we peered through binoculars, trying to discern what lay fallen and follow the action – but our efforts were in vain. There was little to be gained by lingering.

We looped around Lake Magadi on a course similar to the one we had taken the morning before. This time there were no grazing animals near the freshwater inlet. We soon found out why. On a stretch of beach splotched white with soda deposits lay five lionesses panting in the heat – five big predators with bulging bellies that fit handily into our imagined scenario for the kill we had left a mile or two back.

Although there is nothing to prevent herd animals from entering and leaving the crater, even migrating with their brethren for a change of scenery, there is also no incentive for them to do so. Within the caldera ecosystem, food and water are plentiful all year round – and apparently even a wildebeest is bright enough to choose paradise over nomadic privation and a perilous trek. But even paradise has its drawbacks. A yearlong abundance of food for herbivores equates to a yearlong abundance of food for carnivores. As a result, the Ngorongoro Crater has an exceptionally dense population of lions – about a hundred adults split among five main prides that hold dominion over specific territories that are generally smaller than those found in less bountiful regions.

The long-term prognosis for this multitude of lions is unclear, however. Because the crater is naturally isolated, and because generations of pride males have fiercely and successfully defended their territories, male immigration has been largely nonexistent. Consequently and inevitably, significant inbreeding has taken place over the years – and cumulatively taken its toll – weakening the collective gene pool and contributing to reproductive dysfunction and a decline in the overall birth rate. There is also evidence to suggest that this diminution of genetic diversity has rendered the crater lions more susceptible to certain ailments. A viral infection in the mid-nineties temporarily reduced their numbers by two-thirds. If, through inbreeding, all of the crater lions were to inherit the same genetic predisposition to disease, a particularly virulent outbreak could wipe out the entire population.

But the lionesses before us were blithely unaware of such weighty matters. Well-fed and content, they lazed near the water as a handful of cautious zebras hung back, eyeing them from a distance, unwilling to venture closer for a drink. Midday was approaching, however, and it was getting hot. Soon the sleepy cats would go in search of a shady spot in which to escape the heat of the day – no small task in an open habitat where shady spots are few and far between. I was reminded of another hot morning in the crater, during my previous visit with Gregg, when we stopped behind a parked Land Rover whose occupants were watching a pride of lions lolling in the grass nearby. As we did so, three of the cats rose sleepily to their feet, stretched and yawned in unison, then ambled our way. What they wanted was soon apparent. Two of them collapsed in

the shade of the Land Rover, and the third crawled halfway underneath. That vehicle was going nowhere until the lions decided to move – and a lion in shade could be set for the day. Before our current subjects had a chance to formulate a similar plan, we decided to part company, relinquishing our choice vantage point to another safari vehicle – one of far too many now converged on the site and jockeying for position.

As the day wore on and we continued our survey of the crater and its wonders, it struck me as odd that we had yet to see a rhinoceros. At least as far as I was concerned we had not. Aware that Rachael, in particular, was keen to find one, Gervas had been keeping his eyes peeled – and in fact had pointed out a rhino or two on a few occasions. These were no more than gray specks, however, and we had to peer through binoculars even to confirm what they were. Rachael seemed pleased to have even a distant glimpse of these great behemoths teetering on the brink of extinction, but the rest of us were disappointed for her. My feeling was that if high-power optics were needed to distinguish something as large as a rhinoceros, it hardly counted. Gervas apparently agreed. Determined to give Rachael a memorable rhino sighting, he headed us toward the Lerai Forest as the sun made its afternoon descent. He explained that the reclusive beasts, which disperse over the crater floor to forage during the daytime, usually seek refuge in the woodlands at night. His plan was to situate us on the road leading past the forest and wait to see what happened. Maybe we would be lucky and one would appear before the park closed to visitors at sundown.

We cruised up the frontage road and pulled to a stop. Gervas lifted his binoculars and soon zeroed in on a pair of rhinos snuffling through the grass a mile or so away. Though browsers by nature, black rhinos have adapted to grazing within the crater, where browsing options are limited. Further away were three more rhinos, one lying down. Such peaceful proximity reflected another adaptation peculiar to the crater, since almost anywhere else in its much-reduced range, the adult black rhino is solitary and territorial. None of the five within sight seemed in any hurry to head toward the forest.

Up a ways we noticed a small herd of zebras, two of whose members were engaged in spirited combat. We moved forward to get a better view,

and watched as the two young stallions darted and feinted and bit at each other, reared up with front legs flailing, then dropped to their knees seeking leverage. One sat down to deflect a biting assault from the rear. It was not a serious fight – or so it seemed to us – but it went on uninterrupted for a good twenty minutes. None of the other zebras seemed interested – but for us it was lively entertainment while we waited for the rhinos to come our way.

As we sat watching and waiting, the sun dropped below the crater rim, casting a shadow that quickly engulfed us and swept across the plain. It was time to leave. We were 45 minutes from the eastern park exit and there was just enough time to make it out by curfew. Not one of the rhinos had taken so much as a step in our direction.

Our exit route took us back past the Gorigor Swamp where we were awarded a more than adequate consolation prize. Prowling along the roadside was a serval – a small spotted cat rarely active in the daytime. In nine trips to Africa, I had seen one only once before. Among the feline predators, cheetahs almost never venture into the Ngorongoro Crater and leopards tend to keep to the woodlands and forested rim areas – competition from lions and hyenas is simply too intense. But the serval, which subsists principally on prey too small for the larger predators to bother with, occupies a niche that allows it to thrive in the grassy region adjoining the marsh. Even with no time to spare, Gervas could not resist giving us the opportunity to enjoy this rare sighting for a few minutes. We watched as the serval moved silently through its range, stopping to sniff perfunctorily at a number of small holes and burrows. We knew if we waited long enough it was bound to hunt – leaping high into the air to pounce on an unsuspecting rodent or bird – but there was simply no time to linger.

Gervas fired up the Land Cruiser and pushed forward into the gathering dusk, driving well over the unposted speed limit to make up for lost time. It was an act wholly out of character for one as respectful of the wildlife and mindful of park regulations as he, but from it we concluded that crater authorities took an exceptionally dim view of late departures. We made it to the ascent road uneventfully, and near the top Gervas pulled to a sharp stop and hopped out. Quickly he examined the front of the vehicle – to make certain that no low-flying birds with terminally poor timing had splatted incriminatingly on the grille, we later learned – then jumped back in and made it to the guard post with less than a minute to spare. The ranger on duty waved us through, pointed to an imaginary watch on his wrist, then pushed the gate closed and padlocked it.

Last out, first in. At sunup we were back at the same gate waiting for the same ranger to open up. Hoping for another opportunity to enjoy the antics of the black-backed jackal puppies, we headed straight to the place we had seen them the morning before. The pups were there – adding weight to our assumption that the den was nearby – but so were the parents. It was clear that the puppies had transgressed the previous day – and knew it – because in the presence of mom and dad, they made no move to approach us. The adult jackals, wary and protective, rounded them up as soon as we came to a stop, and the entire family trotted off into the tall grass. We considered ourselves fortunate to have found the youngsters unsupervised during our first encounter.

We headed to the lake where we came upon a golden jackal hunting along the shoreline. We took it to be one of the pair we had seen the day before since it was in the same vicinity and jackals, like most predators, are highly territorial. Moving slowly and ever so carefully through the grass, as though treading on paper-thin ice, the animal froze in mid-step and listened for the sound of scurrying rodents. All of its senses came to focus on a spot several feet away. Suddenly it made a great leap and plunged into the turf, emerging with a squirming mouse clenched in its teeth. A couple of quick chews and the rodent vanished down the hunter's throat. Without so much as a self-satisfied pause, the jackal was back at it – stalking, stopping, listening, pouncing – but his next several attempts went unrewarded. He scratched at the ground, uncovering a few insects or seeds, then spotted something darting into a hole. The jackal thrust his muzzle in after it and commenced digging with abandon, soon emerging with another mouse that promptly joined the first. There was certainly no shortage of food in the area – and this jackal was a master of the hunt, wily and intelligent and nimbly athletic. Before moving off he made three flying leaps in quick succession, like a stone skipping across a pond, and for his parting effort earned a final tasty morsel.

No other vehicles were yet in sight, so we headed on down the lakeshore with the idea of photographing the flamingos before too much traffic pushed the skittish birds out of range. Several hundred were trolling near the freshwater inlet and we inched our way slowly to the water's edge so as not to disturb them. Even so, they began drifting away almost at once, finding the edible microorganisms a bit further out just slightly more appealing.

Engrossed by the panoramic display of flamingos and other water-birds, we were oblivious to all else until Rachael happened to glance behind us and saw zebras heading our way – hundreds of them marching toward the lake for an early-morning drink. Although the initial impression was of a single mass of animals, closer observation revealed distinct family units – up to a dozen or so mares and foals led by a single stallion – walking together in single file. Without the slightest acknowledgment of our presence, the first group of zebras strode past our Land Cruiser and into the water where they promptly began to drink. Others followed, passing us on either side, and fanned out along the shoreline, some wading knee-deep into the water as others pressed in behind them. We were engulfed in zebras. As though obeying some precept of equine etiquette, the bulk of the procession laid back, waiting for the first arrivals to finish drinking. Some nibbled on whatever coarse grass happened to be nearby. A couple of young stallions engaged in mock combat. Most just waited their turn. In the distance, other zebras were still filing in. A cloud of dust hung over the gathering herd.

As those at the waterline got their fill, they turned and trudged off, making way for others to come in and take their places. For more than an hour we were in an ever-shifting kaleidoscope of black and white stripes. Even though crater animals are accustomed to vehicular intrusions, had we arrived on the scene while the zebras were drinking, they would have dispersed or at least been wary of our presence – especially if we had tried to get close. But somehow, since we were already there when they began to arrive, they paid us no mind. We were simply part of the landscape.

Enthralled by the spectacle and unwilling in any event to disrupt it, we remained until the last of the zebras had come and gone. Then, awash in the glow of this indelible experience, we moved off down the lake. In the distance we noted what looked like two large boulders near the water. We knew they were not, however, because we had driven this route before and there were no boulders near the water. They could only be hippos.

Rarely is a hippopotamus sighting cause for excitement. Almost anyplace in Africa with a river or a lake worthy of the name will have hippos in abundance, so finding them is no great achievement. Finding them out of water – especially up close – is another matter. These two had apparently decided to sun themselves on shore before slipping into the lake for the day. We approached them cautiously and in small increments, aware that without some finesse we might frighten them off or, worse, provoke an attack. Not that we had much to fear inside our Land Cruiser, but we had no desire to put these heavyweights in a position where they felt that attacking us was an appropriate response to our presence.

The hippos were lying head to head, their fleshy bodies spilling shapelessly over the short grass. We judged them to be cows, based on the absence of combat scarring indicative of bulls. A pair of wattled starlings balanced precariously atop the heaving forms, plucking insects and parasites from the leathery skin and eliciting an occasional twitch from the accommodating hosts. One of the hippos pushed herself up into a sitting position, stared at us with disinterest for a moment or two, then rose gracelessly to her feet. Instead of making for the water as we expected, however, she merely shifted her weight and flopped back down. A while later, both animals struggled to their feet. After nuzzling each other, the two bulldozed a parcel of grass and chewed it open-mouthed, expelling great clumps of dirt in the process, then moved at last to the water's edge and eased themselves in.

An hour or so later we were driving along a meager stream feeding into the crater from the east when we came upon three lions under a bush just off the road. The sun was high in the sky and the crater was cooking. The lions were doing what lions do to weather the heat. Two were attempting to snooze – a large female and a subadult male sprawled on his back with a hind leg draped ridiculously over a low branch. Though bedeviled by countless flies, many skittering over their faces and probing their eyes and nostrils for moisture, the half-asleep duo responded only with reflexive flicks of their ears and tails. The third lion, another young male, was sitting apart watching a small herd of zebras a hundred yards away. We thought he was showing considerable interest, but doubted

that he would act on it at this time of day. When two other vehicles pulled up behind us, we were sure of it.

As we were close to the road leading up to the Sopa, we decided to forego the pleasure of our customary box-lunch rations – anorexic chicken, cucumber sandwich, hard-boiled egg, overripe banana – and go topside for something a bit more elegant. Why not? It was our last day and we deserved it.

The spacious dining room, with its high-beam conical ceiling and wraparound windows, was practically empty. Hardly anyone leaves the crater at midday. We took a table by the window where we could admire the enormity of the volcanic wonder below us. Over a fine lunch and several ice-cold drinks, we reflected on the high points of a safari that had too many of them to recount. In my experience, every trip to Africa surpasses the last – or seems to at the time – but this one had truly been extraordinary. Thanks to an exceptional and tireless guide, we had seen and done just about everything. Gervas was indomitable. Even at the end of a twelve-hour game drive, when the light was gone and we were stuporous with exhaustion, there was always one more thing he wanted to show us. He just never gave up.

We considered staying at the lodge for the rest of the afternoon, taking in the view and enjoying our final hours there in pleasant contemplation. It was a heretical notion to be sure – a gross departure from the dawn-to-dusk game drives of the last three weeks – but we thought we could handle it. Then again, maybe not. There was Gervas to consider. Could we live with ourselves knowing we had deprived him of his last chance to find Rachael one of those damned elusive rhinos?

The sun was already on the descent by the time we rolled out onto the crater floor for our final bit of Ngorongoro game viewing. In the thinning woods at the base of the rim, we stopped for a while to watch the antics of a bustling troop of baboons. Further on we inched past clusters of wildebeest and gazelles grazing contentedly as a pair of secretary birds stomped through the grass rousting lizards and snakes. Somewhat later we came upon three hyena puppies, several months old, who tumbled onto the road and approached us with a curious and confident air. A few dozen yards away, a couple of adults were rounding up four other youngsters who had wandered off in another direction. But, for the most part, it was a quiet afternoon. By the time we circled back to the spot where we had left the lions before lunch, they had moved away from the shade tree and were lying in the open. The zebras had long since disappeared and the cats showed no sign at all of stirring. We decided to call it a day.

No one was disappointed – except perhaps Gervas. A mile or two up the road we intersected with one of the main arterials in the crater. To the left was the exit route leading up to the Sopa. Gervas eased to a stop, hesitated for a moment, then turned the wheel sharply and headed right. With less than an hour to get out of the crater, we were tearing off in the opposite direction toward the Gorigor Swamp. We thought Gervas must have seen something, but no – he was operating on instinct and intuition. Ten minutes down the road he turned onto one of the crossroads spanning the open plains between the swamp and the lake, drove out a ways and pulled to a stop.

We lifted our binoculars and scanned the horizon. At first we saw nothing. Then, a long way off, we picked out the unmistakable shape of a rhinoceros walking west toward the Lerai Forest. Even at that distance we could tell it was a cow, because close on her heels was a young calf. Unless they altered course, the two would pass right in front of our posi-

tion. Rhinos have sharp hearing, but terrible eyesight, so we sat quietly and watched as they advanced upon us. The sun slipped below the crater rim, blanketing us in gray twilight. It was getting late. Still the rhinos came on. Soon we could see clearly without the binoculars. The cow was a large one – with long, rather thin horns – and the calf was about two years of age. It would be another two years before it was old enough to manage on its own.

The mother halted at the edge of the road – just a dozen yards ahead – and peered suspiciously in our direction. We doubted she could see us, but thought she might be able to sense our presence – perhaps even hear our excited whispers. After a few moments, she crossed the road, her offspring right behind, and continued her march toward the forest sanctuary, passing close by some Thomson's gazelles that paid as little attention to her as she did to them. We waited until the rhinos were a distance away before breaking our silence. Then Rachael exploded with a whoop of delight. The vehicle rocked with laughter and overlapping exclamations. Gervas had done it again. In the final minutes of our final day, he had found not one rhino, but two. Gervas cranked the starter on the Land Cruiser, pulled a deft U-turn on the narrow road, then set off toward the east rim exit in a plume of dust. Even in the gathering darkness we could tell he was beaming.

CAPE BUFFALO IN MORNING MIST
Ngorongoro Crater, Tanzania

BLACK RHINOCEROS AND CALF
Ngorongoro Crater, Tanzania

137

BABOON TROOP
Ngorongoro Crater, Tanzania

VERVET MONKEY
Ngorongoro Crater, Tanzania

CROWNED CRANE
Mount Kenya Safari Club, Kenya

LESSER FLAMINGOS
Ngorongoro Crater, Tanzania

LIONESS
Serengeti National Park, Tanzania

LIONESS WITH TOPI CALF
Serengeti National Park, Tanzania

LILAC-BREASTED ROLLER
Serengeti National Park, Tanzania

HAMERKOP
Serengeti National Park, Tanzania

BLACK-HEADED WEAVER BUILDING NEST
Lake Manyara National Park, Tanzania

OSTRICH
Serengeti National Park, Tanzania

OSTRICH COURTSHIP
Ngorongoro Crater, Tanzania

OSTRICH AND CHICKS
Serengeti National Park, Tanzania

BLACK-BACKED JACKAL
Ngorongoro Crater, Tanzania

HIPPOPOTAMUS
Ngorongoro Crater, Tanzania

ZEBRAS
Ngorongoro Crater, Tanzania

CAPE BUFFALO
Ngorongoro Crater, Tanzania

ELEPHANT
Ngorongoro Crater, Tanzania

ZEBRA
Ngorongoro Crater, Tanzania

SPOTTED HYENA
Ngorongoro Crater, Tanzania

LION IN TREE
Serengeti National Park, Tanzania

JACKALS AND VULTURES ON ELEPHANT CARCASS
Ngorongoro Crater, Tanzania

Mountain High

A few miles northwest of the Ngorongoro Crater, on the way to Serengeti National Park, an easily missed signpost marks a byway into the prehistoric past. At the end of a washboard road sits a nondescript building housing a small museum and visitor center overlooking Olduvai Gorge, one of the world's preeminent archaeological sites. Though bone-dry most of the year, the gorge is a conduit for seasonal runoff from the southern Serengeti plain and nearby mountains, which over countless millennia has produced a deep cleft through two million years of volcanic deposits.

It was at Olduvai Gorge that celebrated archaeologist and anthropologist Louis Leakey, acting on an educated hunch, began searching for traces of early man in 1931. Although rewarded early on with the discovery of stone tools and other primitive artifacts, the underfunded effort progressed intermittently without dramatic note for a quarter of a century until Mary Leakey, a dedicated field archaeologist who had long toiled in the shadow of her more illustrious husband, unearthed the fossilized skull fragments of a possible human forebear determined by carbon-dating to have roamed the region some 1.75 million years ago. Her later discovery of a second hominid species, thought to be even more closely linked to modern-day humans than the first, coupled with her attendant discovery of fossilized footprints that proved these beings walked upright, created a furor of academic debate as to which, if either, was the true progenitor of modern man. These findings, and others that followed, formed the basis of the Leakeys' then-controversial theory that these early hominids had diverged from their lesser primate cousins on the plains of East Africa, and from there migrated on foot across Europe and Asia, evolving over time into Homo sapiens.

The legacy of Louis Leakey extends well beyond his discoveries and theories regarding the origin of man. His interest in primatology spanned the ages, and it was through his initiative that three of the longest-running studies of primate behavior in the wild were undertaken. Convinced that women with a passion for the subject, but with no formal training or academic background, were the ideal candidates to conduct long-term observation and evaluation, he recruited a trio of untested but enthusiastic researchers to expand the world's heretofore limited knowledge of the great apes, the primates most closely related to human beings. All three were captivated enough by their subjects to make the project their life's work. For more than forty years, Jane Goodall has studied and championed chimpanzees in Tanzania. For some thirty years, Biruté Galdikas has done likewise with orangutans in Borneo. And for the last twenty years of her life, Dian Fossey strove to preserve and protect the mountain gorillas of Rwanda.

Of all the great apes, the gorilla has most insinuated itself into worldwide popular culture. Although overwrought accounts of great hairy man-beasts, preternaturally strong and aggressive, had been trickling out of Africa since the earliest days of European visitation, the gorilla did not officially enter the scientific record until the mid-nineteenth century. Even then, not much was known of it. Gorilla studies were largely of the postmortem variety, offering clinical data as to anatomy and physiology, but little in the way of information or insight into the life cycle and behavior of the planet's largest primate. Published memoirs by explorers and hunters – many predisposed to embellish their exploits – only perpetuated the gorilla's baseless reputation for unprovoked ferocity. Popular literature and Hollywood movies did little to alter that lurid perception. Of the early iconographers, pulp novelist Edgar Rice Burroughs – who never once set foot in Africa – probably came closest to divining the true nature of gorillas in his enduring series of Tarzan adventures, about a shipwrecked infant adopted and raised to maturity by a family of nurturing apes.

Shy and essentially peaceable, more inclined to flee danger than confront it, gorillas are, nonetheless, immensely powerful and can respond explosively if aroused or threatened. Most gorillas live in polygamous family units ranging in size from just a few members to more than thirty. At the head of each family is a dominant male silverback – so named for the saddle of white fur that comes with sexual maturity – who will typically have undisputed dominion over two to five breeding females and an assortment of offspring. Silverbacks are formidable leaders, tasked with protecting the family from outside threats, including hostile takeovers by would-be usurpers, as well as maintaining discipline and harmony within the group. For this reason, and because strength and fighting ability are essential to attracting and retaining breeding partners, sexual dimorphism among gorillas is the most pronounced of all primates, with fully mature males standing a foot taller and weighing nearly twice as much as their female counterparts.

Gorillas inhabit the equatorial rainforests of central and western Africa. Although tens of thousands of eastern and western lowland gorillas are dispersed throughout the region, all of the world's few hundred mountain gorillas live on or near the Virunga Mountains, a cluster of eight volcanoes – two still active – that serves as a natural and political boundary for the converging nations of Rwanda, Uganda and Congo. Mountain gorillas have longer and more copious hair than their lowland cousins – an adaptation to the ofttimes freezing climate in which they live – as well as other distinguishing characteristics less apparent to the untrained eye. They are also less arboreal as adults. Although indigenous Africans were certainly aware of their existence, mountain gorillas were unknown to the outside world until 1902, when a German military officer and explorer discovered and shot two of them. Many more would suffer similar fates.

Though the idea of a safari honeymoon is far from unappealing, if a bit nontraditional, I suspect only a select few brides-to-be would see the romance in inviting eleven friends along to share the experience. Fewer still would consider, after putting most of those eleven on a plane home at journey's end, staying on and plunging deeper into the wild for a vigorous trek through mountain forests and a face-to-face encounter with gorillas. Estelle was one of those few.

Not long after our first trip to Africa – we were still in withdrawal – I heard from Jerry Dale, who had just returned from another of his grand adventures. When not ferrying safari groups to and from Kenya, as he had for more than a decade now, Jerry was diligently working his way through wilderness regions elsewhere in Africa, seeking personal fulfillment and possible destinations for his clients, many of whom were repeaters looking for something new and unusual. He and a couple of traveling buddies had just returned from Rwanda, and though he considered it a bit much for the average tourist, he had nothing but glowing reports of climbing the Virunga volcanoes and visiting a group of mountain gorillas. My interest was piqued.

I began reading everything I could find on gorillas, beginning with Dian Fossey's stirring account of her years spent in their midst. Although Fossey was not the first to study mountain gorillas – George Schaller had spent a year amongst them in the early sixties – she was certainly the most recognized. Upon her arrival in Rwanda in 1967, she threw herself into the work with all-out commitment, hiring local guides and a small staff and establishing the Karisoke Research Center high in the Virungas. Over time, and with much patience, she managed to habituate four gorilla groups to her presence, allowing her to be among them without appreciably affecting their natural behavior. In the years to come, her observations and writings would contribute immeasurably to world recognition and understanding of these highly social creatures, and she formed a close personal bond with her subjects, rejoicing in every birth and mourning every death. To her growing dismay, mountain gorilla numbers, never high, were in steep decline. Confronted with rampant poaching for trophies and bush meat, instances of entire gorilla families being slaughtered so that infants could be captured for zoos, and a national bureaucracy indifferent or hostile to the plight of gorillas, Fossey soon concluded that her true mission was not to study the mountain gorillas, but to save them. Her motives were pure, but her methods extreme. In a zealous fury, she waged a personal war on those who threatened her gorillas – interrogating and torturing poachers, shooting at others, even kidnapping some of their children. Wracked by emphysema and recurring pneumonia, often in an alcoholic stupor, she isolated and alienated herself from all around her, eventually becoming a thorn in the side of the Rwandan government and an embarrassment to the conservation organizations funding her work. In 1986, under circumstances still clouded in mystery, Dian Fossey was murdered in her cabin at Karisoke.

A sense of urgency had always attended the Virunga field research. Even before it commenced, Louis Leakey had voiced his concern that the mountain gorilla might be rendered extinct in the same century it was discovered. There was little to counter this fear at the time. The mountain gorilla population, estimated at between 400 and 500 individuals in 1960, had, by 1973, plummeted to between 260 and 275. By the late eighties, however, through the efforts of Dian Fossey, and others who followed more judiciously in her footsteps, it looked as if the mountain gorilla was recovering and would indeed see the dawn of the new century. But the species was still perilously endangered with only 320 members as of the latest census. The desire to see them for myself was both compelling and pressing.

Estelle felt the same. When she and I decided to marry, there was little doubt we would honeymoon in Africa. No other option was even discussed. But with gorillas now in the mix, the two-week Kenya reprise we were contemplating soon grew to include another week in Rwanda. And so it was that we found ourselves on the twice-a-week Kenya Airways flight from Nairobi to Kigali, the tinderbox capital of Rwanda, where we spent a day and a half providing sustenance to the local mosquito population before heading out by van toward the volcanic highlands to the west. Making the trip with us were Jerry Dale – who had organized it all – and Searle Turner, a physician who traveled often with Jerry, and who had accompanied him on his first Rwanda outing. Also in the group were John Van Vliet and Katherine Kean, co-owners of a Hollywood animation and visual effects company, who had been with us on the just-completed Kenya safari. John, a master cartoonist with a sly sense of humor, was seldom far from his sketchbook, and his witty scribblings never failed to perfectly send up the best and worst of the safari experience.

Our drive through the Rwandan countryside was a study in contrasts to similar jaunts we had made throughout Kenya, beginning with the roadway itself, a two-lane strip of unblemished blacktop that was startlingly unlike the derelict steeplechase courses that passed for highways in Kenya. When I remarked upon that to Victor, our driver, he observed that the road had been built some years back by the Chinese. I wondered what quid pro quo had been exacted or expected for that display of international philanthropy. And was a highway even needed? For most of our three-hour journey, we had the road entirely to ourselves, save for an occasional overstuffed bus and a few lumbering trucks. Passenger cars were a rarity.

Which is not to say the road was empty. A stream of pedestrians claimed the margins, coming and going in either direction, even along the most remote stretches where it was hard to imagine a point of origin or destination within walking distance. A few ancient bicycles wobbled amongst them. Men on foot were typically empty-handed, although some wrangled livestock or led makeshift donkey carts piled with goods. Walking women, however – many with babies strapped to their backs – often carried items of considerable weight and size, from sacks of produce to jugs of water to bundles of firewood or charcoal, all balanced deftly on their heads. Young girls, in training for adulthood at a tender age, bore lighter loads in identical manner.

Mount Kenya and the Rift Valley notwithstanding, the impression I retained from my drives through rural Kenya was that the country was largely flat and featureless – not to mention thinly populated. Open spaces abounded. Exactly the opposite was true in Rwanda. Here the topography ranged from gently hilly to steeply mountainous, creating a sense of confinement – and there were people everywhere. Rwanda was the most densely populated country in Africa. To support the crush of humanity, the entire countryside, even the deepest ravines and steepest hillsides, was cultivated. Goats and donkeys, neither requiring much grazing space, were the most common livestock, but there were also longhorn cows with awesome cranial endowments. Family homes, invariably small, ranged from traditional mud and stick huts to more substantial brick and plaster constructs. Roofs were of thatch or corrugated metal, or sometimes even tile, with the common denominator being that none seemed to have chimneys. We drove past many a dwelling where meals were being cooked inside over open fires, and smoke was seeping out from every crack and crevice.

After about three hours, having climbed steadily past thousands of small farms and homesteads interspersed with expansive tea and banana plantations, we arrived at Ruhengeri, the nearest town of consequence to our final objective, the Parc National des Volcans and its star attractions. From there we turned southwest, away from the park, and drove another hour or so to Gisenyi, a small resort community on the northern shore of sprawling Lake Kivu, where Jerry had arranged accommodations at Le Méridien Izuba. The Méridien was an unexpected oasis of luxury in this part of Africa, a spacious and charming hotel with a terraced architectural motif that, intentionally or otherwise, seemed to echo the countryside through which we had wended our way since morning. We had a pleasant meal in the dining room and retired early in anticipation of the day ahead.

After an hour-plus drive through gathering daylight, we entered the Parc National des Volcans early the next morning and proceeded to the park headquarters, a cluster of small brick and stone buildings splayed across a well-tended stretch of grass and flowers surrounded by dense forest. Beyond lay the beckoning peaks of the Virunga volcanoes.

We presented our climbing permits – purchased months earlier – and were given our assignments. We would be visiting Group 11, one of four mountain gorilla families designated for visitation by tourists. These were not the four habituated by Dian Fossey. Those groups were still being observed by researchers at the Karisoke Research Center. Fossey, in fact, had been virulently opposed to the notion of tourists traipsing up and down the mountains disrupting her gorillas. Over her objections, however, a consortium of conservation organizations, in partnership with the Rwandan government, founded the Mountain Gorilla Project in 1978, acting upon the conviction that gorilla tourism, properly administered and regulated, would actually improve the gorillas' chances for survival. Not only would it heighten world awareness and generate much-needed revenue for the hiring and training of park guards, it would also provide an economic incentive for local people to take an interest in the gorillas and their well-being. One of the first items on the project agenda was acclimating new gorilla groups to the presence of tourists.

Since the natural response of gorillas to humans is to run away, the process of habituating them to visitation is a slow and laborious one, requiring not only prize tracking skills and immense patience on the part of the facilitator, but also the grit to withstand intimidation charges by the dominant male until he is convinced that the intruder intends his family no harm. That can take a year or more – as it did with the designated tourist groups. But once the task was completed and gorilla tourism commenced, it seemed to produce all of the results the founders of the Mountain Gorilla Project had anticipated – plus a few they dared not hope for. Within the first year or so, gorilla poaching skidded almost to a halt – as did a host of other transgressions – a result of increased tourist traffic and attendant support presence throughout the park.

It was not the intent of the Mountain Gorilla Project, however, to substitute gorilla harassment by poachers with gorilla harassment by tourists. Strict controls were in place to minimize the disruption of the apes' daily routines. Principal among these were limiting the number of tourists visiting each gorilla group to only six per day and limiting the

duration of these visits to just one hour. Tourists were allowed in the mountains only in the company of expert guides whose job it was to find the place where the gorillas had been seen the day before and then track them to their current location. Seldom would the gorillas not be found – it was simply a matter of how long it took.

After signing in at park headquarters, we drove for another half-hour to a rustic outpost at the base of Mount Visoke where we met our guide and the others who would be accompanying us, including an armed park ranger and four porters assigned to carry beverages and lunches and any personal items we chose not to tote ourselves. Also joining us at that point was an Italian couple. As there were already six in our party – the limit for a gorilla trek – we had expected to have Group 11 all to ourselves. I considered it impolitic to ask why there were now eight, presuming that an influential palm or two had been greased somewhere along the way, but learned later that the Rwandan government – intent upon boosting gorilla revenue – had endeavored to increase the tourist group sizes to twelve, but backed off to eight in the face of severe opposition from the Mountain Gorilla Project. Since the climb would be rigorous and the altitude high – upwards of 9,000 feet – our guide suggested that we surrender as much of our belongings as possible to the porters. I elected to hold onto my cameras to document the ascent.

Clutching issued bamboo walking sticks, we set off on foot toward the trail head a few hundred yards away. The going was level and easy at first, leading, in fact, through neatly planted fields of beans and potatoes. Women tending these crops – neither friendly nor unfriendly – stopped and watched as we passed. Just another bunch of crazy tourists. Had we taken this same route twenty years earlier – before the government annexed forty percent of the national park and cleared it for cultivation – this would all have been wild and wooded land. But no more. A mere sixty square miles of parkland remained. At the far end of the fields, we passed through a gated fence and into the forest.

A well-worn trail wove through a skirt of tall bamboo on the lower slopes of the mountain. The incline was gradual and the air was moist and cool. Advised that the climb would be difficult, Estelle and I had trained for weeks in desert heat on the rocky mountain behind our

Southern California home – and in my mind there was no comparison. This was going to be easy. Or so I thought. A few minutes into the ascent, my heart was racing and I was panting. The starting point of our trek had been well above 8,000 feet in elevation, and my sea-level body was voicing its objections to the thin air. Anxiety swept through me. Perhaps all of those insistent warnings about how tough this was going to be were not as overstated as I supposed. We had barely begun. Would I be able to make it when the climbing got tough? I glanced around to see if any of my companions seemed similarly apprehensive. No one was wimpy enough to voice a complaint, but our formerly tight formation was now strung out over several dozen yards.

I trudged ahead, determined to focus on other things – like the carbine slung over the shoulder of our ranger, who passed me on the trail as I stopped to catch my breath. The weapon looked to be of World War II vintage, with a chipped and splintered stock, and I wondered if it had been fired in living memory. Was it to protect us from buffalo – the only dangerous animals known to frequent the mountain slopes – or from poachers or insurgents who, if armed at all, were probably toting AK-47 assault weapons? Almost certainly, it was *not* to protect us from gorillas. Even if the normally mild-mannered apes were to take a severe disliking to us, what were the chances of a ranger shooting one of the world's last 300 mountain gorillas to preserve one of its 6 billion humans?

Hardly buoyed by such ruminations, I soldiered on as we left the bamboo forest and entered what in my youth would have been called a jungle but was now, in contemporary terminology, a tropical rainforest – a more precise appellation, to be sure, but somehow less colorful and evocative. The vegetation was more dense and varied here, but there was still a clearly defined trail, and we proceeded with surprising ease up and down slopes and across open meadows. Our guide had little to say, but at one juncture stopped to point out a cluster of knee-high plants with heart-shaped pointy leaves. He identified them as stinging nettles and warned us to stay clear of them. I suppose I should have paid closer attention, but I figured the last thing I needed to worry about was a plant. I was wearing tall hiking boots, heavy denim jeans and leather work gloves. I was prepared. Besides, nettles have been used medicinally for centuries and gorillas consume them as part of their day-to-day diet.

How bad could they be? I found out a few hundred feet up the trail when I brushed against one of them and a hot slap of pain seared the side of my leg like a branding iron. Only later did I learn that the stems and leaves of the stinging nettle are covered with thousands of tiny hollow needles through which the plant injects a virulent potion of formic acid and ammonia when touched. Clearly denim was no defense. Nor was total avoidance an option, as I was to learn on several more occasions. The nettles grew in profusion, and it was impossible to miss them all.

My experience was by no means singular. Over the next hour or so, up and down our ragged line, other yelps of surprise and pain rang out at intervals, usually accompanied by a choice expletive or two. Jerry suffered the worst of it when he stumbled and pitched face-first into one of the noxious plants. The burning sensation, though severe at first, diminished over time – and within an hour or less, registered as only a mild irritation. At least it provided a diversion. By the time we passed through the nettle zone, I took pause to note that even though the climb was now steeper and more rigorous, I was finding it less exhausting than I had an hour before. Evidently my body was becoming accustomed to the altitude.

Which was a very good thing, because about ninety minutes into our ascent we left the trail and plunged into the forest. From here on out there would be no straight lines ahead and no flat surfaces underfoot. Trees of all shapes and sizes grew everywhere, draped with vines and mosses, and we had to pick our way through them as though on an obstacle course. Ground-level foliage was thick and wet, and often we were crawling on hands and knees through tight passageways slashed into the wall of green by our guide, who wielded a panga – the local equivalent of a machete – with speed and precision. It was difficult to tell exactly what we were walking on, but it was seldom terra firma. The ground was covered with interwoven layers of exposed roots and creepers, and atop everything was a thick carpet of leaves decaying into black muck. There were times when our walking sticks sank a foot into the ooze without hitting anything more solid than a fallen branch or buried vine. I glanced back to see how Estelle was faring, and noted that one of the porters – a young man in bright-orange rubber boots – was solicitously assisting her over the rough spots. A few steps behind, another was tending to

Kathy. Whether chivalry or chauvinism – we guys were on our own – it was comforting to know that I could tend to my own stumbling progress without worrying much about how Estelle was managing.

Perhaps I should have. Through one particularly tangled stretch, she found herself trooping along behind John – sans porter – somewhere in the middle of our drawn-out procession. After stopping for a moment so the Italian woman ahead of them could tighten her boot lace, the three took a slightly wrong turn through the pressing undergrowth and wound up lost and disoriented less than thirty yards from the rest of us. Wisely, they stopped when they realized they had gone astray, called out to announce their plight, and we managed to talk them in. It was a scary moment, even though we knew it was highly unlikely that anyone could get seriously lost with an expert guide and tracker in our midst. Everyone stayed a little closer after that.

For at least the past hour we had been hacking our way through the rainforest. Every inch of our advance was at the expense of some living thing. But anytime I was tempted to worry about the environmental consequences of our clumsy assault on this pristine wilderness, all I had to do was turn around and look to assure myself that in minutes there would be little evidence we had even been there. Hewn vegetation seemed to be growing back even as we moved through it. At least, I convinced myself, we were unlikely to run into buffalo. Only creatures of superior intellect would willingly choose such a route through the forest. But what about other things? Like snakes. It was impossible, crawling on hands and knees through this claustrophobe's nightmare, not to imagine an eye-level meeting with a cobra or a mamba or whatever other vipers inhabited the region. Or maybe there were no snakes at this altitude. Why had I not thought to ask? As it turned out, the slitheriest things we came upon were earthworms – enormous white ones a foot or so long and as thick as your finger. Creepy, but harmless.

About three hours into our climb we passed through a munched and mangled expanse that our guide identified as the place where he had found and left the gorillas the day before. How he had made his way back to this particular spot, through dense forest growth with minimal visibility and few apparent landmarks, was one of the great wonders of the journey – but it was something that he and his fellows managed to do virtually every day. A few dozen yards beyond, we came upon another trampled area, where the gorillas had spent the night. Scattered around the site were bowl-shaped sleeping nests, made of loosely woven vines and branches, that the gorillas fashion each night to insulate themselves from the damp forest floor, then abandon in the morning. I knew we had to be near the end of our quest. Mountain gorillas rarely travel more than a few hundred yards per day.

To this point, I had been so intent upon brooking the climb that I had scarcely given thought to our objective, denying myself the opportunity to consider, perhaps, that ours might be the one sorry group out of a hundred, or a thousand or whatever, that would somehow fail to locate the mountain gorillas. That now seemed quite unlikely.

As we moved forward, slowly and quietly, my mind replayed the briefing we had been given before our departure. Once we found the gorillas, we were to remain quiet and keep together, crouching or squatting to ensure that we never stood taller than the group silverback. This was important, because the silverback weighed upwards of 400 pounds, was stronger than a dozen men, and was the absolute lord of his domain. Best not to make him think you were challenging him. Sustained eye contact was also considered threatening. Best to avoid that as well. We were not to point. Or show our teeth. Or make sudden movements. We were not to get closer than fifteen feet to any gorilla. This was to prevent the transmission of human diseases, particularly of a respiratory nature, to which the gorillas are especially susceptible and ill-equipped to combat. Most important of all, if the silverback decided to charge us, we were not to run away. The apparent attack would, in all probability, be a bluff display intended only to intimidate us. If we were to flee in response, however, that would likely provoke an aggressive reaction. An aggressive reaction would almost certainly be hazardous to our health. In the event of a silverback charge, we were to drop to the ground and – if not in a dead faint – engage in nonchalant submissive behaviors such as pretending to eat leaves and simulating gorilla grunts. Although we did not practice these potentially life-preserving measures, I was confident that I could improvise a fine semblance of submission if the occasion arose.

Suddenly our guide halted and signaled for silence. The gorillas had to be close, though we could still see nothing ahead but a wall of vegetation. Our porters distributed cameras they had been hauling for most of our group members, and relieved us of our walking sticks, which could be construed as weapons by the gorillas. They then remained behind with the ranger as we crept forward with our guide.

I smelled them before I saw them. It was a strong musky *eau de gorilla* kind of smell – the kind of smell one might expect from big hairy beasts with a reputed aversion to water. Our guide beckoned us forward into a tight group. Then, with a slight theatrical flourish, he parted a curtain of foliage – and there was a mountain gorilla, not twenty feet away.

The gorilla – a subadult male sitting in a cloud of buzzing insects – barely glanced our way as we eased forward into the small glade where he and his family had settled in for the morning. With the practiced hands of an itinerant crop picker, he worked his way through the smorgasbord of delicacies within easy reach, harvesting fistfuls of fresh mixed greens and packing them into his mouth. Nearby, an adult female was similarly engaged, though her foraging was less focused, as it was continually being interrupted by a tussling infant whose interests lay more in play. When the persistent youngster climbed onto her back, she rose on all fours and knuckle-walked into a thicket, where her rider dropped off and scampered up a tree. Elsewhere in the greenery, I could detect indistinct patches of black signifying the presence of other gorillas. We were right in the midst of them.

The gorillas of Group 11 were among the first habituated to tourists, almost ten years before, though visits had been minimal during most of that time as Rwanda was barely on the radar for anyone planning a wildlife adventure in Africa. Only during the past two or three years had gorilla awareness peaked and tourism begun to flourish. At the time of our visit, the dominant silverback of Group 11 had a family comprised of four adult females and their two male offspring – one almost three years old and the other about fifteen months. The group also contained the subadult male – or blackback – and three subordinate silverbacks, ranging from twelve to almost fourteen years of age.

In many species, maturing males are driven from their natal families by the dominant male to preclude future challenge and possible takeover, but this is not always the case with gorillas. Adult females within a given family are rarely related, as females generally transfer out of their birth groups upon reaching sexual maturity – an instinctual safeguard to minimize inbreeding. Without blood relationships, social bonds among adult females are weak, so the death of a dominant silverback will often result in the severe disruption – perhaps even disintegration – of the group. Although aging silverbacks can be ousted from a group, either from within or without, the peaceful succession of power is often secured by the dominant silverback's permitting a sexually maturing subordinate to remain and mate within the group, thus accounting for a significant incidence of gorilla families having multiple silverbacks. Other maturing males may leave the family, voluntarily or involuntarily, to travel alone or with bachelors of like situation until they are physically strong enough to take over an existing group or establish a new one by attracting emigrant females.

We were being directed toward a small clearing that offered a reasonably unobstructed view of the assembled gorillas. The only accessible route took us right past one of the young silverbacks – well within the fifteen-foot restricted area – but our guide nodded that it was all right and led the way, stationing himself between us and the gorilla as we passed close by. Every few seconds our guide would make a low grunting sound, somewhat like a belch, intended to mimic the primary vocalization of a calm and contented gorilla. The rhythmic utterances must have been adequately reassuring, because we managed to edge past the silverback without his giving us more than a casual glance. It was evident that the meal of leaves and bark he was stripping off a slender tree branch was of far greater interest to him than we were.

Though the adults seemed largely indifferent to our presence, the youngsters were unabashedly curious, sometimes stealing glances from behind tree trunks or veils of leaves, sometimes advancing a step or two in our direction and eyeing us with bold directness. One even stood upright and beat a quick tattoo on his chest – a bit of comic bravado in imitation of his elders – then dropped back down and scampered into the undergrowth.

Mostly they played. Together and singly, they scaled vines and branches into the canopy, leaping skillfully from handhold to handhold – an activity older gorillas learn to forego once their weight surpasses the tensile strength of the treetop jungle gym. One of the youngsters, after shimmying up a slender tree trunk, reached out and clasped another nearby with a single hand and foot, straddling the void in between. Clinging to the swaying uprights like a clown on stilts, he then climbed, spread-eagled, a few feet higher aloft before releasing one of the trees and riding the other gently to the ground as its slight trunk bowed under his weight. A more graceless return to earth followed when the budding gymnast attempted a repeat performance and the overtaxed tree snapped in two.

I was so engrossed by the youthful antics that I almost failed to notice an adult female ambling my way. Was I supposed to step aside or stand fast? I read nothing hostile in her body language, so I dismissed the cowering and groveling option as reactive overkill. I suppose I could have looked to our guide for an indication of what to do, but I was unable to take my eyes off the approaching gorilla. Evidently no one had informed her about the fifteen-foot rule. With long fluid strides, she continued toward me, then veered slightly to the side, brushing against my pants leg and angling on to a spot some ten feet behind me where she spun around and sat, then commenced dining upon whatever it was that had attracted her to the particular tangle of greenery. By no means was our physical encounter one of those Michelangelo hand-of-God moments that Dian Fossey shared with her soulmate silverback – but it was close enough for me.

As I watched the female enjoying her morning repast, a large dark shape stepped into my field of view – a large dark shape with a splash of white across its muscled lower back. This was the dominant silverback. Though I have no doubt he had been acutely aware of our presence from the instant we entered his domain, I had not been aware of his until just that moment. He plopped himself down within reach of the female and, like the others in his family, began plucking leaves and grasses and folding them into his mouth. Unlike the others, however, this gorilla wrangled foodstuffs only with his left hand. His right was entirely missing.

All the mountain gorillas in each of the study and tourist groups had been assigned names. While the urge to christen wild animals has always seemed to me oddly presumptuous – undignifying in a way – the practice does offer a convenient means to distinguish one individual from another and record the various activities and behaviors of each. The Group 11 silverback was Ndume.

Ndume had been a young subordinate silverback at the time Group 11 was habituated to human visitation in 1979. Sometime prior to that, presumably as a youngster, he had encountered a poacher's snare, a painfully simple trapping device consisting of a loop of wire attached to a piece of tautly bent bamboo. When an animal trips the snare by stepping into it, the bamboo acts as a spring and the wire snaps tight around its leg, slicing deep into flesh and bone as the quarry struggles to pull free. Gorillas were not the intended victims of these cruel devices, but snares by the dozens were regularly placed along game trails by poachers seeking to trap small antelopes, such as duikers and bushbuck, for meat. Any gorilla caught in a snare was usually strong enough to yank itself free, or be pulled free by its companions, but the wire often remained embedded in the arm or leg, producing wounds that sometimes turn septic and fatal. The suffering endured by Ndume in freeing himself from the wire noose, at the cost of his right forearm, is painful even to contemplate. But the wound had long ago healed and the surviving portion of the limb seemed remarkably functional even though it terminated just below the elbow in a scarred and calloused stump. Ndume was not alone in his disfigurement. Two other members of his family, also maimed, attested to the severity of the poaching problem that had once plagued Group 11's home range. Happily, the introduction of tourism to the area, and the consequent regular visitation by guides and rangers, had heightened the risks for poachers and dramatically reduced the number of wire snares strewn around the park.

One of the shortest hours of my life ended just after noon that day when our guide raised his arm and pointed at his watch. I checked my own in disbelief. Sure enough. Right to the minute.

Midday for gorillas is a time of rest. Though the youngsters were still tearing about and playing, the adults were abandoning their culinary pursuits and beginning to settle into makeshift nests where they would relax and snooze through the steamiest part of the day. Closest to me

was an adult female who eased herself into a leafy thicket that supported her bulk like a well-worn recliner. She lay there for a minute, gazing dreamily into the canopy above, then turned her head slightly in my direction. Our eyes made contact. There was nothing hostile in her look, or fearful or anxious – or even curious really. Rather it was the kind of relaxed, comfortable look I get from our family dog when he is content and curled up at our bedside at night. I wondered what the gorilla was reading in my eyes, for there was no doubt she was reading something. After our brief shared moment, her eyes shifted away from mine and closed. That simplest and most understated of acts seemed to me an extraordinary display of trust – one undeservedly extended to a representative of a fellow primate species that has mutilated and murdered and driven these gentle giants to the threshold of extinction.

Time to leave. Reluctantly we withdrew and commenced our descent off the mountain. Only a few paces up the trail we had blazed hiking in, I paused and glanced back, hoping for one last glimpse of the gorillas. It was not to be. Already they were swallowed up by the forest, free to pursue their routines without further disruption – for another twenty-three hours at least. I wondered if the gorillas derived some sort of pleasure from the daily appearance of human strangers in their midst. It would be nice to think so.

Our climb off Mount Visoke was largely uneventful, though somehow I had supposed that it would be much shorter and less arduous than it was. We were, after all, heading downhill and there were no gorillas to be tracked. The descent took almost as long as the ascent, however, and by the time we returned to park headquarters and then to our faraway hotel, the sun was slipping below the mountaintops past Lake Kivu. The day's double-whammy of strenuous exercise and unaccustomed altitude left all of us a blink or two shy of asleep on our feet, but showers were rejuvenating and we excitedly revisited every moment of our adventure over dinner.

Jerry had wisely planned a down day between our two gorilla climbs, which was more than welcomed by me since I had pulled a groin muscle on the descent off Mount Visoke and it had tightened painfully overnight. Nonetheless, Estelle and I joined John and Kathy for a stroll into Gisenyi

to see what little there was to see in the town. Concerned that anything further might jeopardize my climb the next day – and a bit worried that I might not be able to manage it in any event – I then hobbled back to the hotel where I spent the rest of the day reading and relaxing on the verandah overlooking the lake.

The sun had not made an appearance by the time we pulled into the Parc National des Volcans parking area the next morning. Nor was there any sign it was likely to. The sky was cold and gray, and heavy dark clouds hung low overhead. Rain had teemed throughout the night – accompanied by lightning and sleep-shattering thunderclaps – and though it had ceased some hours back, even my abiding optimism gave me little assurance that our second gorilla trek would be completed without another major downpour.

Today we were slated to visit Group 13. Like Group 11, this gorilla family had been acclimated to humans a decade before, and was noted for being a calm and receptive group under the leadership of a particularly mellow silverback named Mrithi. Only a month or so after the group had been habituated – when Mrithi was still a young subordinate, just beginning to develop his saddle of silver fur – the group's dominant silverback had been shot and killed by poachers. It was a traumatic and terrible blow to the family – which under the circumstances might have been expected to fracture and disperse – not to mention the mountain gorilla population at large, which was then estimated to have no more than thirty silverbacks in the entire breeding pool. But Mrithi, inexperienced and unprepared though he was to assume his predecessor's role, managed to hold the group together with support from one of the ranking females. Group 13 now consisted of thirteen members, including five adult females and their seven offspring, ranging from infants to near-adults, all sired by the amorous young silverback.

After checking in at park headquarters, we headed off in a different direction than we had two days before, northeast toward Mount Sabyinyo on whose western flank Group 13 could usually be found. Though not the tallest volcano in the Virunga chain, Sabyinyo is the most distinctive in appearance, topped by a crown of jagged peaks carved from the rim of its long-dormant cauldron by a million years of heavy rainfall.

We reached our departure point after a twenty-minute drive, met up with our guide and armed ranger, selected a few porters from the many eager prospects seeking work, and prepared for our second excursion into gorilla country. Joining us on the climb were Mark and Mimi, a young American couple that Estelle and I learned, in one of those 'small world' introductory exchanges, hailed from a town not forty miles from where we lived. Mark and Mimi were making their first ascent. The rest of us were seasoned veterans.

Walking sticks in hand, we set out along a slender pathway transecting the cultivated farmland encroaching the park, passed through a flimsy gate in the boundary fence, then plunged into the bamboo woodlands at the base of the mountain. Almost from the start, Sabyinyo proved a more challenging climb than Visoke – at least from our respective routes of ascent – consistently steeper in grade and with fewer open areas where we could relax into a walk. My pulled muscle, which at the start of the day seemed much improved, soon reminded me that it was not yet fully healed. I was determined not to be sidelined by a minor injury, however, so I tried my best to ignore it. Armed with the knowledge that Group 13 had been found the day before only an hour and a half from the start point, I was certain I could tough it out. Plus I had learned the wisdom of entrusting my camera gear to the porters. The minor apprehensions, rooted in the unknown, that had accompanied me on the first ascent were no longer present. I had done it before and I could do it again. I suppose all of us on our sophomore climb felt much the same. Only Mimi was visibly unenamored of the experience.

In addition to being steep and uneven, the tangled surface underfoot was slick and muddy from the all-night downpour, making graceful passage a challenge. The vegetation hugging our route was sopping wet, and great globs of icy water, puddled on the leaves above, spilled onto our heads and down our necks as we pushed through it. Once we got into the rhythm of the climb, however, the experience was anything but unpleasant. The air was brisk and invigorating, the scents fresh and sweet. And every so often, through rents in the cocoon of foliage that embraced us, we gazed out upon vast panoramas of rugged peaks and verdant slopes still draped in morning mist. Only an expanse of advancing black clouds added a disquieting element.

Already curtains of grayish rain were sweeping across the highlands to the west. Would we be hit or spared? There was no way to tell. At least I could hear no thunder booming across the range. That was something. But what would a full-blown storm be like up here? Would we have to turn back short of our objective? I was toward the rear of the group, unaware of what our guide might be imparting to those up front, but a glance at my watch confirmed that we had been climbing for more than ninety minutes. We had to be close. Please let us find the gorillas.

And then we did. Just ahead and slightly above us, on a slope covered in waist-high vegetation, were several dark shapes, indistinct but definitely not part of the natural topography. Quickly we broke out our camera gear, left our nonessentials with the porters, and crept forward for a closer look.

The first gorilla to squarely catch my eye was the group silverback. Mrithi had been seated like a rotund buddha, but as we approached, he rose on all fours and eyed us. He was a magnificent animal, the very picture of a mountain gorilla, with a massive crested head and perfect features. In evident counterpoint to his reputed placidity, however, Mrithi seemed to be scowling. Even as I noted that, I recognized the absurdity of my trying to interpret gorilla mood based solely on human cues, but it was difficult not to in view of their common countenance and uncannily human demeanor. I wondered if the gathering storm had colored his disposition.

Suddenly I realized that I had neglected the edict about not maintaining eye contact with a silverback. Mrithi seemed to take no offense at this breach of protocol, however, and soon ambled up the hillside a few yards, affording us a fine view of his broad back emblazoned with short white fur denoting his dominant rank within the group. Spotting something of epicurean interest, he parked himself near one of the adult females and commenced to feed with a practiced two-handed style that made it easy to understand how an adult gorilla can consume more than sixty pounds of vegetation per day.

The female was similarly occupied, though with less efficiency since her right arm was engaged in cradling a tiny bundle of scruffy black fur, identified in whispers by our guide as the youngest member of Group 13, a male born five months earlier. Again I was struck by the behavioral

similarities of gorillas and humans. Though the infant was fussing and squirming, his mother held him tenderly, as caring and solicitous as any human mother — and the pose they struck was universal across the species. On average, females of mating age give birth at four-year intervals. As with humans, gorillas are born helpless, wholly dependent upon their mothers for every need. Suckled from birth, the babies are slowly weaned onto plants after about four months, though nursing usually continues for another three or more years. For the first six months or so, gorilla mothers carry their young everywhere and sleep nestled with them to insure their warmth and safety. Only after the first year are infants encouraged to leave their mothers' sides and participate in play activities with other young gorillas.

I was edging forward, angling for a better look and a photo less obstructed by vegetation, when I felt the first drops of rain. A skyward look revealed darkest gray in all directions. Estelle and I exchanged glances. Unlike some of our more pessimistic companions who had brought along serious rain gear, we had gambled on fair weather and opted to travel light, carrying only photo vests and hooded nylon windbreakers. If we got wet, we got wet. No big deal. The rationale for that decision seemed less compelling as we stood splattered by the first of what promised to be a great many raindrops, a good two-hour hike from the nearest anything that might offer shelter.

Reluctant to holster my camera, I draped it with some plastic I had brought along, just in case, and continued shooting. Within minutes, however, I realized it was pointless, and packed it away. The volume of rain was increasing, the light was below optimal exposure levels, and the gorillas, which had been active just prior, were now immobile, hunkering down to wait out the storm. Suddenly the skies opened up and the rain came down in torrents. Within just a few moments, the scant barrier my garments afforded was thoroughly breached. The vest beneath my windbreaker became a cold compress, then a soggy wet sponge, and my soaked denim jeans lay plastered against my legs.

The gorillas seemed to be faring somewhat better. Most of the group members, scattered across the open slope, were seated with their backs to the blowing rain, hunched over with arms crossed to preserve body temperature. Exposed to hundred-plus inches of rain per year, this was a practiced activity for these mountain denizens. As best I could judge, the rain seemed to run off their thick fur rather than penetrate to the skin. Although most of the gorillas stayed still once the storm began, at one point early in the downpour, Mrithi rose and clambered up the hillside, ousting a subordinate family member from a choice piece of semi-shelter beneath a great tree. Rank hath its privileges.

We were, at most, fifteen minutes into our allotted hour with the gorillas. On one side of the clearing sat thirteen gorillas, looking wet and miserable. On the other side of the clearing crouched eight tourists and a guide, looking wet and miserable. It was almost comic – a John Van Vliet cartoon begging to be drawn. All of us except Kathy, who had brought a weatherproof video camera, had stowed our camera gear. The gorillas were doing nothing. We were doing nothing. Yet no one deigned to suggest that we might want to head back. We had come halfway around the world to spend this particular hour with these particular gorillas. After another fifteen minutes of unabated rainfall, however, it became clear to even the most stubborn of us that this was no passing shower. Eventually, resistance gave way to resignation. It was time to leave.

As wet and slippery as the ascent had been, it was nothing compared to the descent. Every step was an invitation to comedic pratfall.

Even our guide and porters labored to remain afoot as we sloshed over ultraslick terrain and through muddy streams of rainwater sluicing down hillsides and trails. Our visibility was diminished by the incessant downpour and our eardrums throbbed with the machine-gun splattering of raindrops on leaves. All of us were now thoroughly drenched – our best rain gear and our worst being equalized over time – and even waterproof boots were defeated when water spilled in over the tops. At least no one could say we missed out on the full Rwanda experience.

Once I realized that I could throw myself into Lake Kivu without getting any wetter than I already was, the rain ceased to matter to me. Who cared if it stopped? I was liberated. Somewhere around the halfway point, I slipped on a muddy decline and lost my footing. My left leg skidded through the muck and my right leg shot skyward like a place-kicker's going for long yardage. John, who was walking behind me, caught my arm and kept me from falling, but not before my kicking foot laid a boot-wide strip of gloppy black mud, from calf to neck, up the back of poor Mimi, who was just ahead of me being helped down the slope by one of the porters. She never even noticed. John took one look at her and started to laugh. Then I started to laugh. Pretty soon everyone was laughing, though for reasons individual. Everything was suddenly just ... funny. We laughed all the way to the bottom. And it never stopped raining.

SERVAL HUNTING RODENTS
Serengeti National Park, Tanzania

IMPALAS ON ALERT
Tarangire National Park, Tanzania

LEOPARD WITH DISMEMBERED IMPALA
Samburu National Reserve, Kenya

ELEPHANT MUD BATH
Tarangire National Park, Tanzania

GIRAFFE COMBATANTS
Lake Manyara National Park, Tanzania

ROCK HYRAX
Serengeti National Park, Tanzania

FLAMINGOS
Lake Bogoria National Reserve, Kenya

ELEPHANT NURSING CALF
Amboseli National Park, Kenya

ELEPHANTS GATHERING PALM NUTS
South Luangwa National Park, Zambia

MATING ELEPHANTS
Samburu National Reserve, Kenya

HIPPOPOTAMUSES
Lake Manyara National Park, Tanzania

SUPERB STARLINGS
Serengeti National Park, Tanzania

IMPALAS
Chobe National Park, Botswana

LESSER FLAMINGOS
Lake Bogoria National Reserve, Kenya

WHITE PELICANS
Lake Manyara National Park, Tanzania

BANDED MONGOOSE
Chobe National Park, Botswana

DWARF MONGOOSES ON TERMITE MOUND DEN
Samburu National Reserve, Kenya

NILE MONITOR

Dog Days

The best places should be hard to get to. Without a doubt. Otherwise they become like Yosemite or the Grand Canyon on any summer weekend. Too many people. Too many cars. Too little opportunity to enjoy what draws one there in the first place. Such is not the case with Africa, where invading hordes and vehicular gridlock have yet to diminish the wilderness experience. Access is simply not that convenient. Remote throughout history and still wild at its core, Africa remains unspoiled by run-amuck tourism.

But even wildest Africa can seem crowded at times – not in any true sense, to be sure, but only because those of us who venture there so want each experience to be singular, a one-on-one with nature, unblemished by the presence of others of our species. Anyone who has witnessed the encircling of a lion or a cheetah by a throng of jostling minivans cannot help but find the sorry spectacle repugnant. Yet it happens in the more popular game reserves in Africa – most often in Kenya with its long tradition as the destination of choice for safari goers. In response to such aversion stimuli, those who are drawn to Africa again and again – those with the narcotic of bush and savanna in their souls – tend to push on into places less traveled. Like junkies on a quest for the ultimate high, these khaki-clad recidivists crave ever more intense safari experiences – more wildlife unaccustomed to human observation, fewer vehicles and roads and people, a truer evocation of Africa the way it must have been. Moving south, scouring the continent for the quintessential wilderness fix, the indomitable wind up, sooner or later, in the Okavango Delta.

Situated in northern Botswana – squarely within the vast Kalahari Desert which blankets some eighty percent of that landlocked country – the Okavango Delta is a sprawling waterworld of grassy plains and woodlands that supports an astonishing profusion of plant and animal life. Although the region has its own period of moderate rainfall in the summer months spanning December and March, its principal influx of water arrives somewhat later, originating in the highlands of Angola where torrential seasonal rains gorge the Okavango River which courses southeast through the Caprivi Strip of Namibia and into Botswana. There the surge is checked by the thirsty Kalahari whose sandy mantle consumes the prodigious flow and disperses it through an ecosystem unlike any other in the world. While the upper reaches of the Okavango Delta are permanent wetlands with scattered islands and narrow winding waterways, the lower regions are dry during much of the year, except when vitalized by the gentle flood waters that traverse the delta between March and July before receding into scattered pans and then vanishing altogether in the blistering sun. It is this cycle of renewal – withering drought opposed by regenerative irrigation – that gives the Okavango Delta its singular character and makes it a prime habitat for heterogeneous wildlife.

Southeast and just beyond reach of the seasonal floodwaters is the town of Maun. On the map since 1915, when it was established as the tribal capital of the Batawana people, Maun enjoyed for many years its reputation as a remote and rugged frontier settlement. Only two decades ago, its main thoroughfare was impassable without four-wheel drive. Passage in and out of town was treacherous. But the character of the place has changed under the pressure of expanding tourism into the region. Seldom a destination, but invariably a springboard for any-one venturing into the Okavango Delta, Maun is now an active regional center with the busiest airport in all of Botswana.

Although ground travel past Maun is possible – a range of condi-tions permitting – distances are daunting and roads are seldom more than ruts in the rough. Most visitors bound for the region's far-flung safari camps elect to be flown in by bushplane. Aware that Estelle is a reluctant flyer, even under the most ideal of circumstances, I considered it imprudent, in planning our first excursion into the Delta, to inquire in her presence exactly what a 'bushplane' might be. My own mental image, however, was of a sputtering antique not unlike the one that plucked Indiana Jones out of a Peruvian jungle as he was about to be skewered by natives. I hoped I was wrong – because, otherwise, short of an equally pressing incentive for Estelle to board such a conveyance, I feared there might be some last-minute changes to our itinerary.

Weight being a critical factor with light aircraft, we stowed all but the most essential of our belongings at the airport terminal and hiked across the flight line toward a pair of single-engine Cessnas that looked reassuringly contemporary and well maintained. Dozens of these sturdy workhorses provide aerial taxi service to and from camps throughout the Okavango and beyond. As the Cessnas were five-passenger aircraft, and there were six in our party, Estelle and I were split off and paired with a young couple being dropped at another camp. Sharing passage on the other plane were Jerry Dale – who had scouted our destination the pre-

vious year – and Searle Turner, who had traveled solo on our gorilla trek, but was now accompanied by his wife Patti and daughter Rachel. All of seven years old, Rachel was on her second African safari.

With little more than the customary anxiety she demonstrates upon boarding even the most airworthy of commercial jetliners, Estelle hoisted herself into the plane designated as ours – and within minutes, we were airborne en route to Mombo Camp. All signs of civilization van-ished beneath our wings within moments after takeoff. Creeping tenta-tively into the dusty wilderness past Maun were a few austere dwellings, but even those feathered out to zero-density as the Cessna climbed to a thousand feet and leveled off on a northwesterly course. Not long into our thirty-minute flight, the barren wasteland over which we were pass-ing commenced a gradual transformation as islands of vegetation swept into view and sunlight glanced brilliantly off patches of standing water. We were over the southernmost reaches of the Okavango Delta. As we proceeded, both vegetation and water became more abundant. Stands of towering palm trees stretched toward the sky and silvery waterways flanked by greenery meandered crazily through expanses of arid hard-pan. Overlaying all was an intricate spider's web of game trails worn into the terrain by generations of wandering wildlife. On occasion, we spotted clusters of antelope – too far below to identify more precisely – as well as communal groupings of giraffes and elephants, unmistakable from any altitude. We were experiencing a vast ecosystem in miniature.

With the roar of the propeller quelling conversation, I allowed my mind to wander to an article Jerry had clipped from the Air Botswana in-flight magazine a year or so before. The subject was Mombo Camp and its environs, and what had struck me most about it was a full-page photo of African wild dogs, which the text professed were resident to the area – at least at times. Though packs of wild dogs once ranged widely throughout much of the continent, they are now Africa's most endan-gered large predator. Sightings are so rare in the safari belt of East Africa, once a stronghold for the species, that they are presumed to be virtually extinct there. I had certainly never seen one. On my first trip to the northern Serengeti, there was posted in the lobby of Lobo Wildlife Lodge a wild dog photograph accompanied by a written plea urging any-one having sighted these imperiled creatures to forward all details to a researcher engaged in studying them. Despite our best game-spotting efforts, we left the area with nothing to submit on the topic of wild dogs. My disappointment was salved somewhat on a subsequent visit when I learned from the hot-air balloon pilot flying out of Seronera Wildlife Lodge to the south that the researcher in question had been funded for a full year, during which he had not once had a personal encounter with the subject of his study. The population was that depleted. But a sixth of the world's surviving wild dogs – some 800 in number – was said to reside in northern Botswana. Would fortune smile upon us?

Our pilot landed expertly on a generous airstrip hacked out of the coarse vegetation indigenous to the region. Preventing that vegetation from reclaiming the strip is an ongoing concern for those it services, as are repairs occasioned by flooding during the rainy season. Short on equipment and supplies, but long on ingenuity, the Mombo Camp maintenance crew patches washed-away sections of runway by grinding up termite mounds, then adding water to produce a mending compound that hardens like cement.

Awaiting our arrival was an open Land Rover dispatched to convey us to camp. Unlike the safari vehicles we were accustomed to in Kenya and Tanzania – which have pop-tops for panoramic viewing, but are otherwise enclosed – the Land Rovers in service here had passenger seating on a tiered flatbed that afforded unrestricted viewing in all directions. It also – as we would discover – afforded an exquisitely vulnerable vantage point from which to observe lions or elephants up close.

Mombo Island is located just off the northwestern tip of Chief's Island – the largest permanent land mass in the Okavango Delta – and depending upon the time of year and the extent of seasonal flooding can be either connected to its giant neighbor or a small island unto itself. Nestled on it in a wooded glade overlooking a broad floodplain is Mombo Camp, as intimate as it is remote, with ten spacious tents and a lounge and dining room under thatch. Our arrival occasioned a warm greeting by camp manager Annie Grimm, a young Australian, who acquainted us with camp procedures and outlined what to expect of the region. Hoping for an optimistic reply, I inquired as to the likelihood of our seeing wild dogs. Her response was unequivocal – we would see wild dogs. By pure

dumb luck, our August appearance at Mombo had coincided with the denning season – the only time wild dogs will abandon their perpetually nomadic lifestyle and settle into one location for an extended period. A pack of twenty-six adults was raising twenty-one pups only ten minutes from camp.

We had barely settled into our tents when booming tribal drums summoned us for afternoon tea – a light repast of sandwiches and cake that serves as the traditional kickoff to the afternoon game drive. There we met Gert Brits, our guide and driver, an affable South African with a naturalist's grasp of animal behavior and a schoolmaster's passion to impart it. Aware of our intense interest in the wild dogs, Gert proposed that we begin our drive with a visit to the den, cautioning us that there was likely to be little activity at that time of the day.

Our route took us through terrain as singular as any I had encountered in Africa. Everywhere there was evidence of a divine perversity at work, with dusty flat plains adjoining marshy wetlands adjoining islands of plants and trees curiously intermingled. I confess with little pride that the osmotic effect of my travels has failed to instill in me any discernible capacity to distinguish one type of tree or bush from the next, but even the botanically challenged could not help but notice that the acacia woodlands and thorn scrub that abound throughout much of the continent have here been infiltrated by tropical palms.

Termite mound sightings rarely occasion much excitement, but their profusion and size in this region are extraordinary. Barely a few dozen yards can be navigated in any direction without encountering at least one of these monuments to insect industry. Mature mounds a dozen or more feet in height are not at all uncommon, and structural diversity is the norm rather than the exception. I wondered, as we maneuvered around these towering constructs, why some were built like sprawling condominiums and others like skyscrapers – why a flamboyant few even seemed patterned after medieval castles, with two, sometimes three, distinct turrets emerging from stucco battlements. Evidently there are competing schools of termite architecture.

Below each active mound is a colony of termites numbering into the millions. From the profusion of mounds in evidence, I can only suppose that there are more termites in a single square mile of Okavango wilderness than there are people on the face of the earth. More than any other creature, the lowly termite has shaped and altered the topography of the region. When flood waters spill into the lower Okavango Delta during the winter dry season each year, all but the hardiest plants and trees perish on the submerged flatlands. But when the waters recede, termites drawn to the vegetal residue move in and establish colonies whose nascent fortresses are able to withstand the next onslaught of water, thus providing a dry haven for young plant life sprouting on and around them. As the years progress, both mounds and vegetation increase in stature, and deposits of wind-blown topsoil accumulate at their bases. Additional plants take root and propagate. Alate termites colonize proximate frontiers. Over the course of time, an island with mounds at its core will have arisen out of the floodplain – a permanent sanctuary from the seasonal submersions that keep much of the adjacent expanses barren except for annual grasses.

We reached the wild dog den site with barely a pause en route. Dominating a dusty clearing in an otherwise forested area were the jumbled remains of a large jackal berry tree – so christened for its fruit of which jackals are reputedly fond. Felled by disease and long ago stripped of its leaves and bark by elephants, the tree and its immediate surroundings had become a refuge and nursery for the litter of pups being raised there. Two adults snoozing on perimeter detail rose to acknowledge our approach, but demonstrated no apparent anxiety – these animals were, after all, accustomed to vehicles and visitors. In addition to being a popular attraction for tourists in residence at Mombo Camp, the pack had been under months-long scrutiny by a film crew from *National Geographic*. Dismissing our intrusion as nonthreatening, the canine sentries flopped back onto the ground and, within moments, resumed their disrupted napping. The other adults were not about.

Roughly the size of a Doberman pinscher, the African wild dog – known also as the Cape hunting dog or painted wolf – is lean and long-legged, with huge rounded ears and a patchwork coat of black and white and mustard-yellow. Though black muzzles and white tufted tail tips are universal, each individual is otherwise uniquely patterned. Masterful pack hunters, wild dogs are successful in up to eighty percent of attempted

kills – as compared to lions, for example, which are successful perhaps twenty percent of the time. So why is the most proficient predator in Africa teetering on the brink of extinction? Though the reasons are varied and interwoven, man is a component in all of them.

Like the coyote of North America and wolves throughout the world, the African wild dog has a sad history of being indiscriminately slaughtered for little reason other than that it is feared and misunderstood – and occasionally exercises poor judgment in preying upon domestic livestock. Scant evidence exists, though, to suggest that wild dogs have ever posed a measurable threat to farmers and ranchers, economic or otherwise. Yet for many years, and throughout much of the continent, these efficient predators were ignominiously relegated to vermin status. Until a few decades ago – astonishingly, even in the game reserves of East Africa – entire wild dog packs were routinely shot by hunters and park rangers, ostensibly to protect populations of prey animals, though no such sanctions were in force against lions or other large predators. Aggravating the wild dog's public relations dilemma was its manner of killing, considered cruel and loathsome by many. While the big cats of the realm tend to dispatch their quarry with a clean stranglehold, the much smaller dogs attack in numbers and literally tear their prey to pieces. Though unpleasant to behold, it is a practice born of necessity – one presumably no more traumatic for the victim than slow suffocation – yet it has contributed to the dogs' reputation as wanton killers deserving of eradication.

Placement of the wild dog on the endangered species list has curtailed the most grievous injustices inflicted upon it – but wild dog numbers are still in serious decline. Loss of habitat is a factor – and wild dogs require lots of habitat. Excepting the three months each year when the pack settles into one locale to raise puppies, these tireless nomads are forever on the move. Often they will traverse fifty miles a day, in good weather or bad, over home ranges – sometimes overlapping those of neighboring packs – comprising 700 square miles or more. Very few protected areas are large enough to sustain such resolute wanderers. Of the thirty-four countries over which wild dogs once ranged, only six are now thought to have survivable populations. Loss of habitat generally has a corollary – human encroachment – and human encroachment

appears to be a component in yet another scourge that has bedeviled the wild dog. Highly communicable canine diseases, most notably distemper and rabies, have in years past destroyed entire populations of wild dogs in the Serengeti and Masai Mara. Although jackals and hyenas can also carry these deadly viruses, domestic dogs are thought to be main transmitters. Since wild dogs are intensely communal and affectionate, a single stricken animal is almost certain to infect others in its pack – maybe all. Extermination results. To date, the sparsity of human settlement within the vast Okavango Delta has served to insulate its resident wild dogs from these killer contagions – which explains why the region is one of the last strongholds of this critically imperiled species.

Gert eased our Land Rover past the dozing adult dogs and inched up to the den where we could see the tiny puppies clustered together under a fallen tree limb. Most were emulating their napping elders – but a rowdy few were engaged in spirited play-fighting, clambering with abandon over slumbering littermates largely oblivious to the tussling and tumbling around them. Although infant mortality is high among wild dogs – as it is among most animals in the wild – these youngsters stood a better chance of survival than most, belonging as they did to a large and thriving pack, certainly among the largest in Africa. A century ago, hunting bands of a hundred or more were reliably reported – but today, an average wild dog pack numbers only about eight to twelve.

No one in our troupe of six safari veterans had ever seen wild dogs – even Jerry Dale, who at the time had been taking tour groups to Africa for twenty years – and I suspect we would all have been content to park ourselves by the den and watch them do nothing for the duration of our stay at Mombo. But Gert assured us that more engaging diversions were certain to be found nearby and that we would return to the den early in the morning when activity was virtually guaranteed.

We drove the dusty roads looking for game. Mostly what we found were antelopes. Wildebeests and impalas – old acquaintances from our travels in East Africa – were here intermingled with tsessebes and red lechwes and others we had not before encountered. Although annual floodwaters had peaked and were already beginning to recede, expanses of shallow water still stretched over many of the floodplains, affording drink and fresh forage for a range of browsers and grazers – which, in turn, provided sustenance to the region's many predators. Near one of these seasonal lakes we came upon a lioness and her three subadult offspring engaged in every lion's activity of choice – which is no activity at all. Aside from a nasty bite wound on the flank of the adult female – probably from an altercation with another lion, or perhaps a hyena – the cats looked healthy and fit, but without the distended bellies that signify recent feeding. Since the sun was getting low, we decided to wait until dusk and see if they showed any inclination to embark on a hunt. There was no rush to leave. Night game drives were permitted here.

About thirty minutes into our vigil, the still silence was ruptured by a squawk from the Land Rover's radio. Another of the camp's game drive vehicles had happened upon the wild dog pack heading out to hunt. Rough directions spilled from the speaker – and with barely a thought to the contrary we abandoned our slumbering lions to pursue their evening's activities unobserved.

Guided by landmarks that only one intimate with a region could hope to recognize, Gert put us on an intercept course with the other vehicle and the dogs. Radio contact was maintained as we closed the distance, but our first indication that we were drawing near came with the sighting of a half-dozen spotted hyenas loping unhurriedly, but purposefully, across a dusty plain. Though formidable hunters in their own right, hyenas are no match for wild dogs in efficiency and often will trail a hunting pack in hopes of stealing an easy meal from their smaller competitors. This unabashed freebooting is not without its perils, however, as wild dogs, in sufficient numbers, can and will bestow razor-jawed punishment on any marauder incautious enough to linger within range.

By the time we at last encountered the dogs, the sun was hovering behind a phalanx of trees on the far horizon. Counterweighing it from the opposite direction was an ascendant full moon. Everything in between was a crosshatch of dwindling light and deepening shadow. Almost at once the action began. Across an expanse of open marshland, we watched as a dozen or more of the wild dogs – only part of the pack – ran headlong into a small herd of impalas. From wildlife documentaries, I knew what to expect. Working like a crack combat unit, the dogs would identify the

most promising target animal and then run it to ground in a full-throttle sprint that could last up to three or four miles. So much for expectations. What took place before us could most fittingly be characterized as chaotic. The startled antelopes bolted in all directions – and the dogs did pretty much the same.

Most of the impalas spun away from the water, charging hard into shoreline vegetation which narrowed our perception of the chase to stroboscopic flashes of hide and fur. As we peered into the palms, straining for a glimpse of anything at all, one of the impalas suddenly burst back into view and leaped into the marsh, running full tilt through the shallows with a single wild dog close on its heels, seemingly unslowed by the fluid drag. Predator and prey splashed through the water for several dozen yards and then veered off into the enveloping underbrush once again.

An eruption of dust through the trees across the way prompted Gert to surmise that a kill had been made. Though only a scant sixty yards separated us from the spot, it was sixty yards of marsh water – uninviting even for a Land Rover – and circumnavigating it took about ten minutes. By the time we arrived, the dust had settled and the pack had moved on, leaving only two of its members behind to pick over the tattered remnants of what had, just minutes before, been an impala on the run. Wild dogs – featherweights in the predatory arena – consume their kills with awesome swiftness as a best defense against having them stolen by heavyweight opponents such as lions and hyenas.

A few hundred yards away, another impala had given its all to sustain the wild dog pack. It, too, was scarcely recognizable by the time we arrived, mere minutes after its last breath and heartbeat. Here again, most of the pack had eaten and run, leaving behind a few stragglers to polish off the leftovers. With darkness now upon us, Gert produced a spotlight and plugged it into the dash, directing its powerful beam on the trampled clearing. The dogs – evidently accustomed to such phenomena – appeared unperturbed by the flood of artificial illumination. With barely a glance in our direction, they went about their business with dispatch, three of them picking morsels of flesh from the now-scattered remains while two others stood watch, peering into the darkness in anticipation of the party-crashers they knew would soon arrive.

And arrive they did. We perceived them first as fleeting shapes at

the outer limits of our spotlight's reach. Hyenas. The sentries darted forward a few menacing steps, and the forms retreated in the darkness. The other wild dogs continued to feed. A minute or two passed. Then a hyena bolted into the clearing and confronted one of the dogs which was gnawing at the antelope's spinal column. The wild dog stood and growled, holding its ground, and the interloper withdrew. Moments later, the hyena approached again and the dog leaped forward, leaving its meal untended for just a moment – but a moment too long. A second hyena lunged out of the darkness, grabbed the prize and ran for cover, screeching its species' distinctive laugh – seemingly apropos, but actually a vocalization of terror and alarm – as several of the wild dogs chased after it.

Other skirmishes followed – mostly minor, since neither the dogs nor the hyenas appeared to regard what little remained of the impala as worth the risk of injury – until the last of the skeletal remnants was trotted away by one side or the other and the parties dispersed into the African night.

We drove about for another hour or more. Although each of us harbored hopes of some grand encounter – our lions on the hunt, perhaps – nothing of the sort was in store. We were, however, rewarded with sightings of some of the region's denizens of darkness – creatures rarely, if ever, observed during daylight hours. Most revealed themselves simply by looking in our direction. While our spotlight allowed us to see only a few yards into the inky blackness, its illumination penetrated well beyond that, reflecting back pairs of glowing orbs from ofttimes considerable distances. Found in profusion were springhares – hopping rodents looking like a cross between a rabbit and a kangaroo – that emerge from their burrows only at night to forage on roots and grasses. Discovered on a tree branch was a genet, a small predator, catlike in appearance and nature, that subsists principally on mice and insects. Also sighted was a honey badger digging voraciously for rodents or grubs. It was a magical experience – a rare one for the average traveler, since night game drives are not allowed in most of the continent's national parks and reserves. Little did we know at the time that it would be our last such experience at Mombo. When we returned the following year, we found that the region – which had only recently been absorbed into the sprawling Moremi Game

207

Reserve – now had to comply with regulations in force throughout the Botswana park system. Night game viewing was no longer permitted.

Some of those nocturnal creatures were still about the next morning when we piled into our Land Rover and set course for the wild dog den. Darkness was just beginning to surrender to a glow on the eastern horizon. Although all of us were savvy enough to know that August in the southern hemisphere meant wintertime, none of us was prepared for just how frosty Botswana mornings could get at that time of year. Botswana is, after all, Africa. But with mid-forties air temperature driven below freezing by the wind chill attributable to our open-air conveyance, we might as easily have been looking for wolves in the Yukon as wild dogs in the Okavango. Huddled beneath piles of woolen blankets – provided by a camp staff accustomed to ill-prepared visitors – we peered into the gathering light through plumes of flash-frozen breath.

We arrived at the den just as the first rays of sunlight pierced the adjoining woodlands, casting slender shadows over the toppled jackal berry tree and the dusty clearing surrounding it. Gert had apprised us that early mornings were generally the most active times at the den, especially when the adults returned from a successful hunt to feed the hungry and excited puppies. Wild dogs customarily hunt in the daylight hours around sunrise and sunset – and with forty-seven mouths to feed, this pack was particularly assiduous in its quest for sustenance – but sometimes they will hunt by night if there is adequate moonlight. Since there had been a full moon the night before, we hoped that the two impalas downed the previous evening had been sufficient to keep the pack satisfied and asleep until daybreak. A successful night hunt might have deprived us of the chance to observe the puppies feeding.

We need not have been concerned. Only four adult dogs were at the den, keeping watch while lying together in pairs to conserve body warmth. The puppies, in a hollow beneath the fallen tree trunk, were just beginning to stir in anticipation of breakfast and the wonders of a new day. Before long, they were up and at play, chasing about, stalking and pouncing on one another, tugging on stray ears and tails, and generally exploring age-old scenarios of dominance and submission that would be carried into adulthood.

Ranging in age from six to eight weeks, the twenty-one littermates were the issue of at least three different mothers – an atypical situation for a tight-knit hierarchical community in which only the dominant female maintains the right to breed. Females of reproductive age either defer to this prerogative or leave the pack to form family groupings of their own. When transgressions occur within the pack, the dominant female will usually kill the offspring of her subordinates, or, if pup-rearing resources are plentiful, adopt them as her own. In this situation, the balance tilted in favor of adoption. The fact that multiple births were in evidence, however, coupled with the unusually large size of the pack, led to speculation by those knowledgeable of such things that the Mombo pack was due to split.

Like children at a pet shop window, we delighted at the pups' playful interactions for nearly an hour before the first of the hunters returned. Weaving through trees as if on a slalom, the three in the lead – bloodied muzzles proclaiming the success of their mission – sprinted the last dozen yards to the den and burst into the clearing. Immediately they were set upon by a score of boisterous puppies.

The civil division of food among wild dogs is an essential component of pack cohesion. Unlike other predators, lions and hyenas in particular, which hunt cooperatively but then fight amongst themselves over the spoils, wild dogs feed swiftly and voraciously, but without rancor. When accompanied by juveniles not yet of age to participate in the hunt, adult dogs will defer to the youngsters, allowing them their fill and settling for what remains. Among pack members there is also a near-obsessive compulsion to share. Puppies still confined to the den area during weaning are proffered portions of meat disgorged by returning hunters of both sexes and all ages. While regurgitation is not uncommon in the animal world, wild dogs are among the only species to provision fellow adults – those remaining behind with the pups, as well as the sick and disabled – in this solicitous and altruistic fashion.

More often than not, ritualized begging precedes the disgorgement of food. The supplicants – adults as well as puppies – will approach the returning hunters with whines and high-pitched squeals, nudging them and licking their faces and acting impassionately submissive until the donors comply with their none-too-subtle demands for a handout. With twenty-one puppies, the ritual was perfunctory. Like a wave, they washed over the lead returnee, twittering like birds, leaping and jockeying for position. Almost at once, and with a convulsive heave, the adult deposited an offering of meat on the ground and vaulted out of the fray. Clambering over one another, the tiny gluttons fed greedily until the last morsel was consumed, then sprinted en masse to the next returnee who was similarly induced to reapportion the bounty of the hunt.

During the next half hour or so, the ritual was repeated several times more as additional members of the hunting party returned to the den. Most of the dogs – seemingly aware that delay was an invitation to mobbing – regurgitated almost as soon as the puppy horde descended upon them. Since youngsters are particularly vulnerable at mealtime, the adult sentries were especially alert, facing outward from the den and scanning the tree line for predators. The only incursion was from within, however. Resident to the den area were a dozen or more hooded vultures for whom the wild dog denning season was a time of plenty. Perched on low branches or shuffling about on the ground, these dedicated scavengers – among the smallest of the African vultures – were forever on the lookout for tidbits of food overlooked or dropped by the puppies. Often they would sidle up to the feeding pups – larcenous intent clearly in evidence – but almost without fail these furtive advances would elicit a rebuff from one or more of the adult dogs which would leap high into the air and snap at the fleeing thieves. In most instances, it seemed more like sport than a response to any real threat.

Although some of the adults engaged in play with the tireless youngsters, most eventually found a quiet spot in which to rest. Unwilling to relinquish their grasp on the still-new day, the puppies continued to play-fight and chase each other about. Some approached to within a few feet of our vehicle and peered up at us inquisitively. The boldest gnawed on our tires. Anything at all could become a coveted prize. On several occasions, we watched as one pup or another picked up a stray stick or a bone and ran with it, pursued at once by several littermates intent upon seizing the trophy. Three puppies trotted past us carrying a vulture feather like a parade banner. Aping their elders, a few even stalked and darted at the ubiquitous vultures, deriving no small pleasure, I am sure, from the fact that the startled interlopers flapped away squawking, just

as they had from the adult vanquishers. It was a sublime morning for the young dogs – and for us.

We saw little else of Mombo on that visit. Most of our time we spent parked at the den, marveling at our good fortune in being able, in one brief stay, to observe so much of wild dog life and behavior, from hunting and fending off opposition, to feeding and nurturing their young.

First experiences tend to be ones that remain most vividly in mind, and when I think of the wild dogs, my strongest recollections are of that first visit to Mombo. But there were further encounters. We returned to Mombo the following August, hoping that the lure of the familiar would have brought the dogs back to their former denning site – and it had. As predicted, the pack had split, though the faction that returned was undiminished in numbers due to the influx of yearlings from the previous season's bumper crop of puppies. Again, more than one female had given birth, and during our stay, we had the pleasure of watching the last of the litters make its first foray into sunlight.

A couple of years passed before our next visit to Mombo – in April this time, so we had no reasonable expectation that the far-ranging dogs would be around. But they happened into the area on the day we arrived and remained until we left, affording us an opportunity to witness the twice-daily ritual of exuberant bounding and nuzzling by which pack members psych each other up for the hunt. We even tagged along with them a couple of times – unconcerned that our presence would disturb the proceedings since wild dogs make no pretense of hunting by stealth – and felt like participants as the dogs led us on a wild chase after a lechwe they had targeted for dinner. Defying the odds, the lechwe evaded death by charging belly-deep into a marshy lagoon. Wary of crocodiles, and lacking the supreme motivation of the antelope, the dogs chose not to follow.

I imagine that one of the great satisfactions of doing field research in Africa is the opportunity that prolonged observation affords to really get to know animals as individuals and as group members. This sense of communion with the wild almost never occurs in the context of a safari where each experience is a brief encounter, a moment of time recorded in recollection, unconnected to anything in the continuum. It struck me as I watched our wild dogs disappear into the gathering darkness that this was something more than the norm. On previous visits we had seen two generations of puppies carousing around the natal den. Now some of those exact same animals were stalwarts of the pack, hunting and parenting and following instinctual imperatives refined over countless millennia, unburdened by the awareness that their survival as a species hangs by a thread.

Our paths would cross yet again.

Two years later, near the end of a long safari marking our tenth wedding anniversary, Estelle and I returned to Mombo during the wild dog denning season. Once again, we were with Bill and Sally Snyder. It had been four years since we last visited Mombo at that time, but we were hopefully optimistic that our luck would hold and we would again see the wild dogs. It was not to be. The once mighty Mombo pack had split, then split again, into tighter groups of twelve to fifteen which had dispersed throughout and beyond the original unit's broad territory. One of the splinter packs still included the Mombo region within its home range, and the dogs' nomadic natures brought them back to the camp area from time to time, but they had not denned nearby for several years. Seeing wild dogs at Mombo was no longer a certainty. Much more distressing was news that the resident pack had lost all of its offspring for the past two seasons – no one could say for sure whether through predation or disease. Though we were well into the denning season, the current den had not been located and the condition of the pack was as unknown as its whereabouts. During our three days at Mombo – abundant as ever with predators and prey – we kept an eye out for tricolor coats and big round ears, hoping the dogs would make an appearance as they had during each of our previous visits, but there was to be no wild dog fix on this particular stay.

From Mombo we flew south over delta wetlands to the final stop on our itinerary, Chitabe Camp. Newer by a dozen years than Mombo, Chitabe is an eight-tent camp whose luxury accommodations are situated on raised wooden platforms connected by elevated walkways – an architectural style finding favor in Africa because of its minimal impact on the environment. Though erected within a glade of ancient leadwood

and sausage trees, the entire camp complex required the cutting of just a single tree branch during the course of its construction and could, on very short notice if the need arose, be dismantled and removed without a trace.

The terrain around Chitabe – a vast intermingling of woodlands and marshes and grassy plains – looks much like Mombo. Although deep inside the Okavango Delta, the region and the camp are not within the Moremi Game Reserve, but rather in an adjacent private concession area designated by the government as a natural buffer zone for the unfenced park. While still a protected area, the concession is free of park restrictions limiting off-road driving and night game drives. Animals wander freely between the park and the concession area, and in recent years one of the splinter groups from the original Mombo wild dog pack had taken up residence in the Chitabe area. We hoped to reacquaint ourselves with some of our old friends. But here, too, we were disappointed to learn that the dogs had not been sighted in many weeks.

Our guide at Chitabe was Newman Chuma, widely regarded as one of the two best trackers in the country, a native Botswanan who for seven years had honed his prodigious skills shepherding naturalists and film crews studying wild dogs. On our first afternoon with him, driving along a dusty road far from camp, Newman abruptly slowed the Land Rover and pulled to the side, peering down and pointing out to us several sets of wind-smudged tracks left earlier in the day. Wild dogs. He continued on, following the tracks until they headed off the road and into an expanse of mopane woodland. As it was already late in the day, there was no point in trying to follow any further. But Newman suspected there was a den somewhere about, and we voted at once to return in the morning and try to pick up the trail.

We left the camp at first light and drove for an hour or so to the area where the dog tracks had been spotted the afternoon before. Along the same stretch of road Newman found fresh evidence that our quarry was still around. With mounting excitement, we followed the signpost markings of overlapping paw prints that could not have been more than a few hours old. When the tracks veered abruptly into the bush, we did the same.

Spread out before us, as far as we could see, was a vast expanse of mopane woodland. Ubiquitous throughout the region, the mopane – whose distinctive butterfly-shaped leaves are a favorite food of many browsers – can grow to heights of eighty feet or more. In less than optimal environments, however, the mopane manifests itself in a shrub-like form that rarely exceeds a tenth of that height. It was this stunted variant that lay before us, and though, for the most part, individual trees were sufficiently spaced to allow passage of our vehicle, it was going to be a serious obstacle course. Moreover, the sandy clay from which they grew was not nearly as fine an impression medium as the road we had just left. Tracking would be difficult.

At this point I knew what to expect. We would thrash about in the bush for a while, long enough for our guide to justify having brought us all the way out here, then give up and see what else we could find. It was a common safari scenario. Everyone played along.

Not Newman. Acting every bit as though he knew exactly where he was going, he set course and plunged into the woodlands, weaving his way skillfully through the mopane maze, slowing every so often to scan the ground for wild dog spoor or prevent those of us topside from being sliced and diced by whiplashing branches. At times he would lose the faint trail, but never for long or by much. Always he would pick it up again and, with a silent hand gesture denoting the direction the quarry had taken, resume the hunt. We were in awe. Whether we found the dogs or not hardly mattered at this point. It was a privilege just watching a master at work.

By now, we were a half-hour or more from the road and the mopane was closing in on us. No longer was it possible to skirt every tree and bush, but Newman was not to be deterred in his quest. If there was no passage around a bush or small tree, he simply drove over it. Tree after tree yielded to our Land Rover's bulldozer might, disappearing beneath the oversize bumper and noisily raking the undercarriage. Convinced we were raping the wilderness, I turned with unease to survey the swath of destruction in our wake – and saw virtually none. Trees emerging from the underside of the vehicle simply sprang back upright as though made of sprung steel. From the evidence on hand, we might have been airlifted to this spot by helicopter – the woodlands, largely undisturbed, looked uniform in every direction. Which begged a question. Where the hell were we? Only half-kidding, I asked Newman if he had ever gotten lost. With merely a hint of amusement, he assured me he had not.

About mid-morning we emerged into a clearing. Newman pulled to a stop and looked around. He knew this place. Though we had come to it by an altogether different route – presumably a much less direct one – he recognized it as being in the same area where the wild dogs had denned the previous season. How he could distinguish one small clearing from any other in the midst of endless square miles of woodland was beyond me – but there was no doubting him, even if we had been inclined, because within seconds of his pronouncement we all gasped and pointed as one. No more than forty yards ahead, near the opposing tree line, a wild dog lay with its head erect in perfect profile. Noticing us as we noticed it, the animal turned to meet our gaze, showing little concern or surprise in its demeanor. Clearly it was acquainted with Land Rovers and considered them no threat.

As we edged forward, the wild dog rose and moved into the trees. In the dappled shadows beyond we spotted a second animal – then a third. We had found the Chitabe pack. And more. A few feet in from the clearing, amidst a cluster of scraggly mopane, was a low mound of dirt with an excavated hole at its center. We had found the den. Since no puppies were in view we assumed that they had skittered unseen into their subterranean sanctuary upon first sighting us across the clearing. We approached to a respectful distance and Newman cut the engine. Cameras at the ready, we waited quietly to see what developed.

It did not take long. Within minutes, two Mickey Mouse ears and a small head popped into view and peered at us over the rim of the den. Detecting no cause for alarm in the relaxed demeanor of the adult dogs on babysitting detail, the youngster scrambled fully out of the burrow. Soon a half-dozen brothers and sisters had done likewise. Though they remained close enough to the opening to dart to safety should the need arise, the pups seemed remarkably unperturbed by the first-ever appearance of a mechanical behemoth at their doorstep – not to mention the curious creatures on board.

Just when it looked as if the pups might make a tentative move in

our direction, a trio of adults returning from the morning hunt burst into view, and the puppies, joined instantly by others we had not even seen yet, raced to greet them in joyful expectation of breakfast. The twittering reunion took place in the underbrush, largely out of view, affording us only occasional glimpses of the feeding frenzy we knew to be in progress. Other adults returned, and the rowdy scene was repeated. As young and old ran in and out of view, like stage actors in a frantic farce, we did our best to determine a count. Though when last seen the Chitabe pack had numbered fourteen adult members, only nine were in evidence this morning. But the pack had now been enlarged by the addition of eleven puppies – about a month and a half old by Newman's estimation.

Having consumed every regurgitated morsel presented to them, the youngsters returned to the proximity of the den and renewed their interrupted interest in our presence. At first, none strayed far from the security of the group. But then, emboldened by curiosity, one of the pups broke ranks and took a few steps in our direction. After a few moments several others followed, taking up position next to the leader. It was an extraordinary encounter. We were the very first human beings these dogs had ever seen. They gazed at us. We gazed at them. Then an unknown something spooked one of them and they all scampered back to the den opening. A short while later it started again. This time the pups got a bit closer before turning tail and retreating. Before long they were back. In the end, all eleven puppies ventured to within ten feet of the vehicle and peered up at us with intense interest. Happily, the nonstop clicks and whirs of our cameras seemed not to frighten them – but then the ill-timed clink of a dropped lens cap startled them all the way back and into the den.

At this juncture we decided to depart so as not to overstay our welcome. Eager to spend more time with the dogs, we proposed returning in the afternoon, but Newman countered by suggesting instead that we head out very early the next morning and try to intercept the adults in the process of hunting. Should we fail in that, we could always push on to the den and wait for their return. It seemed a capital idea.

Word of our good fortune spread like wildfire through the camp, and it came as no surprise when we learned that the other two guides and their guests were planning to pay the dogs a visit during the afternoon game drive. Our own plan was to head off in another direction. Midway into the drive, a call came crackling over the radio from one of the dog-hunting teams. The wild dog den had not been located despite Newman's having given his fellow guides specific directions on how to find it. Newman reiterated the route, and the radio fell silent. Twenty minutes later there was another request for help. Newman explained again. The calls kept coming in. It was incredible. Here our guide had managed to track wild dogs straight to their den over exceptionally challenging terrain while these others – clearly less experienced – were unable even to track our four-ton Land Rover over the same course. I found it amusing in a perverse sort of way. Newman continued to do his best to put his comrades on target, but the sun was getting low in the sky and it was apparent, at least to me, that the other camp guests were not going to see the wild dogs – at least not that day.

The next morning, like commandos on a secret mission, we slipped out of camp before anyone else was even awake. The plan was to head toward the wild dog den and look for signs of the adult pack members on the hunt. It was a much shorter journey this time, as Newman, now aware of the den's location, was able to take a less circuitous route. The sun was barely up when we reached the site, but it was evident right away that something was amiss. No adult dogs were on watch and no youngsters were about. Newman announced his conclusion that the dogs had moved to another location.

Our first guilty thought was that the animals had moved because we had found them, but Newman assured us that was most unlikely. The adult members of the pack were thoroughly habituated to human presence and would have felt no threat from our visit. He explained that wild dogs often change dens midway through pup rearing for reasons relating to the accumulation of waste and irksome parasites within and around the site. It was, in his opinion, a coincidence that they had chosen yesterday to make such a move. He would try again to pick up their trail.

We set about crisscrossing an expanding circle of terrain looking for fresh spoor that would lead us to the new denning location. Every once in a while, Newman picked up what appeared to be fresh tracks, sometimes even puppy tracks, but none rewarded us with decisive information. After an hour or more, he announced that it was time to give it up. The area surrounding the old den had just too many sets of to-and-fro tracks to afford us a clear indication of where the dogs had gone.

As we wound our way back to the main road, my initial disappointment faded with the recognition that, once again, we had been rewarded with a very special wild dog experience. After many weeks of not having been sighted at the two prime wild dog locations we had visited on this trip, the dogs had presented themselves – to us and us alone – on our next-to-last day in Africa. It had been a gift. In the company of a master guide who had found the wild dogs where others had not and could not, we had shared a few moments with these rare and noble creatures. Then, like phantoms, they had vanished into the boundless Okavango.

OKAVANGO VISTA
Moremi Game Reserve, Botswana

ZEBRAS AND GIRAFFES

IMPALA
Chitabe, Okavango Delta, Botswana

WILDEBEEST
Mombo, Moremi Game Reserve, Botswana

GIRAFFES AND ZEBRAS
EYE RESTING LIONS
Mombo, Moremi Game Reserve, Botswana

AFRICAN WILD DOGS
Mombo, Moremi Game Reserve, Botswana

WILD DOG PUPS AT PLAY
Mombo, Moremi Game Reserve, Botswana

CHEETAH HUNTING
Mombo, Moremi Game Reserve, Botswana

CHEETAH CUBS
Mombo, Moremi Game Reserve, Botswana

LIONESS
Mombo, Moremi Game Reserve, Botswana

AFRICAN WILD DOG
Mombo, Moremi Game Reserve, Botswana

CHEETAH
Serengeti National Park, Tanzania

LIONESS AND CUBS
Mombo, Moremi Game Reserve, Botswana

BLACK-BACKED JACKAL
Serengeti National Park, Tanzania

LEOPARD AND CUB
Chitabe, Okavango Delta, Botswana

SPOTTED HYENA AND CUBS
Mombo, Moremi Game Reserve, Botswana

WILD DOGS REGURGITATE FOOD FOR PUPS
Mombo, Moremi Game Reserve, Botswana

WARTHOGS
Mombo, Moremi Game Reserve, Botswana

ELEPHANT CREATING MUD WALLOW
Mombo, Moremi Game Reserve, Botswana

ELEPHANT CHARGE
Mombo, Moremi Game Reserve, Botswana

CHACMA BABOON
Victoria Falls National Park, Zimbabwe

LIONS AT WARTHOG BURROW
...abo, Moremi Game Reserve, Botswana

Heaven and Hell

One of the extraordinary things about elephants is the stealth with which they move through dense bush and woodlands. With scarcely a wavering leaf or a snapping twig to announce them, an entire herd can appear out of nowhere at a waterhole, enjoy a rowdy session of drink and play, and then vanish in a whisper as though at the bidding of a master illusionist.

When we first began traveling to Africa, the phenomenon of vanishing elephants was far from illusory. The African elephant was, in fact, vanishing off the face of the earth at a rate so alarming that many observers feared it would be virtually extinct in another generation. In the decade prior to our maiden safari, fully half of the continent's 1.3 million elephants had been systematically slaughtered by poachers, often working brazenly within the boundaries of national parks and reserves.

Ivory poaching was nothing new. What had once been a cottage industry, however, was now big business thanks to the exceptional killing power of military assault weapons diverted from a succession of post-colonial conflicts. Park rangers trying to preserve and protect the wildlife in their charge were routinely outnumbered and outgunned in the field, and, with remark-ably few exceptions, the governments for whom they worked, and sometimes died, showed neither the capacity nor the resolve to combat the problem. The war against poaching would not be won with firepower, but by the elimination of its economic incentive. To that end, a worldwide ban on ivory trade was proposed, but global consensus was slow in coming and not at all assured. The slaughter continued. If the elephant could not be saved, what hope was there for Africa's — or the world's — less charismatic creatures?

Having nothing to compare it with, and expecting the worst, I was frankly thrilled by the numbers of elephants we saw on our early trips to Kenya and Tanzania. That initial euphoria at seeing elephants in the wild — any number of them — was tempered, in time, by the somber acceptance that the great herds that had once roamed the savannas and bushlands of East Africa were no more. To see elephants as in days of old, we would have to journey south to Botswana, which has resisted the scourge of poaching and where populations of elephants were still robust.

An astonishing 60,000 elephants — roughly a tenth of Africa's surviving population — were said to inhabit Chobe National Park, a sprawling tract of pristine wilderness in northern Botswana. Along the Chobe River, which defines a segment of that country's border with

Namibia, sightings of hundreds at a time were not uncommon, especially in the dry season when water elsewhere tends to vanish and the giants congregate en masse around the region's only year-round source.

Our first visit to Chobe was during the rainy season – not the best time for game viewing – but as we were planning to be in Victoria Falls, just ninety minutes away on well-paved roads, we decided to reconnoiter the area. With assurances that Chobe would not disappoint, whatever the season, Jerry Dale booked us into the only permanent accommodation in the park. No disappointment. Located on a prime stretch of riverbank, the posh Chobe Game Lodge, all stucco and tile and arches, was a charming retreat with sweeping views and all the amenities.

Even better were the activities. After two weeks of dusty game drives, we were now in the realm of motorboat game viewing. That was an altogether new experience – sensational in the root sense of the word. With wind in our faces, and occasional spray, we zipped up and down the river, stopping at intervals to observe hippos and crocodiles – the most dangerous of Africa's water denizens – from an eye-level perspective both up-close and fresh. And though elephants by the thousands had abandoned the river for the season, drawn by ephemeral water sources and the lure of greener pastures, we still saw them in numbers that would have been exceptional anywhere else.

Our most memorable encounter was with a lone bull we found wading in the shallows. He was an impressive animal, well in his prime, with deep-creased skin and furrowed trunk, and tusks worn to stubs by years of use and abuse. Adept at reading body language and behavioral cues, our boat guide eased up to the old tusker, closer than I would have considered prudent, then cut the engine. The churning rumble of the outboard motor – strangely comforting in context – was abruptly and unexpectedly silenced, supplanted by the quiet lapping of water against the side of the boat. Momentum carried us to within twenty feet of the elephant, who stood attentive, yet relaxed and composed, ears flapping rhythmically as we gazed up and into his eyes. He was totally in his element. We were totally out of ours. I contemplated how many elephants had perished at the hands of hunters and poachers. Had this one borne witness to the dark side of human nature? Clearly it was within his power to wreak terrible retribution upon us, exposed as we were in our puny boat, but on this fine day he was content to look past the ignobility of our kind and return our gaze with equanimity. There was an openness in the moment, an intimacy, an interspecies connection unlike any I had known in a land vehicle. Or so I convinced myself.

We returned to Chobe two years later, this time during the dry season. I was eager to get back on the water, but our midday arrival via bushplane precluded our securing a boat that first afternoon, so we settled for a game drive in one of the lodge's open Land Rovers. As there were seven of us traveling together, we were given our own guide and vehicle – always a godsend for those in fear of being outnumbered by pathological bird-watchers intent upon identifying even the most nondescript species or, worse, their polar opposites for whom ninety seconds and a snapshot are all any encounter warrants. Best to travel with like-minded companions. Ours on this occasion were Sally and Bill Snyder, who had been on our introductory visit to Chobe, safari neophytes Lynne Wolf and Kathy Burns, friends of ours with a shared interest in wildlife and exotic travel, and John Ruffner, a colleague of Kathy's.

Our drive took us northeast, along a sandy track that fronted the river, and within minutes we came across our first elephants. A dozen or more were in view, bathing in the water or browsing nearby, and we pulled to a stop near a group of four approaching a wallow just off the main channel. Three were adults and the fourth was a year-old calf – the rule of thumb being that an infant can walk beneath its mother's belly until about that age.

The matriarch stepped into the wallow, plunged her trunk into the ooze, drew it out and blew a burst of mud and water up and over her head. The slurry landed on her back with a great splash, sending spattered shorebirds scurrying out of range. Gloppy runoff was still pouring down her flanks when she repeated the maneuver, this time swinging her trunk wide and to the rear, and unleashing a stream of muck that blanketed her hindquarters. The other elephants – even the calf – followed her example. Within minutes, all were festooned with overlapping swaths of glistening mud.

What looks like a childish game is actually therapeutic for elephants. A thorough application of mud or water, typically followed by a dusting of dirt, helps keep the animal cool in the sun and provides a measure of protection against parasites. Any notion we may have harbored, however, that this peculiar bathing ritual was strictly business was expunged at a subsequent wallow, where we watched for some time as a solitary bull amused himself by sloshing mud and kicking it about long after every inch of his body was covered. His enthusiasm for the activity far exceeded his need. This was fun.

The elephant plays a complex role in the ecology of Africa. As the world's largest land mammal – with cows topping three tons and bulls more than twice that – its hunger and thirst are prodigious. An elephant spends up to sixteen hours a day consuming an eclectic mix of grasses, leaves and twigs, bark, fruit and seeds. Though elephants have a reputation for trashing their habitat, in a balanced ecosystem, their extreme browsing techniques, which include tree toppling and bark stripping, are generally offset by new growth fortuitously promoted by their regular pruning. Overgrowth is seldom a problem in elephant country.

Elephants serve fellow denizens of the wild by establishing bush trails and keeping them open, and by depositing copious amounts of dung wherever they go. Since elephants absorb only a small percentage of the nutrients contained in their diet, most of the 300 pounds they ingest each day is quite literally left behind, unprocessed, providing an abundant source of food for various birds and insects, as well as some mammals. Monkeys and baboons, in particular, are fond of picking through elephant droppings. Animals are not the only beneficiaries. Undigested seeds dispersed by elephants often take root and grow well outside the reproductive range of the parent plant – as evidenced in places like the Kalahari Desert where ancient elephant trails are delineated by narrow rows of palms and other trees found running through areas otherwise devoid of them. Indeed, certain species of trees produce seeds that will germinate only after passing through the digestive system of an elephant. So the elephant is an agent of both destruction and creation.

It was destruction that was most in evidence as we drove along the river's edge and into the adjoining woodlands. Although Chobe is one of the largest national parks in Africa – a third larger than any in the contiguous United States – there is a limit to the number of animals any habitat can support, especially during the dry season when drought compresses them into narrow greenbelt stretches near permanent water. The elephants of Chobe were pushing that limit. We passed dozens of trees laid waste in recent weeks. Some were uprooted and torn apart. Others, still standing, were dying by degrees after immoderate bark stripping ravaged their vascular systems. This was nothing new or unusual. The wizened remains of past-season casualties, countless in numbers, now served as lookout posts for vultures and birds of prey.

We stopped for a while to watch a family of banded mongooses rooting for insects and grubs near a termite mound they had excavated for a den. One of the two dozen pack members was on sentry duty, sitting upright to gain a few extra inches of height and scanning the ground and skies for predators, ready in an instant to sound a chirping alarm that would send the others darting for cover.

Further along, we came upon a small herd of elephants standing watch over a calf – perhaps two years old – lying motionless near the road. Although adult elephants usually sleep standing up, youngsters typically lie down, so we took this one to be napping after a wearying day of feeding and playing. Young elephants, like young children, need plenty of rest. After a while, however, we began to wonder if the calf was sick or injured – or worse. Many minutes had passed without so much as a twitch. Was she even breathing? We peered through our binoculars, voicing concern. Our driver laughed in response and assured us the youngster was fine – and, indeed, a few moments later, she stirred at last and got shakily to her feet with a helpful boost from one of the adults.

The elephants took to the road and ambled on ahead in no particular hurry. We crept along behind them. Through the foliage flickering past on either side of the vehicle, I caught zoetrope glimpses of other elephants browsing amongst the trees and thickets, and wondered how many were actually out there. Hundreds? Thousands? We paused as a huge troop of baboons chased through our field of view, then continued on. Suddenly and unexpectedly, an enormous elephant – a herd matriarch – strode out of the bush and onto the road just ahead. Our driver reacted at once, applying the brakes and bringing us to an abrupt halt. As anyone in Africa will affirm, elephants have the right of way. With scarcely a glance in our direction, the cow crossed in front of us, a mere car-length away, followed by a dozen others close behind. They were heading for the river, where elephants were said to congregate in huge numbers during the waning hours of the day. Tomorrow we would see.

Breakfast was on the verandah overlooking the river. Anywhere else in the world, I might have been tempted to spend the morning there, enjoying the view and the ambiance. But this was Africa. The river was beckoning. And if anything could match the intoxicating thrill of driving through the Serengeti in an open-top vehicle, it was cruising the Chobe River in a motorboat.

An aluminum skiff awaited us at the boat landing – as did our guide for the morning. A local with years of experience on the river, Stanley Maruza welcomed us on board, advised us to keep any extremities we hoped to go home with out of the water, and promptly pushed off. Any thoughts we might have had that this would be a tranquil little outing were quickly put to rest when Stanley opened the throttle and took off as if he had a water-skier in tow.

Whipping past on one side of us was Botswana. Whipping past on the other was Namibia – the aptly named Caprivi Strip, to be precise, a slender finger of land protruding from the northeast corner of Namibia that should, geography and logic would argue, more rightly be part of modern-day Angola and Zambia. But for more than a century, this carto-graphic oddity has stood as testament to the enduring legacy of the colonial superpowers that appropriated and apportioned nearly all of Africa in accordance with individual and shared objectives.

In recent decades the Caprivi Strip – remote and unprotected – had hosted numerous regional conflicts, with government and insurgent forces from neighboring nations using it as a communal combat zone and accessway. Even now, with armed conflicts resolved, there was a military presence beyond any seeming necessity, with Namibian troops encamped as a show of force in a lingering dispute with Botswana over which chan-nel of the Chobe River defined the border between the two countries. Stanley cautioned us not to photograph any of the military outposts and added that it was pointless to survey the Namibia side of the river for elephants. Poachers were active in the Caprivi Strip – and elephants were smart enough to make themselves scarce there. A safe haven lay

just across the river. Small wonder, then, that much of the Botswana side of the waterway was dry and depleted, while the Namibia side, a hundred yards away, was lush and pristine.

With the lodge far behind, and not another boat in sight, Stanley eased back on the throttle, slowing us to game-viewing speed. Although elephants were the region's star attraction, they were far from being the only draw as the river was a magnet for all manner of supporting players. We drifted past warthogs and waterbuck drinking at the marshy shoreline, as well as exotic waterbirds such as the African jacana, whose large splayed feet allow it to trot across lily pads as though walking on water, and the fish-spearing darter which characteristically swims with only its head and neck above water and then perches with wings out-stretched to dry its feathers. On a low branch at the river's edge, we were treated to an up-close view of Africa's most majestic bird of prey, the fish eagle, usually seen perched atop a tall dead tree, scanning the river with telescope eyes for a target unwary enough to be lingering near the surface.

The resident fish population had more than just raptors to worry about. Like most freshwater habitats in Africa, the Chobe was home to crocodiles – a profusion of them, judging from the numbers we saw adrift in the shallows or sunning on the riverbanks. Although the giants of the species are renowned for predating on antelopes and zebra – even humans – meals of such bounty are infrequent for even the most profi-cient of these lie-in-wait hunters, and fish are a dietary staple for crocs of all sizes. Most that we saw were of average length – eight to ten feet – but an occasional few were exceptional. Crocodiles can live a hundred years and, with abundant food supply, grow up to twenty feet in length and weigh more than a ton. They are the most widely distributed preda-tor in Africa and – despite rampant hunting for skins that once endan-gered them – are thought to outnumber all other predators combined. Spotting an impressive specimen lying in a patch of short grass at the water's edge, Stanley eased over toward it. A slight cutaway on the riverbank allowed us to get within six feet of the reptile, which looked to be about fifteen feet in length. It was the closest I had ever been to a crocodile in the wild, and it was difficult, at first, to focus on anything past the drowsy eyes and bear-trap jaws, closed but with jagged teeth

visible behind what looked like a sly smile. After enduring our scrutiny for several minutes, the great beast elevated itself on stubby legs and slid into the water, gliding past us with a lateral stroke of its tail and vanishing into the depths.

While the crocodile is easily the ranking carnivore of the African wetlands, it shares its habitat with an equally formidable herbivore, the hippopotamus. Prone to overheating and dehydration in the sun, hippos tend to spend their days in the water, lazing and interacting in small territories vigorously defended by quick-tempered males with gaping jaws and twenty-inch tusks. At night, they emerge from the water and disperse along well-worn paths, ranging up to three miles inland to forage on grasses. In the morning they lumber back a hundred pounds heavier. Although hippos appear sluggish and ungainly on land, they are remark-ably quick and agile when motivated, able to chase down most humans on foot, and have little to fear from predators, who generally respect their prickly disposition and capacity for mayhem.

We came upon our first herd of these amphibious giants bobbing in the river near the mouth of a small lagoon. There appeared to be about twenty in all, adults and calves, though a reliable count was hampered by the fact that several were submerged and moving about at any given moment. Hippos can remain underwater for three to five minutes at a stretch. Stanley slowed the boat and circled the herd, watchful of the dominant male, who was quick to challenge our intrusion by lifting his head and surging powerfully in our direction. We motored out of range. Hippo vocalizations – reverberant honking guffaws – battered our eardrums as others in the herd voiced collective displeasure. We longed to remain and see what would unfold, but there was no question that our presence was unwelcome and that one disgruntled hippo could easily overturn our small watercraft. Time to go.

After more than two hours on the river, we returned to the lodge having seen exactly none of the myriad elephants said to be massed along the dry-season water source. Stanley explained that it was com-mon for the elephants to forage deep in the bush during morning and midday hours, then convene at the river to drink and bathe as the day wore on. Our best opportunity to see them in numbers was at dusk. To that end, we could sign on for an afternoon game drive along the river, as we had the day before, or we could opt for a sunset cruise on board a double-decker riverboat owned and operated by the lodge. The river excursion – complete with cocktails and hors d'oeuvres – seemed rather sedate compared to our motorboat outings, but intoxicated by the river and smitten by the prospect of sharing it with elephants en masse, we signed up for it.

With a couple of hours to kill after lunch, and with little interest in the lodge amenities when all of Africa lay just beyond, we sought out Stanley and persuaded him to take us out on the river again before the sundowner cruise. The boats large enough to accommodate our party were already taken, but two smaller ones were still moored at the landing. Stanley rounded up a second guide, and we split into two groups – men in one boat and women in the other. Gender competition was already being voiced before we even pushed off.

While the boats were equal in size, the motors were certainly not. Stanley and the women roared off in one direction, waving and whooping, while we men put-putted away in the opposite. How mortifying. Inching along with what dignity we could muster, we buoyed ourselves with out-size predictions of wonders to be seen by those unhurried enough to embrace them. And, indeed, we were rewarded with lingering views of pukus and buffalo on shore and a group of hippos in tall grass – even a fine pair of elephants at the water's edge. Our humble conveyance was serving us well. With some minor embellishment, we would surely hold our own when it came to swapping accounts of the afternoon's observations.

Hardly. The women got back before we did – no surprise – and were waiting excitedly at the landing. They had been awash in elephants. No sooner had their motorboat cleared the bend just west of the lodge than they came upon a herd of about two dozen drinking and cavorting in the river. Stanley eased in very close – almost within splashing distance – and held his position. After a while, when the herd withdrew and vanished into the bush, an even larger one came forth to take its place. And as if that were not more than sufficient to trump our modest sightings, the women further reported seeing two lionesses and a cub, unnoticed at first, eyeing all from beneath a tree only a few yards away from the milling elephants. Now wait just a minute ...

But it was true. Estelle presented her video in evidence. A profusion of elephants overflowed the frame. Most were compressed at the water's edge, trunks extending and retracting, sucking up gallons of water and spewing it into their mouths. A wobbly newborn, sandwiched among them, cued a chorus of sugary 'awws' on the audio track. A pair of adolescent males squared off in the river, shoving and jousting in mock combat that would one day be waged in earnest if they were ever to challenge a herd bull for breeding privileges. A young cow rolled on the sandy riverbank while another scratched her backside against an agreeably abrasive outcrop. There was so much to take in. Without question, it was the definitive elephant encounter of our current safari – exactly what we had come to Chobe to see – but could there be anything more ironic, or pathetic, than witnessing it second-hand through a camcorder viewfinder in glorious black-and-white?

The water flowing past our lodge would, in a day or less, merge into the Zambezi River – one of Africa's mightiest waterways – and soon thereafter plunge thunderously over a mile-wide precipice that explorer David Livingstone, upon discovering it in 1855, presumed to christen Victoria Falls in honor of his queen. Among the indigenous peoples of the region, this natural wonder already had a perfectly good name, descriptive of its deafening roar and ascendant mist, but that appellation was not to be known by an outside world eager to make Africa its own. Our sundowner boat, however, which in a former life had cruised the calm waters above the great cataract, perpetuated the falls' original name with its own – Mosi-oa-Tunya.

Although powered by twin outboard motors, the Mosi-oa-Tunya was hardly built for speed. Our boat captain backed us out into the main channel and then headed upriver, chugging along at a slow and easy pace that invited relaxation in the waning hours of a nonstop day. With only a dozen passengers on board, everyone gravitated to the open upper deck where we communed over drinks and savored our surroundings as the descendant sun vanished and reappeared behind bands of clouds glowing above the horizon. A pair of bushbucks – shy and seldom seen – watched our passage from the water's edge, as did an assortment of other antelopes. Those drifted from view, and our attention shifted to the hundreds of egrets and herons staking out overnight roosts along the riverbank. Further on, we lingered opposite a stand of tall trees as scores of baboons came streaming out of the underbrush, playing and drinking and quarreling noisily before vaulting into the canopy where they would spend the hours of darkness in relative safety, huddled against the terrors of the night.

But what of the elephants? We had passed a few, alone or in small groups, but hardly enough to burnish Chobe's reputation as the elephant capital of the world. Where were the great herds we had come to see? For the present, that remained a mystery, though later, upon reflection, I concluded that our boat captain, who plied these waters daily, must have known exactly where and when we might find them, animals being as subject to routine as people. Just under an hour into our cruise, the trees and foliage verging the river thinned for a stretch and then parted to reveal a broad floodplain – upon which a herd of thirty-some elephants, young and old, was making its way slowly in our direction. Compounding our good fortune, a second procession of comparable size was following some distance behind. This was no mere happenstance. Without a doubt, this worn and dusty floodplain was a major gateway to the river.

The lead herd was still a few dozen yards from the river when several of its younger members, unable to contain themselves, broke ranks and dashed clumsily into the water. The other more disciplined members completed the trek in an orderly manner, fanning out along the shoreline and commencing to drink and splash. Some went for the baptismal plunge, trudging into belly-deep water and keeling over sideways. A pedaling leg might churn the surface, or a trunk periscope-up for air, but otherwise there was little to suggest that a full-grown elephant was immersed in only four feet of water. Even a few infants ventured playfully into the shallows. Water, for elephants, is both a necessity and a joy.

As the sun dipped, spewing shafts of light through gilded clouds, the matriarch stepped off the riverbank and strode out into deep water. The rest of the herd fell in behind her, and all were soon paddling toward the opposite shore. They were halfway across when the second herd reached the river – and kept on going. There were now more than sixty elephants, in two distinct groups, swimming willfully toward a place we had been told these animals dared not go. Our captain explained that

while the Caprivi Strip was indeed shunned by elephants during daylight hours, some of the more mettlesome herds had taken to crossing over at sundown and then returning before dawn. The reason was evident. The Botswana side of the river was dry and overforaged – a testament to the seasonal crush of herbivores – while the Namibia side just opposite, a mere hundred yards away, was lush with untapped foodstuffs. Poachers be damned. A night of fine dining was worth the risk.

The dusty gray forms that entered the river emerged a glistening black on the other side. The bank was steep and slick, and a few of the younger calves needed a boost to make the grade. An expanse of tall grass – aglow in golden-hour light – grew right to the water's edge, and some of the arrivals commenced eating before they had even topped the embankment. As the second herd was plodding out of the river, the sun surrendered the day with a flourish, and we divided our attention between the browsing giants and the painterly skies.

We were about to head back to the lodge when we heard a trumpeting call behind us and turned to see a young male – about eight years old – on the Botswana shoreline. Somehow – counter to all notions of elephant kindercare – a straggler had been left behind. While elephants much smaller than he had crossed with the herds, this one was clearly afraid to attempt the passage on his own. He paced back and forth, voicing his growing distress, but none of his kin seemed to notice. Then a young female – an older sister or perhaps a cousin – heard his plaintive calls and returned to the riverbank, trumpeting in reply and wading into the water.

On some level, I imagine we all expected her to swim back and escort him across the river or, at the very least, alert the herd adults to his predicament – but, though well-intended, she was no Lassie. She was more the cheerleader type, urging the youngster to overcome his anxiety. Responding to her beckoning, the young bull entered the water, ventured a few yards out, then stopped and turned back. The cow persisted in her encouragement, and the bull made a second attempt before again losing his nerve. The expanse of water was too daunting. The other members of his family – now widely dispersed and absorbed in feeding – remained oblivious to his plight. He had only the female for support. Increasingly

overwrought, he tossed his head and flapped his ears, psyching himself up for his next foray into the water that, like the previous two, terminated at its starting point. How long would this go on? And what would happen if he failed to rejoin his herd before nightfall? A young elephant, alone, would be no match for a pride of lions.

Wholly invested in this small drama, we lingered as long as possible, hoping for a positive denouement, but it was getting dark and we had to get back. We continued to watch as the *Mosi-oa-Tunya* carried us slowly downriver, but neither elephant made a move. They looked like the carved wooden bookends ubiquitous in African curio shops. Then, suddenly – perhaps because his fear of darkness outweighed his fear of the river – the young bull pushed out into deep water and began swimming with resolve. We cheered him on, following his progress through binoculars, until at last he regained his footing on the far side of the river. His trial was over. Reunited, the young elephants nuzzled and twined their trunks in greeting, then clambered up the riverbank and onto the grassy plain. We could all rest easy now.

Discounting the real, though probably slim chance of being poached during nighttime excursions to the Caprivi salad bar, the elephants of Chobe had just about the most idyllic existence imaginable for a species that seemed equally, if not more, at home in the water than it did on land. I gave little thought at the time to the fact that the inviting sliver of Namibia across the Chobe was hardly typical of wildlife habitat elsewhere in that predominantly parched country, and that some 600 miles to the west, elephants were living at the extreme opposite end of the survival spectrum.

Africa lingers in the mind. Months after our return from Chobe, I was still having daydreamy flashbacks to motorboat game drives and aquaphile elephants. We had to go back. And so, before too long, we were again poring over maps with Bill and Sally Snyder, devising an intinerary that would – in part – take our Chobe experience to the next level. Our plan was to start in South Luangwa National Park in Zambia, an area still in recovery a decade after poachers all but exterminated its elephant population, one of the largest in Africa, in a few frenzied years of unchecked slaughter. Tens of thousands of rotting carcasses – ivory hacked off with axes and chainsaws – littered the Luangwa Valley during those execrable times. After sampling that renascent region, we would journey south into Botswana elephant country, spending much of our time there in permanent tented camps along the Linyanti River, just west of Chobe National Park, where visitors were few and off-road driving was permitted. The elephants we had seen at Chobe would be matched in numbers here, and water activities ranked high among the camps' many offerings.

The trip was already planned and booked before I got the notion to add another segment. I had been enchanted by Namibia for years, awestruck by images of its wondrous desert vistas. To date, however, I had resisted the urge to go there. The focus of our Africa travels had always been wildlife, and wildlife was certain to be sparse in that inhospitable land. But with three weeks of intense game viewing a certainty in Zambia and Botswana, what better occasion than this to introduce ourselves to Namibia? The scenery alone would be worth it. When the Snyders opted to pass on this added extravagance, which would extend our safari to more than a month, Estelle and I reconsidered for a minute or two and then decided to do it on our own.

Namibia is a land of open spaces, twice the size of California, but with barely half the population of Los Angeles. Only Mongolia, among the countries of the world, is more sparsely inhabited. A year or two earlier, Jerry Dale had made an exploratory road trip through Namibia, enthralled by its wildlife and scenic attractions, but daunted by the distances between them. To compress his experience into an abbreviated time frame, Estelle and I signed on for a week-long flying safari – a literal overview of the driest nation in sub-Saharan Africa.

I grew up in a region of meadows and streams and woodlands, a wonderland of verdant beauty that, apart from its blemishing towns and highways, looked much as it must have when Washington Irving took quill in hand to evoke its allure in tales of headless horsemen and ceaseless sleepers. So it stands to reason, human nature being ever perverse, that I spent much of my youth enamored of the desert. Not that I ever saw a desert in those days – but the idea of one was immensely appealing. My impressions of the desert, as with many other things in my life, came from books and movies. I was especially taken with westerns – the best of which were shot in the American Southwest – and whenever the camera pulled away from John Wayne or Henry Fonda or James Stewart to reveal the sandy desert vistas that typified the genre, my eyes grew wide as I drank in stark images of rugged canyons and towering buttes that were every bit as alien to the place I lived as Jupiter or Mars. It was probably a surprise to no one that my compass pointed west when I came of age.

Having now spent most of my adult life in California, an hour's drive from the ocean or the mountains or the desert, I will still, seeking an outing and given the choice, set a course for the desert – not with the romanticized expectations of my youth, but with a fuller appreciation of the environment and its stalwart life forms that only real-world experience can provide. I was eager to graft my love of the desert onto my love of Africa.

Our flying safari began in Windhoek, the capital of Namibia, at a general aviation airport in the city. There we met our charter pilot, an affable young Zambian named Mulopu Kaumba, and our companions for the week, Mickey and Shelley Cohen, inveterate world travelers from Manhattan. As with the Snyders, whom we had met under similar circumstances years before, our shared African adventure would pave the way to an enduring friendship. We boarded the Cessna Centurion that would be ours exclusively for the duration of our trip, and were soon winging our way southwest toward Sossusvlei and the Namib Desert.

Africa is home to many of the world's great deserts. Mere mention of the word conjures up images of the Sahara – a sprawling expanse of dunes and desiccation that covers nearly a third of the continent – an area larger than the continental United States. The Namib is minute by comparison – a mere 1,000-mile-long stretch of hyper-arid terrain running the entire length of Namibia, and beyond. Though only a fraction of the size of the Sahara, the Namib is thought to be the planet's oldest desert – which accounts for the singular coloration of its coastal dunes. When I first saw photographs of the Namib's signature sand dunes, I attributed their intense burnt-orange color to lens filtration or darkroom trickery. But no. They are indeed that fiery hue. Millions of years of elemental forces have oxidized trace iron content in the sand, forming rusty incrustations on the silica granules. The older the dunes, the more rust-colored they become.

Mulopu set the Cessna down on a gravel airstrip in the middle of nowhere and taxied to a small parking area where a dusty Land Rover stood waiting. Isaiah Iiyambo, our guide for this portion of our itinerary, greeted us warmly and drove us to Sossusvlei Wilderness Camp, an exquisite accommodation comprised of nine thatched bungalows arrayed on a rocky hilltop, with transcendent views of desert plains and distant peaks that could have been lifted from *Lawrence of Arabia*.

Our camp lay just outside Namib-Naukluft Park – the largest conservation area in Africa – and we set off early the next morning to experience its premier attraction, the Sossusvlei sand dunes, arguably the world's tallest with several approaching or exceeding a thousand feet in height. Once inside the preserve, we proceeded some thirty-five miles along a well-tended road through a dry river valley flanked by the towering dunes, stopping at intervals to hike around and over some of the lesser formations.

Although rainfall is minimal and infrequent in the Namib, varieties of hardy plants and insects are sustained by seasonal fog and dew carried inland from the ocean by prevailing southerly winds. These, in turn, provide nourishment for reptiles and birds – even several species of mammals. In the dry river valley, and on flat clay pans amongst the dunes, we observed ostriches – which seem able to flourish in any environment – and small herds of springbok, mid-size antelope with inwardly curving horns that can survive indefinitely without drinking, deriving what moisture they require solely from the vegetation they forage. Out on the low dunes we encountered gemsbok – or oryx – among the largest of the African antelopes, and, for that reason, the most seemingly out of place in a setting of such meager resources. But the gemsbok – predominantly gray in color, with black and white markings and long pointed horns – is supremely adapted to life in the desert, with inner workings to maximize fluid retention and an air conditioning system that keeps its brain cool and functional, even at body temperatures above the lethal limit for most mammals.

Someone in our party thought it would be fun to climb the tallest dune in the park, a veritable Mount Everest of sand prosaically dubbed 'Big Daddy.' From the road, a third of a mile away, the dune did look inviting – and Isaiah seemed to imply that scaling it was some sort of Namibian rite of passage. So why not? More than once, Estelle and I had watched the sun rise from atop the dunes in Death Valley – and this one did not seem that much bigger. Which was crazy. Big Daddy is nearly four times taller than the largest dune in Death Valley – a fact which became increasingly evident the closer we got to it. From directly below, the upswept face of the dune looked like a titanic wave poised to crash down upon us. We began a frontal assault, moving easily up the initial stretch of treadworthy sand, then with growing difficulty as the grade steepened and the sand, now softer, slid away in tiny avalanches beneath our feet. Two steps forward, one step back. I was cursing my decision to haul my leaden backpack full of cameras and lenses to the top. Three steps forward, two steps back. By the time I dragged myself onto the first lateral ridge, scarcely a third of the way to the summit, my heart and lungs were claiming organ abuse. Isaiah was encouraging, offering to shoulder my gear and assuring me that we had completed the hardest part of the climb. In the end, though, I decided that summiting Big Daddy was an experience I could live without. Either of like mind or merely in support, Estelle chose to return with me to the bottom, while Mickey and Shelley mushed on to the top. Years later, they still needle us about it.

We viewed the area anew the next morning, peering down on it as Mulopu circled the mammoth dunes, sculpted into crescent and star shapes by shifting winds, then headed westward over an undulating sea of sand that grew calmer and paler as we neared the ocean. The dunes here were younger. Our approach to the Skeleton Coast – so named for the many doomed ships and sailors deposited on its fogbound rocks and shifting sand bars by storms and treacherous currents – took us over one of the region's singular sights. Upright in the sand, a full half-mile inland from the present shoreline, stood the *Eduard Bolen*, an ill-fated German freighter that ran aground in 1909. We circled the wreck, buried in drifted sand almost to its deck, and I supposed that one day it would disappear altogether beneath the dunes.

Passing over abandoned diamond mining camps, we proceeded up the coast to Swakopmond, a seaside resort town, where we stopped for fuel and an elegant picnic on the beach. After lunch, we continued northward, flying over an enormous colony of fur seals, before leaving the dunes behind and heading inland past volcanic peaks and craters toward the high-desert Kaokoveld region and Damaraland Camp, where we would be spending the next two days. Here we hoped to find Africa's most extraordinary population of elephants. Mulopu descended over the camp and then set us down gently on an airstrip not far away.

Our flight had transported us from David Lean country to John Ford country. Taking it in as we made the short drive to the camp, I was struck by how much the region resembled the American Southwest. In every direction, sandy plains and low hills stretched out beyond view, backed by layer-cake mountains and mesas striated in browns and reds and blacks, dissolving into hazy purples at the far horizon. The composite effect was hauntingly beautiful, but water was nowhere and vegetation was sparse. How could the planet's largest land animal – a creature of prodigious thirst and appetite – survive here? If the Chobe waterworld was elephant heaven, then surely the Kaokoveld barrens must be elephant hell.

I confess to surprise at my first aerial sighting of Damaraland Camp. Having grown accustomed to the luxury camps that in recent years have become de rigueur on the upscale safari circuit everywhere in Africa, I must have anticipated, on some subconscious level, an oasis of splendor in this hot and thirsty land. At the very least, I expected something more than a few drab-looking tents in a shallow rock-strewn valley with no natural shade and only a hint of native vegetation. A desert internment camp would have looked no less inviting.

My impressions were premature. We were deposited at the camp's reception area, open to the view and under canvas, which also served as the dining room and lounge. There we were greeted with customary offerings of moist towels and chilled fruit juice to vanquish the dust and thirst of our passage. A camp manager briefed us on the area and its principal attraction, reminding us of why we had come there. Any wildlife sighting at all in this inhospitable realm would be a treat, but, with a measure of luck, we could expect to see the rare and endangered desert elephants of Namibia. Fewer than 500 of these hardy behemoths range over an area the size of West Virginia, but sightings were fairly common around Damaraland. Welcome complete, we were escorted to our tents, which proved to be spacious and pleasantly appointed, with shaded over-hangs and camp chairs at the entry, and there we spent the waning hours of the afternoon watching shadows lengthen and colors change, and weighing our prospects for the day ahead.

In the morning, after breakfast, we set out from camp in an open Land Rover topped with a canvas canopy to provide us a measure of protection from the withering desert sun. Damaraland Camp lies just north of the Huab River. Hardly in league with the Nile or the Zambezi, the Huab is a river deprived – a dry sandy channel through which water flows just a few days each year, and sometimes not at all. Nonetheless, it is a lifeline for flora and fauna. What little rainfall anoints the region during the summer wet season is seldom enough to vitalize the river, but seasonal flooding from upcountry catchments, ducted through a network of washes, converges and spills into the river channel where it rushes, often mightily, through the thirsty drylands. In mere days or weeks, the ephemeral waterway delivers a year's worth of nourishment to the hardy trees and bushes that line the riverbank, which, in turn, provide shelter and sustenance for a surprising assortment of equally hardy birds and animals.

Since no visit to Damaraland can be considered complete without an elephant encounter – which must be cause for performance anxiety amongst those charged with providing them – we headed straightaway to the river where our young South African guide, Ryan Brislin, evidently hoped to relieve the pressure by finding some of the region's superstars browsing considerately among the trees along the bank. No such luck.

We did, however, find fresh elephant tracks in the riverbed – which was encouraging. Ryan pulled to a stop and invited us to dismount for a bit of show and tell. Judging from the size and spacing of the tracks, and the crisp definition of the impressions, two bull elephants had passed this way not more than a few hours before. Ryan had us examine the evidence. An elephant's front foot, he explained, is round on the bottom,

while its rear foot is oval – and if the animal is moving at an unhurried pace, as these were, its rear footprint will overlap the front one. Since all four feet are laid down in a line, elephant trails are typically narrow, despite the animal's prodigious girth. Our instructor further observed that since the soles of an elephant's feet are essentially symmetrical, leaving leathery imprints without distinguishable heel or toe impressions, direction of travel can best be determined by noting that the heel strikes first and the toe scuffs a little dirt out ahead. Ryan ended our bushcraft lesson on a computational note by stating that the size of an elephant can be gauged from its tracks by multiplying the length of its stride by a factor of two and a half to determine its shoulder height.

Now qualified for merit badges in elephant tracking, we piled back into the Land Rover and headed south along the riverbed. Reckoning that the two bulls were the known consorts of a breeding herd of nine that wandered in and out of the area on a regular basis, Ryan figured our best strategy was to follow their trail and see where it led us.

Owing to a leaner physique and longer legs, coupled with behavioral traits atypical of elephants found elsewhere in Africa, it was long pre-sumed that the elephants inhabiting this ever-arid region of Namibia – like the forest elephants of central and western Africa – were a distinct and separate species. Not so. Genetic testing has proven that the des-ert elephants of Namibia are no different than the savanna elephants found almost everywhere else in Africa. Their leaner physique, it appears, is a rather obvious consequence of the fact that food is limited in the desert, and their longer legs only look longer because the elephants are slimmer and trimmer. So, alas, there are no desert elephants – except in the popular idiom. For zoologists and others who prefer precision to simplicity, the elephants of this region are known as 'desert-adapted elephants.' And they are not the only desert-adapted representatives of plains and woodland species more commonly found in greener habitats. Small but hardy populations of giraffes, black rhinos, even lions, unaware that others of their kind are living la dolce vita elsewhere on the conti-nent, share territory and resources with species such as springbok and gemsbok that are physiologically more suited to the rigors of this ever-thirsty land.

Behaviorally, the differences between savanna elephants and desert elephants are striking. The average savanna elephant drinks upwards of sixty gallons of water a day and seldom ventures far from a reliable source – which is why elephant sightings are most plentiful during the dry season when herds congregate around rivers and other permanent water supplies. With both water and forage scarce in the desert, and not always co-located, desert elephants often trek a hundred miles or more between far-flung sources of these precious commodities, and can go without drinking for three or four days at a time. As with elephants everywhere, their diet is varied and voluminous, ranging from new-grown grasses during the short rainy season to a wide assortment of hardier vegetation during the lingering dry season. Unlike elephants in more bounteous habitats, however, which demonstrate slim regard for their environment, desert elephants seem to grasp, on some primal level, the concept and importance of sustainable use. While elephants elsewhere are unhesitant about uprooting a tree to access a few choice leaves or seeds beyond their reach, or destroying a tree just as surely by stripping its bark, desert elephants typically limit their browsing to new growth, rarely destroying a long-term asset for short-term gain.

The riparian vegetation is not immune to other perils, however. The river's yearly allotment of water, delivered in flash-flood overdoses as often as not, can be a catastrophic blessing, as we noted while skirting the toppled remains of several large trees whose purchase on the shoreline had been swept away by raging waters long gone. Others leaned precariously over the riverbank, their roots protruding through the receding undercut, awaiting just one more torrent of floodwater to finish them off. In this harsh land, each such loss is a tragedy on a multitude of levels. But though the water's angry passage seems, on the surface, almost too fleeting and too destructive to affect any lasting good, the seasonal floods do replenish reservoirs of groundwater that the resident elephants are adept at divining and excavating, to the lingering benefit of themselves and other less-resourceful inhabitants of the region.

We followed the elephant tracks up and out of the riverbed and onto a sandy gravel road that meandered down a wide valley peppered with wind-smoothed rocks that had once been spewed out of a distant volcano as molten splatters. Although wildlife was by no means abundant,

we were treated to the sight of a greater kudu bull – every hunter's dream trophy – browsing on a stunted acacia a few yards off the road. Magnificent spiral horns, four feet long and with two complete twists, indicated that the antelope was five to six years old and fully mature. In the distance, a herd of surefooted springbok, fifteen or twenty strong, bounded across a rocky hillside. A pair of ostriches strode by. But, as yet, no elephants.

In as fragile an ecosystem as this, where the destruction of even a single plant could have far-ranging consequences, it was important that we remain on already established vehicle tracks. The elephants, of course, had no such imperative. So when the trail of circles and ovals we were following angled off the road after a mile or two, we had little choice but to continue on course, hoping our divergent paths would rejoin up ahead, but thinking it more than likely our quarry had ambled into one of the canyons that branched off at intervals.

We continued on, well beyond the elephants' range if the signpost spoor at the river was indeed just hours old. Our dwindling prospects of coming across these particular elephants – or any others – now hung on the intuition of our guide, who made a succession of directional changes before doubling back toward the river via another route. With low hills all around now obstructing our view, Ryan hopped out and gamely clambered up a prominent rise for a panoramic survey of what lay beyond. What lay beyond were vast expanses of desert. Vacant desert.

We were in the open once more, wending our way back to camp where we would spend the midday before venturing out again. Off to our left, a mile or so away, was the river, its slender course defined by the incongruous column of greenery running through otherwise barren terrain. To our right, sandy flatlands spread away, climbing into tabletop mesas and canyons through which I could picture a stagecoach or a mounted cavalry troop passing, neither seeming the least out of place or out of time. Anywhere but Africa, these unspoiled vistas alone would have been worth the price of admission, but it had been an hour since our last wildlife sighting – a mere springbok, at that – and …

Ryan tossed a casual glance over his shoulder, did a classic double-take, and then skidded to a stop. Behind us, off in the distance, a lone elephant was picking its way down a steep rocky slope into a narrow canyon. We all grabbed binoculars and zeroed in. Under magnification, we could see that the animal was following a well-worn trail, and I marveled at its ability to navigate the sharp decline, which looked to be pitched at about forty degrees. Could a behemoth weighing three-plus tons even do that? But of course it could. Hannibal marched war elephants over the Alps. Certainly any impediment Namibia could offer would be piddling by comparison.

When the elephant descended out of view, Ryan spun the Land Rover around and headed back the way we had come. The canyon opened a few hundred yards from the road, but there was no driving access into it, and its natural curvature prevented us from seeing much past the mouth. Ryan considered it likely that the elephant we had seen was part of the breeding herd, and that the rest of its members were somewhere up the canyon. He was going to check it out on foot.

Our response was unanimous. No way were we going to wait in the vehicle. We were going with him. Ryan hesitated, an objection forming, then said okay. We jumped down from the Land Rover, slung cameras and binoculars over shoulders, and set off cross-country toward our objective. Walking up the canyon was never an option. Much too risky. Instead, we would climb the backside of a mesa overlooking the canyon – some 200 vertical feet – then hike across the summit and along the canyon edge until we spotted our quarry below.

The mesa was principally dolomite – a jet-black rock common to the area – but yellowish sand covered much of the incline. Rather than scale the rock surfaces – extensively fractured, but weathered smooth – we stuck mostly to the sandy passages, which provided surer footing. Some of the larger monoliths were stacked in curious configurations that seemed almost beyond happenstance, as though arranged for some mystical purpose.

We huffed-and-puffed our way to the summit in short order – a testament to the power of motivation – and crossed toward the canyon where we hoped our exertion would be rewarded. A foot-wide path, worn by gemsbok and elephants, extended to the edge of the mesa – and as we neared the drop-off, Ryan instructed us to stay put while he went ahead to make sure the elephants were not climbing out of the canyon in

our direction. A face-to-face meeting might prove unpleasant. He moved carefully to the edge, peered over, and waved us forward.

Ryan had been correct. The entire breeding herd was directly below, shuffling along the canyon floor in file formation like circus elephants on parade. Ryan knew them all by sight and identified them for us, pointing out floppy ears and kinky tails and other distinguishing features. There were five adult cows, including the matriarch in the lead, a young female in her teens, a pair of juveniles – one male, one female – and a tiny infant, only nine weeks old, doing a laudable job of keeping pace with his elders.

The canyon widened as it opened onto the sandy plain, and the elephants moved down a dry wash toward the river, pausing at intervals to sample the foliage growing along the spillway. Seeking respite from the sun, now high in the sky, they advanced on a pair of acacias large enough to provide shade for them all, and set about browsing among the lower branches. Though aware of the irony, I succumbed to the realization that seeking and finding the elephants had, for me, been much more exciting than actually watching them, especially engaged in this most mundane of elephant activities. I was not the only attention-deficit ingrate in our party – to some degree, everyone felt as I did – but our options on foot were limited, and did not include climbing into the canyon for an up-close encounter.

We had every reason to suppose that the elephants would remain in the shade for hours. Forage was ample. Why not? Given that, it made perfect sense to stay where we were for as long as we wished, see whatever there was to see, and then drive back to camp for our own midday meal. Mission accomplished. But there was another possibility – a long shot. What if the elephants abandoned the shade and pressed on toward the river? Almost certainly, they would pass within yards of our Land Rover – a perfect place from which to view them, provided we were in it. Given this scenario, however remote, if we waited for the elephants to make the first move, there was no way we could get off the mesa and back to the vehicle in time to intercept them. We would slip away now.

We retraced our route off the mesa and crossed the open expanse toward the road. Mercurial winds, gusting this way and that, rippled the sand and blew alternating waves of warm and cool air. It was noon by the time we reached the Land Rover. In our rush to abandon it, no one had thought to bring water, so we promptly broke out the beverages and muffins packed in our cooler, and stood about eating and drinking and reliving our morning. All we now had to do was decide how long we wanted to wait around to see if the elephants would make an appearance. They had been out of sight since our descent from the mesa.

The decision was easily made. Barely had we finished our repast when the matriarch, followed by the herd, emerged from behind a low-lying hill and headed toward the road. While they were still a ways off, we repositioned our vehicle nearer to the point we thought they would cross. Several large trees – camelthorn acacias – stood near the road, at the base of a steep black-rock hill, and as the elephants drew near, they fanned out and took positions around them. Suddenly, the behaviors mundane when viewed from afar and above seemed utterly engrossing when viewed at ground-level from a few dozen yards.

The camelthorn's distinctive seed pods were an evident favorite of the elephants, which bypassed leaves and twigs and other traditional fare to harvest and consume the crunchy snacks. This was a regular stopover, I soon concluded, because only the uppermost branches of the trees still bore seed pods. The lower branches, those within reach, had been picked clean on previous occasions. Challenged, but undeterred, the heftier members of the herd put their weight against the stout acacias and shook the trees vigorously until a shower of pods rewarded their efforts. All of the elephants partook of the bounty. Even the young calf participated. Although mother's milk would be his sole nourishment for months to come, the youngster joined his older siblings and the adults in seeking out the fallen pods, principally for amusement and as an exercise in the mastery of his floppy trunk. More than 40,000 muscles are said to be contained within this most unique of elephant appendages –

as opposed to some 600 in the entire human body – but coordinating and applying these muscles in a gainly manner requires much practice. Judging from this youngster's comical attempts to grasp and hold his findings, he still had a long way to go.

Not all of the elephants were inclined to join in this group pursuit. Some of the larger ones, with the longest reach, extended their probing trunks up into the thorny canopy and delicately extracted whatever lower-level pods they could for on-the-spot consumption. One large cow, stretched to her physical limits, gained a few extra inches by lifting her left foreleg off the ground. I recalled a photo I had seen of an elephant reared back on its hind legs, reaching high into a tree with both forelimbs aloft, like a bear or a dog, and I wondered if we were about to witness the same behavior, astonishing in the wild. But no. The elephant reached as far as she could with one leg quivering in the air, but kept her considerable bulk balanced squarely on the other three.

After a half-hour or so, the matriarch determined that snack time was over. Without notice or ceremony, she left her place in the shade and crossed directly in front of our vehicle – barely glancing at us – then continued on down the dusty wash toward the river. The other elephants followed compliantly. The adults – like the matriarch – passed us with placid indifference, but the juveniles eyed us distrustfully and offered up minor threat displays, extending their ears and shaking their heads to make certain we knew who was boss in these parts. Hilariously, when the infant passed by, just ahead of his mother, he presented his own emulative display, ears flapping and trunk waggling as he tossed his head with all the confidence and vigor of a full-grown bull. We laughed in response – not the desired reaction – but with youngsters such as these, guided to maturity by a wise and loving community, I was somehow assured that the next generation of desert-dwelling giants would survive, indeed flourish, in this most harsh and unforgiving of places.

ELEPHANTS
Chobe National Park, Botswana

HIPPOPOTAMUS
Linyanti Wildlife Reserve, Botswana

ELEPHANT
Chobe National Park, Botswana

ELEPHANT RIVER CROSSING
Chobe National Park, Botswana

SADDLE-BILLED STORKS
Mombo, Moremi Game Reserve, Botswana

NILE CROCODILE
Chobe National Park, Botswana

AFRICAN FISH EAGLE
Chobe National Park, Botswana

AFRICAN FISH EAGLE
Okavango Delta, Botswana

ELEPHANTS
Linyanti Wildlife Reserve, Botswana

ELEPHANT
South Luangwa National Park, Zambia

ELEPHANTS
Linyanti Wildlife Reserve, Botswana

ELEPHANTS STARTLED BY
BABY PUKU ENCIRCLE THEIR YOUNG
Chobe National Park, Botswana

ELEPHANTS
Linyanti Wildlife Reserve, Botswana

YOUNG WATERBUCK EVICTED FROM HERD
Chobe National Park, Botswana

CHEETAH AND CUBS
Savuti, Chobe National Park, Botswana

NILE CROCODILES
Serengeti National Park, Tanzania

CROCODILES DEVOUR HIPPO CARCASS
South Luangwa National Park, Zambia

GREATER KUDU
South Luangwa National Park, Zambia

DESERT-ADAPTED ELEPHANTS
Damaraland, Namibia

DESERT-ADAPTED ELEPHANTS
Damaraland, Namibia

ELEPHANT
Chobe National Park, Botswana

Ballerinas and Bodybuilders

ost who answer the siren call of Africa share a common love of animals. And a common compassion for those in the wild whose perils are many. Poaching. Loss of habitat. Drought. Disease. All the big issues. But take these same concerned souls and expose them to the intoxicants of the savanna — the sensorial stew of sights and sounds and scents — and before long they begin viewing even the most enchanting of antelopes as little more than a potential meal for some savage predator. With utter predictability, compassion gives way to a darker impulse. What everyone wants, more than anything, is to see a kill.

Few ever do. Although death on the hoof is an everyday fact of life, and images of it have been implanted in our collective conscious as somehow typifying the African experience, our familiarity with the brutal spectacle comes largely from wildlife documentaries — more often than not, the distillation of months or years of patient field work on the part of an exceptionally dedicated breed of filmmakers. Only the hopelessly naive or incurably optimistic would set forth on a two- or three-week safari with any real expectation of witnessing such an event. Lions and hyenas, the most abundant and voracious of the large predators, hunt principally at night when park regulations restrict visitors to their campsites or lodges. Even in daytime, following a hunt in progress is often impossible since off-road driving is prohibited in so many of the continent's premier game-viewing locales and predators seem largely disinclined to accommodate tourists by killing along the roadside. In places where cross-country driving is allowed, overeager visitors often disrupt the unfolding drama they so yearn to witness by crowding both hunter and hunted. Only the most determined of predators will attempt a kill when dogged by a caravan of tour vehicles bristling with telephoto lenses. But even though everything conspires against it — and the likelihood of seeing a lethal encounter is about on par with sighting the Loch Ness monster on a drive through Scotland — few can resist the urge to scan the horizon in hopeful anticipation. Beholding a successful hunt is, for nearly everyone, the Holy Grail of the safari experience.

Estelle and I consider ourselves most fortunate to have witnessed a lioness stalking zebra in the Masai Mara and a pack of wild dogs running down impala in the Okavango Delta. But nothing quite measures up to the visceral apex of our first excursion into the Savuti region of northern Botswana.

We were drawn to Savuti by a number of splendid *National Geographic* specials filmed there over a period of years by Dereck and Beverly Joubert. Widely known for its resident bull elephants – exceedingly large and remarkably tolerant of humans – Savuti also plays host to an annual migration of tens of thousands of zebras and supports a nonmigratory assortment of antelopes and other herbivores sufficient in number to satisfy the gastronomic demands of its abundant lion and hyena populations.

Savuti is also known for the volatility of its ecosystem. Once a verdant paradise coursing with water regardless of seasonal vicissitudes, it is now, for much of the year, a parched and dusty wasteland whose native animals owe their existence to water pumped from subterranean sources into man-made waterholes. During the long dry season, when rain-fed waterholes in the region turn first to mud and then to hardpan, elephants in particular congregate at these precious man-made reservoirs, milling about uneasily whenever fluid levels decline, probing the exposed inlet pipes with tactile trunks and waiting for replenishment of the life-sustaining liquid. No one knows for certain exactly what happened – though shifts in the earth's crust are a persistent theory – but between 1979 and 1982, the Savuti Channel, which fed water into the region year-round, simply dried up and disappeared. It was not the first time for this phenomenon.

Savuti lies within the Mababe Depression, which for millennia was submerged beneath an enormous prehistoric lake that covered much of northern Botswana. Extending in a gentle arc to the north and west is the Magwikhwe Sand Ridge, thought to be the shoreline of this ancient inland sea. Aside from it, the prevailing flatness of the region is broken only by the Gubatsaa Hills, a scattering of volcanic outcrops which to this day exhibit erosive evidence of the great waves that once crashed against them. A short climb up Small Quango Hill rewards the contemporary sightseer with a display of ancient Bushman rock paintings – still vibrant after 3,000 years – that depict the wildlife of the day in an elegant distillation of line and form.

Through a gap in the sand ridge passes the Savuti Channel – now just a dry wash meandering through the wilderness – which in times of prosperity carries water more than fifty miles from the Linyanti River and disperses it across the Savuti Marsh. When it flows – typically for years or decades at a time – the channel delivers a steady supply of water even during periods of drought. But since missionary explorer David Livingstone first traversed the region in 1849, the capricious waterway has dried up at least four times, for periods ranging from a few years to more than seventy. Each time the consequence to flora and fauna has been cataclysmic. After an interval of healing and ecological adjustment, however, the reappearance of water can be equally as injurious. Scattered everywhere about the former marshlands are the remains of camelthorn acacias – still tall and erect – that sprouted and grew to full height during a protracted dry spell spanning 1880 and 1957, and then drowned when the channel recommenced its flow. Now that the water is gone once again, and has been for 25 years, a new generation of trees has taken root. The cycle continues.

Our first view of this enigmatic wilderness was from several thousand feet as our bushplane winged northeast from the Okavango Delta over vast expanses that grew more and more arid and inhospitable as we neared our destination. Below us were endless miles of empty game trails, converging from every direction on dozens of wet-season waterholes which were now, in late August, long dry and abandoned. Our pilot deposited us on a dirt airstrip where a vehicle waited to transport us to Lloyd's Camp, the oldest and best-known of Savuti's permanent accommodations – a veritable institution which has since been razed to make way for a luxury safari lodge. Owned and operated by Lloyd and June Wilmot, the twenty-year-old camp was indeed austere compared to some of the competition elsewhere in Botswana, but its tents were spacious and comfortable and its culinary achievements superb. Nestled on the banks of the once and future channel, it offered a tree-shaded viewing area from which elephants and other animals, drawn to a regularly replenished supply of water, could be seen almost within splashing distance. Best of all, it was known for having the top guides in the region.

Our group of eight on this particular trip was too large to fit comfortably in just one of the camp's open Land Rovers. So when the time came for our first afternoon game drive, Estelle and I volunteered to join another group, and our friend Lynne Wolf accompanied us. It was a fortuitous decision.

The indomitable Lionel Song was our driver and guide. In his fourth year at Savuti — and with prior time served in the game parks of his native South Africa — Lionel was everything one expects in a safari guide, but rarely encounters. Acutely knowledgeable of the region and its wild-life, he was a consummate tracker and game spotter, charming and witty and doggedly driven to show us the very best of what Savuti had to offer. Not one to stop and smell the flowers, if Lionel were on the trail of a leopard — as he was on our first game drive — nothing short of hippos in a tree would divert him from his objective. Anything less fell well beneath his perceptual radar. It took a while, but Lionel found us that leopard — a young male who gamely abided our presence for an hour or more — and then, in the time remaining before sundown, proceeded to one-up himself by locating a family of cheetahs striding across the dry marsh bed, a klatsch of bull elephants clustered at a waterhole and a pack of wild dogs giving halfhearted chase to a cheeky wildebeest. It was an after-noon to remember — probably a total fluke, we realized, but none of us was about to suggest that we swap guides in the morning.

We set out before sunup and drove directly to the spot where we had seen the leopard the previous afternoon. Rag-doll remnants of an impala carcass had been draped over a tree branch at the time, and there was reason to hope that the cat might still be in the area. He was not. Unwaveringly confident, Lionel refocused on the cheetah family of the evening before and proceeded to the marsh. We probably could have done without a master tracker. Several vehicles parked along the main road drew us quickly to the spotted cats — six of them — which were picking their way unhurriedly across the sandy expanse. We pulled over and watched.

Any cheetah sighting is a rare treat. Finding six together borders on the miraculous. Neither as gregarious as the lion nor as solitary as the leopard, the cheetah is most often observed singly, although coalitions of two to four are not uncommon. Except for the occasional female that has yet to reach sexual maturity, coalitions consist solely of males — usually littermates — that have forged communal bonds in order to hunt cooperatively and defend group territory. Females of breeding age — at least those without cubs in tow — are invariably found alone as court-ship and mating create no lasting ties and sisterhoods among cheetahs

are nonexistent.

Although all six of our animals looked full-grown, Lionel informed us that they were, in fact, a resident family comprised of an adult female and her subadult offspring. Cheetahs reach full size by fifteen months of age, and most separate from their mothers by seventeen months. Certainly these five youngsters fell within that upper age bracket as it was impossible, to the untrained eye at least, to distinguish any one of them from the mother. A remarkable union of good fortune and good parenting was clearly in evidence here. Most cheetah litters number only three or four cubs to begin with — and infant mortality is extremely high. Less than half of all cubs survive past their first three months when they are still essentially helpless and confined to the natal lair. A third to a half of those die during the next three months when they emerge and begin to follow their mothers during hunting. Only one in twenty young cheetahs survives to full maturity and independence, with predation accounting for a good three-quarters of the cumulative death toll. What we were seeing with this mother and her five near-adult offspring was a cosmic defiance of the odds.

The difference between a good sighting and a great sighting often hinges on patience and commitment. Yet the attention span of most tour groups seems to be about fifteen minutes per sighting. After that, the lure of other possibilities becomes overwhelming and they tend to move on. Sometimes that lure can be downright mundane. Jerry Dale once told me of a group he was escorting that elected to leave a pride of lions trying to bring down a buffalo rather than risk missing lunch back at the lodge. Nothing imminently dramatic was afoot with our cheetahs — though a leisurely hunt could be presumed to be in progress — so we had scant expectation of prolonged interest from the roadside viewing gallery of which we were now a part. Sure enough, within minutes of our arrival, waning attention spans were in evidence as tour vehicles coughed into motion and rumbled off down the roadway. A few stalwarts remained until the stately cats at last disappeared into the acacia scrub adjoin-ing the marsh. Then they, too, dispersed in search of other quarry. Lionel waited for the last of them to leave and then pulled off onto a second-ary track and began paralleling the route taken by the cheetahs.

Without crowding our quarry, Lionel kept the cats in view as they moved purposefully, but unhurriedly, through the patchy brush. There was little doubt that they were on a quest for sustenance. Unlike lions and leopards that favor the dark, cheetahs hunt almost exclusively in daylight – presumably to avoid competition – taking prey in morning or late afternoon and laying up in shade during the sweltering midday heat. A family of six would have to feed often, we reasoned, so there was hope that with some cautious trailing we might be rewarded with a kill – or at least an attempt.

Sometimes the cheetahs would be out of sight for minutes at a time, but Lionel seemed to have a sense of when and where they would reappear, and we would be there when they stepped back into view. When their reconnoitering took them deeper into the enveloping vegetation, Lionel left the road and began weaving through the thorn scrub, following the cats at an interval he judged discreet and noninvasive. Before long, we realized that we were not the only ones so engaged. About fifty yards aback of the cheetahs skulked a spotted hyena hoping for an easy meal. If the cats were cognizant of its presence, they gave no indication. As we pulled abreast of them – still at a respectable distance – they continued walking, without apparent objective, stopping from time to time to flop in the shade. When the cheetahs lounged, so did the hyena. I wondered if the hunters were aware of their pursuer and feigning a casual morning stroll in hopes that the hyena might lose interest and move on. It did not, of course – and neither did we.

With the sun now high in the mid-morning sky, and the cheetahs in a prolonged period of quiescence, Lionel announced that it was tea time and started the engine. We protested – the allure of this ritual being obscure to us Yanks – but Lionel assured us we would return. He pulled away quietly and withdrew to a secluded spot where we dismounted and partook of beverages and cookies while Lionel presented an impromptu tutorial on survival in the bush. His discourse on finding predator-proof sleeping accommodations amongst the thorn thickets was reasonably worthwhile. But I confess to misgivings when he began rhapsodizing about the nutritional value of elephant dung, seizing a sun-dried clump of the stuff and breaking it apart like a loaf of bread to display the undigested seeds and other edibles within. Glancing around at my companions, I wondered just how hungry we would have to be before the prospect of

such a repast would seem appealing. I munched a few extra cookies – just in case.

Our lesson completed, we climbed back into the Land Rover and returned to the spot where we had left the cheetahs napping. They were gone. A rush of dismay was promptly suppressed by my realization that an accomplished guide such as ours had only to follow the signposts – which were manifold. Unique in the cat family, the cheetah has blunt un- sheathed claws, so its spoor is distinctive and rather doglike in appear- ance. Within moments, Lionel had picked up the trail and our quarry was once again in view. The cats were advancing with evident purpose, but without a set target in sight or in range. Since prey was sparse in the vicinity, Lionel announced his intention to drive on ahead of the cheetahs and see what was likely to come into range. By selecting the right prey animal and positioning ourselves ahead of the anticipated event, we stood a good chance of witnessing the chase and perhaps the kill, if there was to be one.

In advance of the cats, we struck out in search of suitable prey, driving a quarter-mile or more before coming upon a handful of impalas grazing on sun-crisped grasses. While the cheetahs of East Africa dine principally on Thomson's gazelles, those in the southern regions, where gazelles are not indigenous, favor the somewhat larger impala. We opted to take a chance on our cheetahs discovering the same ones we had. Although scattered thorn bushes precluded an unobstructed view, we selected an optimal vantage point and parked some seventy or eighty yards away so as not to disrupt the proceedings. Then we waited.

Considerable time had passed, and I was all but convinced we had gambled and lost, when the cheetahs at last entered our field of view. Trailing behind a few dozen yards, with an air of nonchalance, was the hyena. It was a charged moment – predators and prey at opposite ends of a vast proscenium, unaware as yet of the roles they would be enacting in a serial drama that has spanned the ages. Our eyes darted back and forth as we wondered which would catch sight of the other first – and to what end. If the fate of the antelopes hung on our whim, I doubt that mine would have been the only thumb pointing down. A surge of bloodlust had washed through the vehicle. It was a Hemingway kind of moment. The real thing. This was the Africa we had come to see.

Advancing in single file through the scattered thorn bushes, the cheetahs eventually drew up and peered intently in the direction of the grazing impalas. The game was now in play – but its outcome was by no means evident. Recognized without challenge as the fastest mammal on earth, the cheetah can out-accelerate a Ferrari and run at speeds up to seventy miles per hour, but it is essentially a sprinter. Any prey not overtaken within the first 300 yards stands a good chance of surviving the encounter. For our cheetahs to launch a successful attack, they would need to close the distance between themselves and the impalas to an optimal fifty yards without being seen. Given a longer lead, the antelopes' agility and stamina would likely carry the day.

Two of the cheetahs crouched motionless in the shade of a bush while the remaining four disappeared from view into the surrounding veg- etation. With six cats accustomed to hunting as a team, we could only surmise that some sort of flanking maneuver was afoot. We waited. The two cheetahs we could see made no move to advance on the impalas, which continued eating in blissful ignorance of what was being planned for them. We imagined the other four creeping into range. What emerged from the tree line behind the impalas were not flashes of spotted fur, however, but a pair of patchwork giraffes intent upon browsing amongst the acacias. That spelled trouble for the cheetahs.

With keen eyesight and natural elevation, giraffes are adept at sight- ing predators – and alerting others to their presence. Just a few days before, on a game drive at Mombo, we were combing a particular area in search of a resident lion pride when we noticed a dozen or more giraffes, interspersed amongst a herd of zebras, standing stock still and staring fixedly at a clump of trees. Driving over to investigate, we found the lions sprawled out and asleep in the shade. Not content with merely keeping the predators in sight, the giraffes would alternate taking a few steps toward the lions, then pause for a while and press forward again. Though an adult giraffe has little to fear from most predators, this confronta- tional display serves as an added deterrent – a crucial one if vulnerable calves are about. By advancing on the enemy, the giraffes were announc- ing that they were aware of the clear and present danger. The element of surprise – essential to any big cat – was compromised.

Just moments before, a kill had seemed likely, if not certain. Now what would happen? Almost at once, one of the giraffes spotted the two cheetahs under the bush. Alert and flagpole erect, it faced in their direction and stared at them. Its companion took the cue and followed suit. The cheetahs froze. The giraffes froze. We froze. The impalas continued eating. One of the gangling sentinels took a few cautious steps toward the cats and froze again. Surely the impalas would have to take notice. How could prey animals this oblivious have lived to maturity? Minutes passed.

When it happened, none of us caught it all. It was instantaneous. Those observing the antelopes saw the impalas and giraffes scatter in flight. Those watching the cheetahs saw them leap to the chase. No one even glimpsed the four others that had disappeared into the bush. We knew only that the trap had been sprung. Lionel slammed the Land Rover into gear and we were off.

I wish I could recount how we witnessed the chase in all of its *National Geographic* splendor – the cheetahs in fluid pursuit, flexible shoulders and spines increasing their stride to that of a racehorse's, running full tilt, adroitly countering the impalas' evasive zigzags with sweeping tail maneuvers – but the fact is, we were left, quite literally, in the dust. I had never seen a cheetah running at full speed, except in documentaries where every detail of the action was invariably conveyed in balletic slow-motion. Compressed into real time, the chase lasted seconds – and much was obscured behind bushes. By the time we caught up, it was all over. A female impala was down and kicking, her throat clasped tight in a classic stranglehold.

Cheetahs are splendidly efficient hunters – second only to wild dogs in ratio of kills to attempts – but they are not fighters, a fact which makes them vulnerable to others that are, particularly lions and hyenas that would rather steal a meal than hunt for one. Since cheetahs are neither physically nor temperamentally suited to resist, many a hard-won kill is relinquished without so much as a scuffle. Even a few scrappy vultures have been known to drive a cheetah from its prey.

Alert to the possibility of thievery, the cheetahs worked quickly and cooperatively to drag the impala toward a cluster of nearby thorn bushes. The urgency of the effort may have had to do with the hyena that had been following them all morning – but not necessarily. If vultures were to sight the downed animal – as surely they would if it were left in the open – their circling and descent would be a dinner call to any marauder within miles.

Those of us conditioned by wildlife films to expect a quick, clean kill had our consciousness raised in the minutes that followed. The impala, one cheetah clamped at her throat, was still alive when the others began tearing at her underbelly and haunches. As though resigned to her fate, the animal did not struggle, but occasional twitches and movements disclosed that the death grip had not yet served its purpose. At last the impala went limp, and the cheetah executing the hold dropped the lolling head and joined in the hurried feeding. Somehow it seemed more watchable now. No longer were we witnessing a living creature being eaten – only a carcass. One animal had died so that others might live – the old 'circle of life' thing. We could deal with it. Then the antelope stirred again. She was still alive! Another of the cheetahs grabbed onto her neck and resumed the stranglehold. But the horror was not yet over. A flash of movement caught my eye as the hyena, just now reaching the scene, burst through the thorn bushes from behind. The startled cats scattered at once as the juggernaut charged into their midst. Then – most incredibly and terribly of all – the impala somehow struggled to her feet and tried to escape. Her underside was a ruptured mess – and as she reeled on unsteady legs, her stomach dropped from the abdominal cavity and hung dangling by a slender strand of viscera. The hyena spun around and snatched the wretched creature, dragging her effortlessly toward the bushes where it quickly completed the task the cheetahs had botched. With dispassionate ferocity, it tore into its plundered prey, extracting huge mouthfuls of flesh and gore and downing them greedily. The impala would stir no more.

The cheetahs milled about nervously. One even made a tentative advance on the thief – hackles raised and with a grimacing expression – but a quick lunge by the hyena sent it scrambling. Why had the cheetahs allowed a lone scavenger to drive them from their kill? Lionel answered with a query of his own. Would six ballerinas stand up to a bodybuilder? This was not an even match. Larger and beefier than the cheetahs, and with jaws and teeth designed to crush bones, the hyena was a more than formidable adversary. A single bite could easily disable a cheetah or curtail its ability to hunt. Were that to happen, death would certainly follow. Surrendering the impala was both prudent and unavoidable.

The drama had climaxed, but it was not yet over. There were other players still in the wings. Above, keen-eyed vultures began to circle – first a few, then dozens. Like jetliners on final approach, they descended one by one and landed, congregating apart from the main attraction, biding their time and waiting for leftovers. Drawn by the aerial display was a second hyena. As it loped to the site, we watched, expecting a conflict to erupt – but there was none. Clearly both animals were of the same clan. Aside from some impolite squabbling, they shared the booty with minimal rancor. A third joined in a while later. Last on the scene was a black-backed jackal, impertinent enough to mark the turf as his own, that circled and crept about ever so gingerly, waiting for an opportunity to dart in and grab a morsel of food.

One of the primal pleasures of wilderness Africa is that it demands to be accepted on its own terms. Value judgments are inconsequent. An hour was all that it took to reduce the impala to a few bones and some tattered skin – and when the gorged hyenas carted those away there remained only a bloody splotch in the sand. The vultures' patient vigil had earned them precisely nothing. We took away much more. We had witnessed a spectacle whose horrors, irreducible by the passage of time, would linger forever in our memories, but which had about it an essential purity and intensity that made it somehow beautiful, as well. Authorities on such matters contend that animals in the jaws of death feel no agony, that trauma shock produces a sort of anesthesia. I would like to think so. But while pain may be countered, I have only to examine one of the photos I took that morning – of the butchered impala trying to flee, wild-eyed and tottering like a newborn – to know that terror cannot be thus obliterated. It was clearly there on her countenance.

We headed back to camp. More than four hours had passed, and we knew that our companions – and a sumptuous brunch – would be awaiting our return. It was a quiet passage. Even the ebullient Lionel was a bit reserved. We had shared an experience that was exhilarating and abhorrent at the same time, and each of us felt the need to sort out our feelings about it in wordless contemplation. Among the conflicting emotions I felt was a swell of regret that our travel mates had missed the terrible sighting – especially Jerry, who in twenty years of leading safaris had never observed a kill. I hoped they had seen something equally as extraordinary – but knew they had not. Mostly, I kept flashing back to the impala – dead, but in denial – trying valiantly to escape the fate that had befallen her. Awash in their own thoughts, Estelle and Lynne offered up a few silent tears.

No one felt much like eating.

SPRINGBOK
Etosha National Park, Namibia

WATERHOLE CONGREGATION
Etosha National Park, Namibia

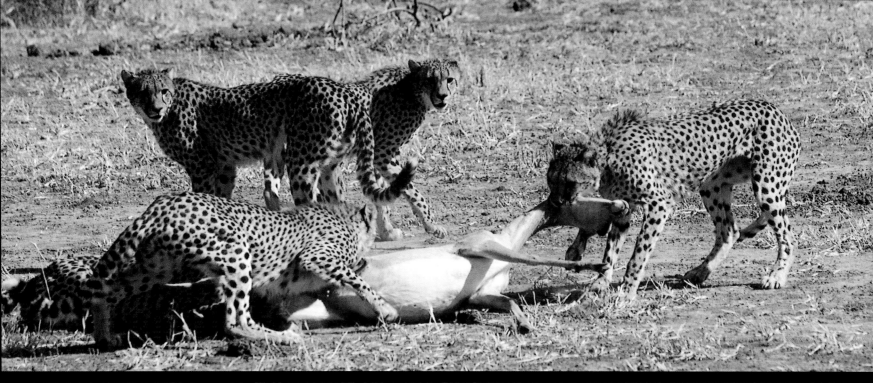

CHEETAHS TAKE DOWN IMPALA
Savuti, Chobe National Park, Botswana

HYENA AMBUSHES HUNTERS
Savuti, Chobe National Park, Botswana

HYENA DEVOURS STOLEN KILL
Savuti, Chobe National Park, Botswana

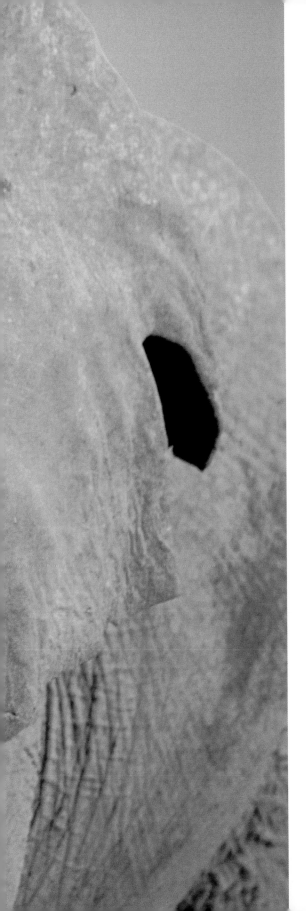

LION
Savuti, Chobe National Park, Botswana

ELEPHANT
Etosha National Park, Namibia

HIPPOPOTAMUSES
South Luangwa National Park, Zambia

PUKU
South Luangwa National Park, Zambia

OXPECKERS
Savuti, Chobe National

Savuti, Chobe National

GEMSBOK
Sossusvlei, Namib-Naukluft Park, Namibia

GEMSBOK
Sossusvlei, Namib-Naukluft Park, Namibia

GEMSBOK
Etosha National Park, Namibia

VERVET MONKEYS WITH INFANT
South Luangwa National Park, Zambia

CHAMELEON
Etosha National Park, Namibia

LEOPARD TORTOISE
Matetsi Game Reserve, Zimbabwe

GIRAFFE AND ZEBRA
Etosha National Park, Namibia

SPRINGBOK FIGHTING
Etosha National Park, Namibia

LIONESS AND CUB
South Luangwa National Park, Zambia

Journey's End

Aside from a few historical references, there are no dates in this book – only accounts of places and events cherry-picked from twenty years of travel and presented without regard to chronology. Dates seemed irrelevant. My intent was to create an evocation of the safari experience. The events I recounted in my chapter on lions in the Masai Mara or in my chapter on elephants on the Chobe River could have transpired twenty years ago or they could have transpired just last week. The safari experience is immutable and timeless at its essence. Which is not to say that nothing has changed over the years. Quite the contrary.

As a young Air Force captain stationed overseas during the Vietnam War, I once volunteered to courier classified documents to Hong Kong, which was a choice perk for anyone with a top secret clearance. Having fulfilled my official obligation, and with several hours to kill before my return flight, I hopped a taxi into the city's high-glitz shopping district and wandered around for a spell. Hong Kong was – and is – a world center for commerce in ivory, and in many of the shops I entered there were exquisitely carved artifacts of every size and sort. Although most were well out of my price range, I happened upon a small ivory sphere, slightly larger than a golf ball, with delicately carved Chinese dragons on its surface and an inner succession of spheres within spheres visible through the latticework intertwining of limbs and tails and serpentine bodies. To this day, I have no idea how it was achieved, but it was all carved from a single piece of ivory – and I had to have it. Never once did I consider the possibility that an elephant might have been slaughtered to provide me with this captivating curio.

A dozen years later, such naiveté would have been impossible. Worldwide public awareness had been slow in coming, but by the time Estelle and I embarked on our first safari to Kenya, in 1987, there was ample evidence to support the contention that the African elephant was at risk of becoming extinct throughout much of its range. Organized gangs of ivory poachers, armed with high-power military assault weapons, had been ravaging the game reserves of Africa since the mid-1970s, slaying upwards of 50,000 elephants per year – cumulatively half of the continent's estimated 1.3 million total in little over a decade. Kenya was one of the countries hardest hit, though we had no personal base line by which to judge that during our first trip there. We saw pleasing numbers of elephants in the Masai Mara and Samburu, and a great many in Amboseli, whose population had benefited from long-term monitoring by

Cynthia Moss and her Amboseli Elephant Research Project. But we saw hardly any in Tsavo, once the country's premier elephant sanctuary with more than 40,000 animals. An aerial survey of the Tsavo region, conducted shortly after our initial visit there, revealed 5,363 live elephants – and 2,421 carcasses. Countrywide, Kenya had lost 70 percent of its elephants. Tanzania and Zambia – which together lost some 300,000 elephants – fared even worse.

The carnage was shocking, but not without precedent. In the early nineteenth century, an estimated 40 million American bison roamed the American Great Plains. Within fifty years, commercial hunting for skins had reduced that number to fewer than 1,000. Wildlife conservationists feared a similar fate for the embattled African elephant.

Removing the commercial incentive for elephant poaching seemed the only solution. In 1989, a month before our second trip to Africa, Kenya focused world attention on the issue by publicly setting ablaze a mountain of some 3,000 recovered elephant tusks worth approximately $3 million dollars on the open market. A few months thereafter, 103 signatory nations belonging to the Convention on International Trade in Endangered Species effectively banned the trade in elephant ivory and skins. A multimillion-dollar market disappeared overnight, and almost at once, poaching dropped dramatically – though not entirely. Contraband ivory still flowed freely through Sudan and Egypt, supplying buyers in China and Thailand mostly, but the pressure was much relieved. Elephant populations could begin to recover.

The ban was not universally embraced, however, even among African nations with elephant populations. Four southern Africa countries had been largely untouched by the poaching epidemic. Consequently, during the same period that elephants were being exterminated elsewhere on the continent, populations in Botswana, Namibia, Zimbabwe and South Africa had more than doubled in size and were now straining the capacity of the wild lands they occupied. All four countries argued for exclusion from the trade ban on the grounds that elephants were not truly endangered – only poorly distributed – and the proceeds derived from the sale of legally acquired ivory and other elephant products would be used to fund conservation efforts and purchase new tracts of land for parks and reserves. A coalition of opponents carried the day, insisting that any

trade, however limited, would lead to further poaching, since legal ivory was indistinguishable from illegal ivory once it entered the market.

Under optimal conditions, elephant numbers will double every fifteen years, making management of the animals an ongoing concern for the ivory-rich nations of Africa. Although some attempts were made to move surplus elephants from overpopulated regions to underpopulated regions – a seemingly elegant solution – capturing and transporting elephants was expensive and time-consuming, and ultimately impractical on a large scale. Various contraceptive approaches were tested, but it was reckoned that three-quarters of all breeding-age females would need to be injected annually to effect a long-term population reduction. Also, there was fear that a predominance of infertile females might undermine the social matriarchy of elephant herds and constrict the gene pool. The most effective – and least acceptable – strategy was culling. Since the mid-1960s – throughout the years when elephants were being pushed toward extinction elsewhere on the continent – South Africa had quietly been killing as many as 600 elephants per year to preserve habitat and bio-diversity in Kruger National Park. Sharpshooters in helicopters would kill entire family groups, including calves, on the grounds that the complex bonds among elephants made eliminating a complete herd preferable to traumatizing survivors by paring selectively from several. Other countries, including Zimbabwe, also employed culling as a wildlife management tool. Amid international pressure, South Africa was the last to suspend the practice in 1996, though a resumption now seems imminent.

A number of African nations, including some ravaged by poaching, have welcomed hunting as a lucrative means of fattening their conservation coffers. Sport hunters from around the world have shown themselves willing to pay enormous fees for the privilege of killing African big game, including elephants in some locales. Though tightly controlled, this practice has come under fire, as well, particularly in the wake of a 1994 incident in which four breeding bulls – part of the Amboseli study group – wandered over the border into Tanzania and were shot by hunters. The elephants were fully habituated to humans, and the killings were considered as challenging as shooting cows in a pasture. International outrage over the incident forced Tanzania authorities to ban elephant hunting in regions adjoining the border with Kenya.

Much of the overpopulation problem relates directly to the creation of national parks and reserves designed to protect the wild animals of Africa. Some parks are fenced and many are unfenced, but only a few fully encompass ancient migration routes between wet-season and dry-season habitats. With Africa's human population having doubled in the past thirty years, farms and communities now obstruct many of these ancient corridors, creating areas of conflict between humans and elephants — many of whom still traverse or reside in unprotected areas. In the past decade or so, a number of African nations, aided and encouraged by conservation groups, have begun forming megaparks, variously known as transfrontier parks and African heartlands, linking multiple conservation areas, often across political borders and through private lands, to reestablish natural ranges disrupted by current national and park boundaries. Fences have come down between overpopulated Kruger and underpopulated reserves in neighboring Mozambique and Zimbabwe, now united in the Great Limpopo Transfrontier Park, and a dozen or more other heartlands are in various stages of development throughout the continent. Although designed for the benefit of all wildlife species, it is hoped that elephants, in particular, will redistribute themselves naturally, as in days of old, moving freely from reserve to reserve, improving the gene pool and relieving pressure on habitats.

Unquestionably, the African elephant is on sounder footing than it was twenty years ago, even though population estimates of 500,000 to 600,000 are still lower than they were when the ivory ban was enacted. Populations in Kenya have more than doubled since the trade ban, and populations in Zambia and elsewhere are on the mend. But populations in some countries — particularly those perennially plagued by civil wars and regional conflicts — have continued to decline. In opposition, the overpopulation of southern African countries — where half of all elephants now reside — remains a persistent and growing concern. Although overall numbers are healthy, the elephant is still poorly distributed in Africa, and a universal solution to that vexing problem is unlikely to emerge.

For tens of thousands of years, another great herbivore coexisted with the elephant. And in a synchronous flash of just two or three decades, it, too, faced extermination at the hand of man — and for much the same reason. Unlike the elephant, however, which was overpopulating some regions even as it was being eradicated in others, the African rhinoceros seemed well on the road to unqualified extinction. At the height of the poaching pandemic, rhinos were disappearing everywhere.

Only half a century ago, rhinos were a fixture on the savannas and woodlands of eastern and southern Africa. Today, one is lucky to see one in the wild. Of the two species native to the continent, the black rhinoceros, solitary and highly aggressive, is a browser with a prehensile upper lip allowing it to pluck twigs and leaves, while the white rhinoceros, social and more docile, is a grazer with a wide square mouth suited to cropping short grasses. Each sports a pair of horns on its snout — a large one in front and a smaller one behind — that are deployed both offensively and defensively. These signature skewers are also, quite literally, worth more than gold — making the animal itself an expendable byproduct.

Rhino horn consists of keratin — a mundane fibrous protein found in hair and fingernails — and for 2,000 years has been ground into powder and used in the Orient as a traditional medicine for the treatment of headaches and fever. Some consider it an aphrodisiac. Rhino horn is also prized in Yemen where it is carved into ceremonial dagger handles denoting status and wealth. Though arguably reprehensible, neither practice posed a threat to the rhinoceros as a species until the 1970s, when the soaring price of Middle East oil created a whole new class of ultra-rich Yemeni eager to display their newfound affluence by accessorizing in style. The demand for rhino horn skyrocketed — and cost was no concern. Quick to respond, organized poachers already ravaging the African elephant population diversified into even more lucrative rhino poaching.

In 1970, there were an estimated 20,000 black rhinos in Kenya — 8,000 in Tsavo National Park alone. By 1987, there were effectively no rhinos left in Tsavo, and barely 500 in all of Kenya. Tanzania, another rhino stronghold, lost most of its 2,000 rhinos in Selous National Park, and all but two of its 700 in the Serengeti. Poachers shot 4,000 black rhinos in Zambia, and then, when there were no more to be found there, crossed into Zimbabwe and slaughtered another 1,400 in the Zambezi Valley. In only seventeen years, nearly 95 percent of the world's black rhinos were massacred in the interest of ornamental indulgence and apocryphal medicine.

The white rhinoceros fared better, by comparison, only because of extraordinary circumstances. Pronounced extinct in 1892 as a result of overhunting, the species was reborn five years later when a handful of survivors was discovered in a remote region of South Africa. Thirty years of watchful management were needed to increase that nucleus population to just 30 individuals. Thirty years after that, however, there were 1,500 – with numbers on the rise. Even during the darkest days of the poaching crisis, when both black and white rhinos were being exterminated elsewhere on the continent, the white rhino population in South Africa grew to more than 4,000.

African nations unable to protect their elephants were equally unable to protect their rhinos. The plight of the rhinoceros was more immediately recognized as critical, but with rhino horns commanding prices in excess of $5,000 per pound in Yemen, the profit incentive for poaching far outweighed any risks the practice might entail – even in Zimbabwe, where a shoot-to-kill order netted more than 50 poachers. The 1976 imposition of an international trade ban on rhino products – a strategy which would later thwart the poaching of elephants – achieved little beyond driving the trade underground.

Desperate times called for desperate measures. Acting upon the assumption that a rhinoceros without horns would be of no interest to poachers, Namibia and Zimbabwe initiated pilot programs to dehorn their imperiled rhinos. Under veterinary supervision, sharpshooters with dart guns would anesthetize a rhinoceros in the wild. Both horns would be painlessly removed with a chainsaw and the animal injected with antibiotics to prevent infection. Then the rhino would be revived and set free. In addition to being a costly procedure – especially in light of its impermanence, since the horns would grow back in time – the practice spawned protest amongst those who considered dehorning unduly stressful to the animal. Others argued that a male without horns would be at a disadvantage when competing for mates, and that a female without horns would be ill-equipped to protect her offspring from predators. Moreover, there was evidence to suggest that dehorned rhinos were still being poached. With rhinos increasingly scarce in the wild, a poacher could easily spend days tracking a single one. If that rhino turned out to be dehorned, and thus valueless, it was sometimes shot anyway so the poacher would not have to waste time tracking the same animal again.

In the years since Estelle and I viewed our first wild rhinoceros in the Masai Mara, steadfast conservation efforts have helped the rhino recover in some regions – nowhere more successfully than in South Africa, where the nurtured population of white rhinos, saved from extinction, now numbers nearly 12,000. Only 500 survive anywhere else. Of the 65,000 black rhinos widespread in 1970, a mere 3,800 remain today – up from a poached-out low of 2,475. Many are remnant populations, too small to be self-sustaining. Black and white combined, only four countries in Africa have populations of more than 100 rhinos.

Those that survive exist under markedly different circumstances than their predecessors. There are few truly free-ranging rhinos anymore. Most have been rounded up and relocated to small national parks and reserves, usually fenced, where their well-being can be more closely monitored. Many have round-the-clock armed guards. A number of countries have adopted programs, pioneered in South Africa, of entrusting rhinos to private ranches and reserves where they can be better protected. Today, more than a quarter of Africa's white and black rhinos are dispersed on private lands. Results of these conservation efforts are encouraging, but the sustained success of low-density populations depends upon rotating the animals within the network of sanctuaries to prevent inbreeding and foster genetic diversity. As to the long term, one can only speculate. Will the rhinoceros ever again range freely through the vast open spaces of Africa? Or must it remain in secure, but almost zoo-like environments, a reminder of the Africa that used to be?

Unlike the elephant and rhinoceros, whose numbers were in sharp decline when Estelle and I first beheld them in the wild, the mountain gorilla was doing rather well – at least for a critically endangered species with only 320 individuals standing between it and total extinction. Mountain gorilla numbers had bottomed out in the mid-1970s when a wake-up field census revealed fewer than 275 adults and young – a reduction of almost 50 percent from a decade earlier. By 1989, however, when Estelle and I made our honeymoon trip to Rwanda, sustained antipoaching and ecotourism initiatives had reversed this grievous trend, and the population had grown steadily by more that 20 percent.

Three years later, the mountain gorilla population would double to slightly more than 600 animals – virtually overnight. The dramatic increase was attributable, not to a reverberant baby boom, but rather a study conducted on another gorilla population some 25 miles to the north in Uganda. Almost 300 gorillas were thought to inhabit the mountains of Bwindi Impenetrable National Park – a rainforest habitat similar to the Virungas – but since those gorillas had shorter hair and somewhat longer limbs than their neighbors to the south, it was supposed that they were a distinct subspecies. However, a DNA study of hairs collected from gorilla night nests led scientists to determine that the Bwindi gorillas were genetically identical to those in the Virungas, and that physiological variances, as well as dietary and behavioral differences, were attributable to the two populations having been separated for more than a century since the woodlands between them were cleared for cultivation.

Given the windfall increase in numbers, the mountain gorilla's prognosis for survival seemed much improved, but with the world's entire population residing in one of the most politically dysfunctional regions of the continent – perhaps the planet – adding a 'happily ever after' tagline to the story was a bit premature.

Even as my companions and I were slogging our way through Rwandan rainforests in search of gorillas, the seeds of catastrophe were germinating just a few miles away in Uganda. Although I had taken pains to acquire a passing knowledge of the gorillas and their mountain habitat, I – along with most of the world – remained complacently ignorant of the country and its people. For hundreds of years, Rwanda and neighboring Burundi had been plagued by ethnic antipathy between the majority Hutus and the minority Tutsis. This ingrained hostility was exacerbated by Belgian colonial governors who considered the Tutsis somehow superior and contrived an institutional caste system that subjugated the Hutus. Eventually, in 1959, Hutu resentment erupted into a succession of bloody riots that annihilated thousands of Tutsis and impelled thousands more to flee the country. When Belgium ceded power in 1962, granting independence to Rwanda, a Hutu government was promptly installed.

In 1990 – a year after our visit – the tide turned again. The Rwanda Patriotic Force – comprised mostly of Tutsi outcasts born and raised in exile – invaded from Uganda and launched a civil war that lasted four years before an accord was reached with the Hutu government. Powerful interests opposed any concession to the Tutsi rebels, however, and backroom plotting began for an extreme response that would stun the world. In April 1994, an executive jet carrying the presidents of Rwanda and Burundi, returning to Kigali from regional peace talks in Tanzania, was shot down over the capital by a hand-held surface-to-air missile – an unequivocal vote of political 'no confidence' calculated to provoke outrage and misdirected retaliation. Within hours, a 'final solution' to the Tutsi problem was set into motion. Hutu soldiers and militiamen – abetted by swarms of machete-wielding civilians inflamed by propaganda – swept through urban and rural Rwanda on a genocidal orgy of unspeakable savagery. Thousands of men, women and children were hacked to death on streets, in homes and in churches, their corpses left to rot where they fell or tossed into rivers.

While the rest of the world grimaced and did nothing – even United Nations peacekeeping forces withdrew – the carnage continued for a hundred days until the Rwanda Patriotic Force seized the capital and routed the Hutu army and its grassroot confederates. By the time a modicum of order was restored, nearly a million Tutsis and sympathetic Hutus had been butchered, and some two million Rwandans, mostly Hutus fearing reprisals, had fled to neighboring nations and were now dying of disease and starvation in squalid refugee camps along the borders. A third of the country's population was dead or displaced.

Estelle and I were in Kenya during the final act of this epic tragedy, and talk of the goings-on in Rwanda, a few hundred miles away, was pervasive at the dinner table. I have a grim recollection of Nile perch – a staple entrée in Kenya safari lodges – being staunchly avoided during this visit. News footage of corpses by the hundreds being swept downriver in Rwanda had begun to be aired, and, whether rightly or wrongly, it was feared that many were flowing into Lake Victoria where the voracious freshwater fish was commercially caught. I was convinced that Rwanda would never recover – at least in my lifetime – and though the human disaster was foremost in the minds of all caring souls, I could not help but worry about the mountain gorillas. What had become of them? What would become of them?

News of the gorillas had been sketchy for some time. From the earliest months of the rebel incursion, the Virungas had been a conduit for insurgents entering Rwanda from Uganda, a dense-cover encampment area, and a regular venue for government and rebel engagements. Gorilla tourism – which was just starting to gain momentum – came to an abrupt halt, thus eliminating daily surveillance of the groups designated for visitation, and ongoing efforts by rangers and researchers to monitor the location and status of the park's other gorilla groups were severely curtailed. Although both sides in the conflict vowed not to harm the great apes, the term 'endangered species' took on a new dimension as armed combatants ranged through their mountain habitat.

Intended or not, there was justifiable concern among wildlife advocates that mountain gorillas would become collateral casualties in a chaotic battle zone where mortars and automatic weapons were often as not in the hands of minimally trained recruits. Trip-wire snares once endemic to the forest – effectively eradicated by antipoaching patrols – were being deployed once again to provision rebel fighters. In the past, these simple devices, intended to trap small game, had proven crippling or even lethal to gorillas. There was also the possibility that traumatic stress induced by gunshots and explosions might cause the breakup of gorilla groups, or that human waste and disease might infect the population at large. Doomsday scenarios were rampant.

In fact, the gorillas managed rather well, following their natural instinct to choose flight over fight when confronted with danger. Even those habituated to humans knew to avoid the humans now prowling the park. But avoidance was not always possible. Some of the gorilla groups abandoned their customary ranges and moved into more placid surroundings in the contiguous reserves of Uganda and Zaire.

Against all odds, in four years of turmoil and conflict, the gorilla population suffered only one confirmed war casualty. Particularly saddening to us, that casualty was Mrithi, the amiable Group 13 patriarch who, as an ill-prepared young silverback, had kept his family intact when its previous leader was slain by poachers. What Mrithi had managed to do, his successor did not. An equally inexperienced young silverback sought to hold Group 13 together, but failed, and the once-favorite tourist group was now fragmented, with some of its members assimilated into other groups.

New perils emerged once the genocide was brought to an end and fleeing government troops drove an exodus of Hutu civilians through the Virungas and into Zaire, planting mines and grenades along trails to thwart their pursuers. In mere days, more than a million Rwandans crossed the border and set up camp, precipitating an immense humanitarian crisis that became an ecological disaster, as well, as refugees clear-cut some 20,000 acres of rainforest for cooking fuel. Hunger and disease claimed 50,000 lives before massive infusions of international aid could relieve and stabilize the situation. Armed militants – swaggering remnants of the Hutu army and militias – ruled the camps with fear and force for more than two years, denying egress to all, until their thuggish stranglehold was broken and the long-suffering refugees returned to Rwanda and an uncertain future.

My prophesy that Rwanda would not recover from its wounds, at least in my lifetime, would prove less than nostradamic. A functional democracy now represents all Rwandans, and national reconciliation initiatives have helped to heal and erase the ethnic divisions of the past. Rwanda is still a poor country, but its economy is on the upswing, helped in no small measure by a resurgent tourism industry, with mountain gorillas once again the foremost attraction. Gorilla groups in Uganda are likewise playing host to visitors from around the world. Only in Congo – no longer Zaire – has tourism failed to blossom, and it is in this lawless country where mountain gorillas are most endangered. Ten of them have been slaughtered there during the past year and a half – and without apparent reason. Still, the overall population continues to prosper, with recent surveys identifying some 720 mountain gorillas dispersed throughout the Virunga and Bwindi rainforests. The species that many feared would vanish in the century of its discovery has survived with brio into the next.

Having spent most of my professional life exploring the intricacies of high technology, one of the things that most appealed to me in the early years of my African odyssey was the lack of technology and the sense of isolation I felt while on safari. Absent the vehicles we rode around in and the cameras we used to document our every sight and deed, we could have been a hundred years in the past.

There were no telephones then. No television or radio. No newspapers or magazines. Emergency communication, if needed, was by shortwave relay from lodge to lodge or camp to camp. Postcards were plentiful, but stamps were not – and any missives we managed to post usually reached home after we did. Our isolation was virtually complete. We could be away for two or three weeks at a time and have no idea what was going on in the outside world – and care not the least. Did it really matter if we missed a few weeks of media yammering about the O.J. Simpson trial or the Monica Lewinsky scandal? Anything of real import managed to filter in from the outside, conveyed via word of mouth as in days of old. On an early trip to Kenya, we returned from a game drive one evening to learn from a new arrival that the Soviet Union had collapsed a few days before. I recall little else penetrating the void until years later when the owner of a remote camp in Zambia drove hours through the bush early one morning to deliver the stunning news that Islamic terrorists had hijacked four American airliners and flown three of them into the World Trade Center and the Pentagon. Anything less cataclysmic tended to be swallowed up in the pervasive isolation of Africa.

That splendid isolation began to diminish a decade or more ago. Perhaps it began when we started flying in comfort from game reserve to game reserve instead of driving the distance over mostly awful roads for hours on end. Africa was a smaller place now, its wonders less removed from the everyday. Or maybe it began with telephones in the rooms at some of the upscale safari lodges. Most were house phones only, but it was oddly unsettling to see them perched on a nightstand as in any hotel or motel in the developed world. Could television be far behind? CNN and DVDs? Then came the word that Internet and e-mail services were now available at many lodges and camps. The outside world was no longer outside. The technological incursion struck me hardest during our most recent visit to Tanzania. We were on the floor of the Ngorongoro Crater, having lunch at the lakeshore picnic area, when one of our travel mates moved apart from the group, pulled a cell phone from his pocket, and placed a call to his wife – in Manhattan. Africa seemed a much smaller place to me now.

In a very real sense, Africa was a much smaller place for its animals. In the twenty years we had been journeying to Africa, the continent's

human population had increased by a number exceeding the present-day population of the United States. So while the elephant and rhinoceros and gorilla were facing extinction at the point of a gun, many other species were facing comparable, if more benign, endangerment as a result of habitat lost in the crush of human expansion.

Unlikely as it may seem, most African animals live outside protected areas, on lands also occupied by human settlement. Although national parks and reserves have been generously allocated throughout much of the continent, these protected spaces are typically insufficient in size to fully satisfy the year-round needs of all resident species, many of which have both dry- and wet-season habitats, often well apart. Fortunately, whether by happenstance or good management, most parks and reserves in Africa are unfenced, allowing wildlife to wander in and out at will in search of food and water. Amboseli National Park in Kenya, for example, covers an area of only 150 square miles – too small to adequately sustain its full complement of nearly 1,500 celebrity elephants – but the reserve itself represents only 5 percent of the elephants' actual range. On any given day, as many as three-quarters of them may be found outside the park, either on adjoining Maasai lands or across the border in Tanzania.

As the density of human population increases – doubling every two or three generations – so, too, does the inevitability of conflict between animals and humans in shared habitats. A poor subsistence farmer, struggling to support his family on a small patch of beans and maize, can hardly be blamed for stoning or spearing an elephant intent upon raiding his crops. Yet, is the animal to be faulted? Both man and beast are simply trying to survive. The impact of habitat constriction is especially severe for large predators, for whom humans have an exceptionally low tolerance. Due principally to loss of territory, and with very little world awareness, the African lion has diminished in numbers from some 100,000 two decades ago to just 23,000 today.

Tourism has long been a driving force for the preservation of African wildlife. Upwards of 20 million people a year infuse African economies with large sums of cash to see zebras and elephants and giraffes in the wild. Until recently, however, very little of this vast revenue stream has trickled down to the African folk who must live with the decidedly mixed blessing of having world-class tourist attractions wandering through their backyards. Government proceeds have typically vanished into general funding – or, worse, numbered Swiss bank accounts – with benefits to the local people seldom extending beyond low-level employment opportunities at lodges and camps catering to foreigners who spend more on a two-week safari than the average African earns in a lifetime. In recent years, governments have begun to see the wisdom of winning the hearts and minds of those most directly able to support or undermine wildlife capitalism, however, and tourism programs now more typically provide a share of revenue to local communities and the people within them.

Education is critical to conservation. Twenty years ago, conservation was irrelevant to the average African, whose world view was defined by more pressing concerns relating to poverty and disease and political unrest. Of what value were wild animals? Few non-rural Africans had ever seen one. In our travels through Africa, Estelle and I have met Britons and Germans and Italians – but never a black African in the role of tourist. Only foreigners could afford that privilege. Sadly, little has changed in that regard, but African schoolchildren are now being taught about their natural heritage and the importance of preserving it. Many of the best and brightest are pursuing careers in conservation – fields formerly dominated by whites – enabled by scholarships and research grants underwritten by international wildlife organizations. With fresh ideas and a native-born sense of the need to sustain Africa's wild lands and wild creatures in a manner compatible with the needs and aspirations of its people, these dedicated young scholars are graduating into important, even top positions in wildlife management and conservation. The brave new world of African conservation is one in which black Africans will fully and capably serve and protect the wildlife entrusted to them – to the benefit of both.

Hardly a day goes by without something reminding Estelle and me of an experience we have shared in Africa. Africa is as much a part of us as anything else in our lives, and our conversations are infused with the things we have seen and done there. Many of our favorite recollections have found their way into this book. But for every incident recalled and recounted, a dozen others, equally cherished and vivid, remain tucked away in our memories.

Most of the chapters focus on a particular species as observed in a particular location during a particular sliver of time. Had the book been structured less rigidly, I would likely have detailed a memorable night in Savuti when Estelle and I, retiring to our tent after a convivial dinner, had to slip past a troop of hyenas that had dragged an impala carcass in front of our tent, and then listen from inside as they noisily devoured it. Or I might have recounted a somewhat similar occasion in South Luangwa when a herd of elephants crossed the river in front of our camp and spent much of the night demolishing the trees directly outside our probably edible thatched chalet. Or I might have conjured up memories of tracking a black rhino and calf on foot through dense bush in Zimbabwe – and then being charged when we finally came upon them. Grand and wondrous experiences – the kind that make good stories – but sometimes wonders can occur on a very small scale.

At the close of an exhilarating safari, Estelle and I have always enjoyed going somewhere special to unwind and pamper ourselves for a couple of days before facing up to the interminable flight home – always much longer than the outbound flight, it seems – and the resumption of our everyday lives. In the early years, when East Africa was our principal destination, that place was usually the Mount Kenya Safari Club, an oasis of luxury on the slopes of Kenya's tallest peak. As guests of Jerry Dale, who was a member, we felt very special indeed. Once our journeys began taking us into southern Africa, however, our allegiance shifted to the Victoria Falls Hotel, a shining example of colonial-era architecture which has maintained its charm and elegance for more than a century.

Victoria Falls is a short walk away. Depending on seasonal variables, the Zambezi River feeding it can be so engorged with water that the spray erupting from the cataract drenches everything within a hundred yards, eclipsing even the chasm rainbows for which the falls are justly famous, or it can be so diminished in flow that one can climb without risk over rocks and surfaces that, a few months earlier or later, would be submerged under raging whitewater about to thunder into the abyss. At either extreme, the mile-long walk along the falls is breathtaking.

Aside from baboons and a great many birds, Victoria Falls is not particularly noted for its wildlife. So, during our third visit there, Estelle and I felt rather pleased with ourselves for having spotted a pair of bush-bucks browsing in the spray-sustained rainforest adjoining the cataract. Though common enough throughout much of Africa, I could count on the fingers of one hand the number of times I had seen one of these shy forest dwellers.

Later, having walked the length of the falls, we were heading back along one of the woodland paths when we happened to hear a slight rustling in the underbrush. Not more than ten feet from the walkway, a tiny antelope calf was tucked in a thicket, left in hiding by its mother who was presumably off feeding somewhere – a common practice among antelopes whose camouflaged young are largely invisible to predators. Slowly, so as not to alarm the creature, I lowered myself to the ground and sat cross-legged on the path. Estelle crouched at my side.

Young calves know to remain still when left unattended. So it was surprising when this one stood up and, on wobbly legs, began picking its way toward us through a carpet of dry leaves. I had been unable to iden-tify it at first, noting only that it had ears many times too large for its tiny head, but once I saw white stripes and spots on its reddish flanks, I realized it was a bushbuck – not more than a day or two old, judging by its gait. The foot-tall newborn came straight toward me, and for a moment I had the strangest feeling that it was going to climb into my lap. Just short of me, however, it veered slightly toward Estelle and stopped, peering up at her. We both held our breath and stayed perfectly still.

Then, unable to resist the urge, Estelle reached out and ever so gently ran her hand along the tiny antelope's back. It did not move away – or even flinch. After another light caress, the newborn turned and tottered back into the brush where it lay down again, ending an encounter more extraordinary than any I could have fantasized.

As we walked back to the hotel, I was reminded of a brief exchange in *Out of Africa*, the first movie we had seen together, and one whose lasting spell, renewed by multiple viewings, may have fueled our grand obsession with Africa. It is midway through the film, and Denys Finch Hatton has persuaded Karen Blixen to accompany him on safari – her first tentative step into his world. Night has fallen, and they sit in the pulsing glow of a campfire sharing wine and conversation under the African stars. In due time, Denys tells Karen that it will be an early day tomorrow, and suggests that she get some sleep. When she inquires expectantly what will happen tomorrow, he replies quite simply that he has no idea.

Having no idea of what the next day will bring is an essential appeal of the safari experience. Africa is not a programmed venue. There are no set performances, only grand improvisations. Any given moment may present the panoramic splendor of a million migrating herbivores or the high-stakes gamesmanship of predators and prey – or even a small and intimate interlude with a baby antelope. Anything is possible. Nothing is certain. I love that about Africa.

Acknowledgments

Beyond her being a matchless travel mate and supportive writing widow, I am indebted to my wife, Estelle, for her exhaustive video documentation of our many Africa trips. Though I have kept sporadic journals and notes through the years, and relied on them and my memory for the broad strokes of this narrative, it was Estelle's compulsive recording of every encounter and incident – fifteen or more hours of video per safari on average – that allowed me to relive our adventures and recount the details with freshness and clarity.

I am grateful to Jody Duncan, writer and editor extraordinaire, whose notes and suggestions from the perspective of one untraveled in Africa helped strengthen the manuscript in its final stages, and to Craig Sholley of the African Wildlife Foundation, whose splendid photography deserves a volume of its own, for reviewing portions of the manuscript relating to his singular expertise in mountain gorillas. I am also in debt to Richard D. Estes, author of *The Safari Companion*, who joined Estelle and me on several memorable game drives in the Masai Mara, and whose essential handbook on wildlife behavior was seldom out of reach – either on safari or at my writing desk.

I profess my gratitude once again to Jerry Dale, a great friend, who introduced us to Africa and orchestrated many of our finest trips. His influence permeates this book. I must also thank Ian Scott of Adventure Travel Desk, a specialist in African travel, who arranged two country-hopping safaris for us that unfolded with flawless precision.

On the continent, our enjoyment and well-being were in the hands of our guides. Some were regulars with whom we spent weeks at a time and developed real relationships. Others – those assigned to particular far-flung camps – left fleeting, if no less indelible, imprints. Among the many standouts not already cited in these pages are Charles Pallangyo, Lucas Mhina, Daniel Mambea and Stanslaus Amara in Tanzania; Peter Allison, Andrew Currell, Graham Hemson, Copper Malela and Kenneth Liwena in Botswana; Huw Jones, Derek Shenton and Phil Berry in Zambia; Bagman Chauke and Zulu Maseko in Zimbabwe; and Stretch Combrink in Namibia. All enhanced and enlivened our safari experiences with their expertise and their fellowship.

Over the years, Estelle and I have induced many of our friends to accompany us on safari, and we have made lasting new friends among travelers we have met along the way. Each has enriched the experience for us: Carol Bauman, Kathleen Brockman, Kathy Burns, Glenn & Patricia Callan, Mickey & Shelley Cohen, David Collier, Pamela Easley & Richard Harris, Howard Green, Michael & Glenis Gross, Arlene Handzel, Brian & Peggy Harris, Gale Anne Hurd, Reggie Jue, Katherine Kean, Bill Lindsay, Dan & Cata Lindsay, Gene & Beulah O'Neal, John & Skook Porter, Mary Rees, John Ruffner, Mike Rybarcyk, Lynne Sher, Craig Sholley, Robert & Barbara Short, Bill & Sally Snyder, Bill & Sara Sparkman, Evelyn Sweigart, Searle & Patti Turner, John Van Vliet, Andrew Velthaus & Wayne Shields, Barry Wall, Cortney Wall and Eric Wall.

My gratitude extends well beyond those who contributed, directly or indirectly, to the writing of this memoir. My longstanding relationship with Valley Printers, owned and operated by René and Anna Vega, has afforded me a level of control over the production of this volume that any author would kill to have. All but the most recent images were captured on a range of evolving film stocks. Master colorist Al Talavera scanned my transparencies and tweaked them to perfection. Technical artist Jason Johnson guided the book through the labyrinthine process of electronic prepress, attending to the countless details beyond my capabilities, and delivered it in turn to Valley pressmen Danny Bell and John Manley for realization on paper. Margie Duncan, my ever-able aide-de-camp, was involved in every aspect of production, from proofreading to press checks. And my son, Gregg Shay – whose love of Africa rivals my own – designed and created the stylish website promoting this long-held dream venture. I salute them all.

I extend my final thanks to Val Warren and Bob Gildersleeve, prized friends since my youth, who long ago introduced me to the fantasy of Africa. I cherish it still.

One of the things I did after my first safari was join several organizations engaged in African wildlife conservation. It seemed a meaningful way to maintain some sort of connection with a place and an experience I was certain would live with me forever. I knew little about any of them at the time. I just wanted to help. Since then, I have gained some understanding of the workings of each, and have narrowed my allegiance and support to those organizations I consider the most vital. At the top of my list is the African Wildlife Foundation.

First and foremost, the African Wildlife Foundation has long understood that wildlife conservation cannot flourish in a vacuum. The needs of African wildlife must be addressed in concert with the needs of the African people. Like many conservation groups, the African Wildlife Foundation had its origin outside the continent it sought to serve. But today, nearly a half-century later, AWF conservation projects and field offices are run principally by dedicated Africans – many with advanced degrees financed by AWF – and the organization has, in recent years, named an African woman as president and moved its world headquarters to Nairobi.

As might be expected, the African Wildlife Foundation funds a range of studies and programs designed to benefit individual species, endangered and not. On a broader front, it conducts joint ventures with African governments and other conservation groups, and is the driving force behind the creation of eight African Heartlands designed to link and restore wildlife ranges and migration routes formerly disrupted by private and political boundaries. AWF also works with rural communities to develop conservation enterprises, such as lodges and camps, to help bring tourism revenue to local people and inspire them to protect and preserve the animals in their midst.

A portion of the proceeds from this book will be donated to the African Wildlife Foundation. I make this pledge knowing that every dollar will be put to exceptionally good use. I invite you to learn more about this worthy organization and become involved in the future of Africa.

www.awf.org